Facebook Advertising

Your Step-By-Step Guide To Generating Quality Leads For Your Business At A Very Affordable Cost

By

Michael Ezeanaka

www.MichaelEzeanaka.com

Disclaimer

This publication is designed to provide competent and reliable information regarding the subject matter covered. However, it is sold with the understanding that the author is not engaged in rendering investment or other professional advice. Laws and practices often vary from state to state and country to country and if investment or other expert assistance is required, the services of a professional should be sought. The author specifically disclaims any liability that is incurred from the use or application of the contents of this book.

Answer Booklet

How would you like to download a booklet that neatly summarizes, all the answers to the end of chapter questions in this book? If you want it, a PDF version of the card is hosted on my website and can be downloaded for free. However, a password is required to unlock the download. Follow the steps below to **retrieve the password**!

Steps to take

1. The password consists of 8 characters (all lower case)
2. Here is the incomplete password: p-z-b-y-
3. The second, fourth, sixth and eight character of the password is missing and is located in random pages of this book.
4. Read this book carefully to locate and retrieve them (they're so obvious you can't miss them).
5. Once you have the complete password go to www.MichaelEzeanaka.com > Free Stuff > Ebooks/Audiobooks > Facebook Advertising Answer Booklet
6. Enter the password, download the Answer Booklet and enjoy!

Books In The Business and Money Series	
Series #	**Book Title**
1	Affiliate Marketing
2	Passive Income Ideas
3	Affiliate Marketing + Passive Income Ideas (2-in-1 Bundle)
4	Facebook Advertising
5	Dropshipping
6	Dropshipping + Facebook Advertising (2-in-1 Bundle)
7	Real Estate Investing For Beginners
8	Credit Cards and Credit Repair Secrets
9	Real Estate Investing And Credit Repair (2-in-1 Bundle)
10	Passive Income With Affiliate Marketing (2nd Edition)
11	Passive Income With Dividend Investing
The kindle edition will be available to you for FREE when you purchase the paperback version from Amazon.com (The US Store)	

Download The Audio Versions Along With The Complementary PDF Document For FREE from Amazon.com or Audible.com

Table of Contents

Introduction

Social media, no doubt, changed the business landscape. People now leverage social media sites like Facebook, Instagram etc. to sell and promote their products and services. Marketing is no longer confined to face-to-face conversations.

Advertising on Facebook and other social media platforms has become the most practical (and arguably cost effective) way of promoting one's brand. Even big companies have recognized the importance of having an online presence.

In this book, you'll discover:

- What the Facebook Advertising platform has to offer your business and why you need to get on board today (**Chapter 1**)
- A concise overview of more than 10 incredible Facebook features including one that allow you to interact with potential customers without sending them a private message or email alert! (**Chapter 2**)
- How to open a secure Business Page using two-layer permission model that allows you to securely maintain and manage your Pages, Ad Accounts and Catalogs. (**Chapter 3**)
- How to leverage the Facebook Ads Manager to create highly optimized and profitable Facebook Ads (**Chapter 4**)
- How to monitor specific actions potential customers take while on your website and, more importantly, how to use the Facebook Pixel to retarget those same people on Facebook (**Chapter 5**)
- How to create a highly effective customer avatar that will boost your conversion rates while keeping ad costs extremely low (**Chapter 6**)
- The A-to-Z of a Facebook Ad Campaign including how to choose the right objective for your ad, add payment methods, set suitable budgets etc. (**Chapter 7**)
- How to set up a highly converting sales funnel, incorporate the sales funnels with Facebook, create a lead magnet and build your email list (**Chapter 8**)

And much, much more!

More importantly, a case study is presented at the very end of this book. This case study will bring together all the concepts discussed and show you exactly how you can leverage the skills and knowledge you'll gain from this book to **make $10,000+ each month with Facebook Advertising**.

It is my sincere hope that what you'll discover in this book will equip you with the skills and knowledge you need to take your business or brand to the next level.

Finally, the screenshots used in this book have been made as large as possible to enhance readability. However, if you find any of it not to be large enough, don't worry. I have created an image booklet that contains an enlarged version of *all the images* used in this book.

To download the booklet, please go to www.MichaelEzeanaka.com > Free Stuff > Ebooks/Audiobooks > Facebook Advertising Answer Booklet. Click on the orange button that says "**Click Here To Download The Image Booklet**"

Without further ado, let's get started!

Chapter 1

Social Media Marketing

Communication is a basic human need. It is just as important to individuals in their personal lives as it is to marketers and entrepreneurs in their businesses. Because of social media, constant interaction has become a major way of life. Social media has indeed simplified communication and with it, opportunities have been created for marketers to reach their target audiences.

Among all the social media platforms, there seems to be one clear winner not just in terms of the number of active users but more importantly, the excellent tools and options it is able to provide for businesses.

Is Facebook advertising worth jumping into? Let's find out as we explore some of the most known benefits and possible drawbacks of using this social media platform for your advertising requirements.

Advantages of Using Facebook as a Marketing Platform

Reach a wide audience

Facebook undoubtedly has the greatest number of active users among all social media platforms. It is unbeatable when it comes to sheer size and number. And, more importantly, these are active users, ready to engage and interact using the platform.

Excellent targeting options

Facebook makes a lot of targeting tools available that allow marketers to reach the right audience. For a marketer, this reduces your chance of wasting a lot of money reaching the wrong people.

Low cost

With Facebook, you can advertise for as little as $5 or even $1 a day. And because of the targeting options, you have a better chance of getting the most value per dollar spent.

Customer loyalty

Facebook allows marketers not only to reach more people and increase awareness. It also provides them an avenue to keep their existing customers engaged in order to build loyalty and long-term profitable relationships.

Flexibility

There are plenty of ad formats available from single image ads to video ads. Advertisers can also use a carousel of images or tell stories about their brand. The possibilities are virtually endless with all the tools at your disposal.

Easy to Use

For the most part, it does not take a rocket scientist to figure out Facebook advertising. Admittedly, it does take some getting used to initially but Facebook provides all the necessary tools and information to assist marketers in navigating the features.

Innovation

The number one reason why this platform has stood the test of time and keeps getting stronger is innovation. The Facebook team constantly comes up with new ways to improve user experience. They also continuously develop new tools that make advertising on Facebook intuitive, easier and much more attractive.

Possible Issues with Facebook Advertising

Lesser organic views

Facebook has changed the algorithm so that brand message visibility is limited. This means that among a fan base, only 8% may be able to view your posts. While this is disappointing for marketers, it's actually a good decision that can be very beneficial in the long run.

What Facebook is trying to do is maintain the *social* aspect of the platform. This is what makes people keep on using Facebook to document their everyday lives, interact with friends near or far, get information from their feeds, etc.

Cost is an issue

Although the minimum cost of Facebook advertising isn't significant, cost can still be an issue for advertisers with a very limited budget. The good news is there are other ways to reach campaign objectives with free tools. Although it will take much more time and more effort, it is worth considering and integrating with paid promotions in order to achieve the best possible return on your investment.

Requires commitment

As with other social media marketing tools, Facebook advertising requires commitment and a lot of effort. Although Facebook provides the platform and the tools to allow you to market and promote effectively, how you leverage these resources at your disposal is entirely up to you. You have to put in effort to learn. This book will help you achieve that objective.

29 Incredible Reasons to Use Facebook Advertising

As you probably already know, Facebook is an incredible social media platform. At the same time, it has paved the way to the success of many business startups. The wide variety of tools made available to marketers and business owners make it possible to reach new customers, engage them to build and maintain a lasting relationship. The best part (and a lot of people aren't aware of this) is a lot of these tools are free.

Ranging from the custom audiences to lookalike audiences, the Facebook marketing tools offer plenty of features and options to connect with a vast network of audiences. Here is a list of Facebook tools and features for businesses.

1. Facebook Page

Packed with features such as Messenger chat and appointment scheduling, Pages is a great way for businesses to connect with potential customers. It can be used for showcasing products and services. Customers can also rate and add reviews about the business. The call-to-action buttons are great for inciting a positive response.

2. Page Insights

This analytics tool is valuable for businesses that signed up with Pages. It tracks and analyzes responses from customers including number of likes. Business owners and marketers can also see exactly where those likes are coming from. Data like content reach, daily post breakdown and visitor demographic profile among others are monitored. It can also tell you which particular sections of your Page people are actually responding to.

3. Pages Manager App

This app allows you to manage and monitor activity on multiple Pages via mobile. You can post updates instantly, as well as, respond to messages and comments. Through this app, latest updates on Page Insights are also much more accessible. The app is available on iOS and Android.

4. Messenger

This is a free app for texting and video calling. It also allows users to send payments. The platform has undergone many iterations and improvements that have proved useful for businesses. Among those updates include Messenger Links to Pages and Messenger codes that can be used for scanning. It also lets businesses create customized notes sent automatically to users who try to connect with them.

5. Canvas

Quality content is important in engaging customers. Canvas makes this possible. Through this free tool, still images can be combined with videos to create interactive content. In addition, Call to action buttons can also be incorporated. Multimedia ads produced with this tool can be opened to full screen when users click on the ads.

6. Power Editor

This is an excellent tool that advertisers can use for controlling ads, campaigns and ad sets. Multiple ads can be edited through the Power Editor and this can be used across campaigns.

7. Ad Creation Tool

This tool can be used for something more than producing ads. It also lets advertisers control which audiences to show the ads according to age, location, interests and other factors. A Facebook ad for instance, can be used to provide store directions. It can also direct a user to download an app, check out videos, add items to cart or any other action on the advertiser's website.

8. Ads Manager

Creating ads is just the first part. Ads Manager allows you not only to manage ads but also to measure its effectiveness. You can check on the performance of each ad or monitor ad sets (i.e. multiple ads grouped together). You also get access to campaign tools like campaign media, audience insights and custom audiences. For large campaigns, you can use the Power Editor.

9. Page Post Engagement Ads

If you want to make sure that more people see, like, comment and share the content on your Page, this is the right tool to achieve those goals. You can create an ad, pick your objective to "boost your posts" and then choose Page Post Engagement. Select the Page and choose which post you want to boost. This Facebook tool also allows you to include website address and send it to people. You can even use a conversion pixel that will allow you to monitor the results.

10. Page Like Ads

This is an incredible tool you can use to boost awareness of your Page. To use it, create the ad, choose **Page Likes** from the ad tool, select the Page you want to promote and begin building awareness of that particular page.

11. Clicks to Website Ads

Driving traffic is one of the most important aspects of marketing. You can use this tool to send more people to your business website through an ad. Upon creating the ad, choose Clicks to Website and add the website address where you want to send traffic. It could be your website homepage, your online store, or a product page.

12. App Installs and App Engagement Ads

If you have an app, this is one of the best ways to promote it. You can use it to drive awareness and encourage people to install your app. Create an ad specifically for your app and through the App Engagement tool, you can link the ad to specific areas of the app from the registration page itself to the online store where visitors can get more information about the app and make a purchase. As the ad makes an appearance on News Feeds of your target audience, you provide them with an easy avenue leading to the app you're promoting.

13. Event Response Ads

Facebook changes the way you promote ads. Instead of creating an invite to your event as an ad, you can use this tool to get users to add your event directly to their Facebook calendar. Once added, they can receive reminders pertaining to your event. You can then monitor the number of people who have responded to the event.

14. Offer Claim Ads

Creating an offer or a promotion through special deals or discounts is a great way to get people's attention. You can do this more effectively with Offer Claim tool. With this feature, you can set the duration of the offer, choose the audience and select the number of people who can make a claim to the offer. To use this feature, create your promo ad and set your campaign objective as "get people to claim your offer" and then select Offer Claims.

15. Video Views

Video ads can be more engaging for the viewers. The challenge is to create memorable ones. This tool proves helpful in this matter. First, create your video ad and set your campaign objective to "get video views." Upload the video and carefully select an eye-catching thumbnail. This is the first thing people see even before they get to view the ads. It's an important part of creating an excellent teaser.

16. Local Awareness Ads

For a more targeted post, this tool allows you to select your locality as well as set the age and gender of the target customers you would like to reach. All that's left to do to start sending these potential customers to your business is to add the Get Directions button.

17. Slideshow Ads

This is a feature that allows you to easily produce video ads and edit them. Because slideshows are generally lighter using less data, they can load faster which makes them more accessible to users. It is an important consideration when users are mobile and connected with low bandwidth.

18. Carousel Ads

Creating a story around multiple products can even be more effective. The Carousel makes this possible. It also allows you to showcase multiple products using one ad. You can take advantage of this feature by introducing the products at various angles and providing important details. To use this tool, choose multiple images in one ad when prompted to select how you prefer your ad to appear.

19. Dynamic Ads

People who have visited your website or Page, checked out your posts, dropped by your Instagram have already shown interest. Dynamic Ads tool allows you to retarget them by presenting these users with relevant products.

There are some prerequisites to start using this feature and they are as follows:

- A product catalog,
- A Business Manager account, and
- Facebook Pixel.

Once you launch Dynamic Ads, you can promote your business on Instagram and Facebook, as well as, use Audience Network to showcase your products exactly where potential customers are spending most of their time.

20. Lead Ads

Facebook has made it easier for users to sign up and get information from various businesses in the form of quotes, special offers and newsletters. This is what Lead Ads are all about. Through this feature, you can build contact forms within your ads with pre-populated contact info including email addresses. This will allow you to follow up on leads more efficiently.

21. Canvas Ads

The Canvas app lets you create multimedia adds combining still images with videos and finishing it up with a call-to-action button. It is a more interactive way of showcasing your products. With it, users can run through carousel of images, view them from various angles and zoom in on them to access the details.

22. Instagram Ads

Instagram has more than 500 million active users. It's a little on the short side compared to the number of Facebook users but a combination of these two in your marketing plan can prove to be highly effective. If you use Instagram, you can manage them using the Power Editor and Ads Manager of Facebook.

23. Business Manager

Security and control are among the things that business owners are concerned about. With Business Manager, you can easily manage your Facebook assets from your Pages to your ad accounts. It puts all these things together (in one place) and the best part is, it doesn't cost anything to set up!

24. Facebook Pixel

One of the most exciting features of Facebook advertising is the Pixel. It is essentially a piece of code embedded on your website which will allow you to build your audience for all your ad campaigns, measure and optimize them. Basically, when a user pays your website a visit, clicks on something or take any kind of action, Pixel records and reports this to you.

In addition, the pixel will try to find and match the action to a Facebook user. In this case, you will not only know that someone went to your website, you will also find out if the user took such action as a response to your Facebook ad. You can then choose to retarget this user using Custom Audience.

25. Hashtags

Phrases and topics can become clickable links on posts either on your Page or timeline. Hashtags make this possible. It will then allow users to locate posts according to your topics of interest.

26. Custom Audiences

Custom Audience can be created to run ads specifically targeted to users you know of. You can start doing this by uploading contacts from a data file or email list. You can either copy and paste them or import those contacts straight from MailChimp, Aweber etc. Assign a name and set a description for your Custom Audience. To run ads for them, choose the Audience field and select the name you created for the Custom Audience.

27. Lookalike Audiences

If you want to grow your customer base, you can use this tool to find more Facebook users that match the traits of your current customers using pieces of information like age, job role, location, gender and interests. To use this feature, proceed to the Ads Manager and choose Audiences. Click on the Create Audience button and select Lookalike Audience. From the Source field, choose the Page, Custom Audience you want to manage and the conversion-tracking pixel.

28. Audience Network

This is a good tool for monetizing mobile apps and websites. It's basically a network of publisher-owned apps and sites where you can show your ads. People spend a lot of their time on Facebook and Instagram. But they are also spending time on other apps and sites.

Audience Network helps advertisers reach more of the people they care about in the other places where they're spending their time. With Audience Network, you can choose from various formats including banner, standard interstitial and custom native units for video and display. Furthermore, Audience Network ads use the same targeting, auction, delivery and measurement systems as Facebook ads.

29. Facebook Blueprint

Facebook offers a variety of avenue for you to promote your business and reach customers. You can learn more about what tools you can use and how to boost your results further by using the Facebook Blueprint. From this, you can select courses and customize your training according to your business objectives.

Congratulations!

The second character of the password required to unlock the Answer Booklet is letter l (l for letter).

Chapter 1 Quiz

Please refer to the Answer Booklet for the solution to this quiz

1. Which analytics tool monitors visitor demographic profile, daily post breakdowns and content reach?

   A) Canvas
   B) Page Insights
   C) Ads Manager
   D) Pixel

2. Which Facebook feature allows you to widen your reach by matching the traits of your current customers or visitors?

   A) Custom Audiences
   B) Lookalike Audiences
   C) Audience Network
   D) Interest Lists

3. Which tool helps ensure that you're delivering the right message to the appropriate audience?

   A) Pixel
   B) Ads Manager
   C) Ad Relevance
   D) Facebook History

4. Facebook offers a variety of avenue for you to promote your business and reach customers. However, you can learn more about what tools you can use and how to boost your results further by using this Facebook feature?

   A) Facebook Blueprint
   B) Facebook Help
   C) Facebook Guide
   D) Facebook Tutorial

5. What are the available formats you can use with Audience Network?

   A) Banner
   B) Standard Interstitial
   C) Custom native units for video and display
   D) Click links

6. Which tool can help you create a quality image for your profile photo and cover photo

   A) Facebook Pixel
   B) Canvas

C) Hashtags
D) Canva

7. With this tool, you can manage and monitor activity on multiple Pages on mobile. You can also post updates instantly and respond to messages and comments immediately.

    A) Multi-Page app
    B) Pages Control app
    C) Pages Manager app
    D) Pages Monitoring app

8. This is an excellent tool that advertisers can use for controlling ads, campaigns and ad sets. Multiple ads can be edited through this tool, which can be used across campaigns.

    A) Canvas
    B) Edit Tools
    C) Power Tools
    D) Power Editor

9. This tool allows you not only to manage ads but also to measure its effectiveness. You can check on the performance of each ad or monitor ad sets.

    A) Power Editor
    B) Ad Creation Tool
    C) Ads Manager
    D) Business Page

10. You can use this tool to send people to your business website through an ad. Upon creating the ad, choose this feature and add the website address where you want to send traffic.

    A) Reach
    B) Traffic
    C) Page Like Ads
    D) Clicks to Website Ads

Did you know?

Video will be more important for social media content marketing than ever. According to Smart Insights, 90 percent of all content shared by users on social media in 2017 was video!

Chapter 2

Facebook Advertising

There are standard Facebook features that most advertisers rely on. Although the tools mentioned in the previous chapter can do wonders for your business goals, there are actually other features that most take for granted. Are you merely scratching the surface with the tactic you're currently using? You probably are if you're not using the tools you're about to see.

You may not have heard about some of them or you're familiar with them but just don't see their great potential yet. Before we go into detail, here's a quick overview.

- For content curation, use Save for Later and Interest Lists features.
- For page management, use Tagging, Pinning, Post Attribution and Filtering.
- For ads management, use Ad Notification, Email Manager and Ad Relevance.
- For competitive advantage, use your competition's top posts and Facebook history.

No, lets talk more about these features.

1. Save for Later

This Save feature can be used for saving music, TV, movies, places and links. There are too many link posts that appear on your news feed on a daily basis. It's quite difficult to keep up with them.

How does this feature help your business? For one, the saved content can help you come up with more relevant content for your target audience. You may find some interesting ones that you can either reuse or rehash. Two, it can also get you more Likes. To save a link, choose a post and go to the arrow at the top right corner. Click on the arrow and select "Save for Later."

2. Interest Lists

This is a feature that will help you be in full control by staying organized. Keeping up with updates, news and info can be challenging if you're working on multiple projects. Interest Lists make it simpler to cope. With this feature, you don't have to go through the task of finding the best Pages whenever you need to. You get them in one place, your Interest Lists. You can create your list according to the following.

- By Interests such as books, movies, sports, outdoors, etc.
- By Medium, i.e., citizen journalism or traditional journalism
- By Industry like consumer goods, aerospace, advertising, etc.
- By City/ State/ Country/ Region

3. Tagging

Tagging is not just for photos among friends, you can also tag users on your Page. It's a great way of interacting with potential customers. You can use the tagging feature instead of sending a private message or an email to alert them. You can also tag an influencer when you share their content. Tagging also works for notifying winners when you're running a promotion.

To tag personal profiles of customers on your Facebook Page, follow the steps below:

- Create a post on your Page.
- View the post and look for the downward-facing arrow at the top right corner.
- Click the arrow and choose Edit Post from the dropdown menu.
- In the textbox, type @ followed by the user's name. Facebook will automatically offer suggestions. If you find the user's name from the list of suggestions, click it. If the user's profile doesn't appear, try typing in the full name.
- Click on Done Editing. This will automatically send a notification to the user.

4. Pinning

To boost visibility, you can pin some posts and keep them at the top portion of your timeline. If you want to drive attention to a particular post, pinning it to the top will ensure better visibility. Follow these steps to start using the pinning feature.

- Go to the post and click on the downward-facing arrow from the top right corner.
- Choose Pin to Top from the dropdown menu.

5. Manage your Fan List.

After Facebook updated user interface for Pages, you can still access and manage your fan list. This will allow you to eliminate fake accounts and pay more attention to the genuine active ones. Follow these steps to access your fan list and weed out the fakes.

- Access your Page Settings.
- Choose Banned Users from the left sidebar.
- Select Banned from the menu.
- Click People Who Like This from the dropdown.

6. Post Attribution

To maintain transparency and credibility, make sure you post on your page with the correct identity. You can do this using the Post Attribution settings. For instance, when you use mobile, set the Post Attribution to your Personal Profile. And when you're on your desktop, set Post Attribution to your Page. To make these changes, follow the steps below:

- Access Post Attribution by going to the Page Settings.
- From the left sidebar, choose Post Attribution and click your preferred identity.

7. Filtering

Manage your post through the filtering feature. It will help you save valuable time. For instance, if you want to access your previous posts, it can take a lot of time to go through your Page. However, if you filter them by type, you will find it easier to find anything you have posted before. To do this, click on the Activity Log found on the left sidebar and select the post type. Page Posts can be filtered using the following categories.

- Offers
- Events
- Notes
- Questions

- Posts by others
- Your posts
- Comments
- Posts marked as spam
- Video posts
- Image Post

8. Ad Notification and Email Manager

Getting a barrage of emails from Facebook for every approved ad, rejected ad, scheduled ad report and the like can be quite a work to go through. But do you know that you can reduce the clutter in your inbox? You can do this by following these steps.

- Proceed to the Ads Manager and choose Settings from the left sidebar to access Ad account settings.
- Go to the Emails Notification section and scroll down.
- Only select the notifications you want to receive.

Find what is necessary for you. For instance, you may still want to be notified about rejected ads so you can quickly address the issue.

9. Ad Relevance

As the name implies, this ad analytic tool measures your ad's relevance and awards a score (from 1 to 10) – the higher the score, the more relevant your ad is. It helps ensure that you're delivering the right message to the appropriate audience. This will let you know if you're ads are under-performing, so you can make the necessary improvements to meet your Return on Investment (ROI) goals.

The relevance score allows you to make a pilot test for your new ads even before you set your budget. If the pilot ad receives 500 impressions, your relevance score is measured and reported to you. Relevance scores also reduce your cost of getting through to your target audience especially in the long run.

To check if you can access the tool, you can follow these steps.

- Proceed to the Ads Manager.
- From the left sidebar, choose Campaigns.
- Click on the name of your campaign and proceed to the ad set.
- Check the fifth column from the right side.

10. Check out top posts from your competitors.

This isn't exactly a tool, but Facebook allows you to get a glimpse of your competition. You can do this within Facebook Insights. Follow these steps.

- Click on Posts tab.
- Choose Top Posts from Pages You Watch.

11. Access Facebook History

Keeping track of your Page's history allows you to review all the posts, videos and images you have shared. By doing so, you also access chat conversations and messages. It will also allow you to review all of your clicked ads, access facial recognition data and check out past information you have shared in your About section.

After downloading your Facebook history, you will get to re-access all the information Facebook has saved for you. Essentially, it will further extend options for your demographic target. After all, there's more to people than just their age and gender.

To download your Facebook history, follow these steps.

- Go to Settings.
- Choose **Download a copy** and **Download Facebook History**.
- You will then get an email that will let you know when you can download your archive.

When used effectively, these Facebook tools can get you more Likes, save time and significantly improve your ROI. There are however, a couple of things you should take note of. Your ads will have to go through the Facebook Ad Review Process. That said, you have to make sure you follow their advertising policies. This is what we will look further into the next section.

Creating a Facebook Page

You've caught a glimpse of the most powerful Facebook features you can use to boost your business. Among the biggest and most essential ones is a business page. Now we look at the benefits of having one.

Why do you need a Facebook Page?

In today's world, a Facebook page is essential for organizations and businesses looking to grow their online presence and reach. Below you will find the top reasons why you need one too.

- **Connect with your target customers.**

A Facebook Page is one of the best ways to connect with your audience. It's like having a focus group that you don't necessarily have to pay for. Your audience will be expecting useful information and that's what you have to deliver. At the same time, you also get to collect useful information from your audience like their needs, pain points, expectations etc.

With the help of Facebook Insights, you get to *mine* more usable data about how they use your page and interact with your content. By interaction, feedback, and comments, they can tell you exactly what they want. You provide them an avenue to directly engage with your brand.

- **Through Facebook Page, you can humanize your business.**

Genuine social connections are what social media is all about. With a Facebook Page, you give your business a name, a face, and a personality that people will be able to relate to. You get to represent your business but also initiate non-business interaction.

❖ **You can build a community.**

In a Page, existing customers and potential customers can give reviews, testimonials and feedback. You allow them to share their opinions and voice any concerns they may have. And you can immediately address them. Building a community around your brand through a Facebook Page isn't rocket science. You can do it in many ways including the following.

- Post relevant, useful, and interesting links to articles, videos etc.
- Initiate conversations by asking your fans for comments, opinions etc
- Encourage them to participate through promotions, giveaways and contests
- Set a section for them to leave feedback and reviews
- Provide incentive for staying active on your Page (i.e. most active member award, recognition, gift cards etc.)

It's a great way to attract new customers and build a relationship with them. If you are successful in bringing them together, you can count on a loyal following that you can keep on growing and nurturing.

❖ **You can also use your Facebook Page for Search Engine Optimization or SEO.**

Creating a page isn't just a venue for you to drive traffic to your blog and website. SEO is a longer-term advertising strategy that you can maximize through your Page. Your links, posts and activities published on the Page are all indexed in search engines like Google. It can contribute to your SEO efforts and attract more traffic to your business. To achieve your SEO goals, make sure to fill your Page with rich and relevant content. These things will help improve your search engine rankings.

❖ **Make your business accessible to customers and clients every single day.**

Most people log in to Facebook every day and plug in to their favorite Pages. This means it is crucial for you to regularly update your status, share videos and links as well as other pieces of valuable information. It will strengthen your connection with your customers.

To date, Facebook has over 2.2 billion active users and the number is steadily growing. There are also an increasing number of users that use Facebook to search for brands, products and services. Your presence in the platform makes it easier for them to find you. When they find you and connect with you, they are more likely to stick with you. When you manage to keep them interested and satisfied, they'd be more than happy to remain loyal and even share their connections with you.

❖ **Your competition has one.**

Why should you create a Facebook Page to represent your business? Why not when your competition has one? Absence in social media leads you to miss out on opportunities. If your competitors have one and you don't, then they have a significant edge over you.

A Facebook Page is one of the most powerful and effective ways to broaden your reach. It is also a cost efficient way to increase awareness of your business. Most importantly, it allows you to build a genuine connection with your current customers, your potential customers and your fans.

How to Create a Facebook Page for Your Business?

This Page will be attached to your Facebook personal profile. It is a separate entity, it works with an independent presence and can be used effectively to promote your brand, business or any cause. There are many features available to a Page that are not accessible to personal profiles. Among them are post scheduling, advertising and analytics. To get started, here's how to create your business Page.

1. Go to your personal profile.

To begin, you have to log in to your personal Facebook profile. Once you're logged in, proceed by clicking on the **Create** button, which you will find next to your name and the **Home** button. In the window that appears, choose **Page**.

2. Enter your business information.

After clicking on Page, you will be prompted to choose between **Business or Brand** and a **Community or Public Figure**. Choose *Get Started* under Business or Brand.

You will then have to fill in the following information.

- Page Name
- Category
- Address (Street Address, City, State and Zip Code)
- Phone Number

You will be given a choice not to show the address. If you choose to tick the box, Facebook will only show that your business is within the city, state region.

3. Upload a profile picture and cover photo.

The next step is to add a profile picture that represents your business well.

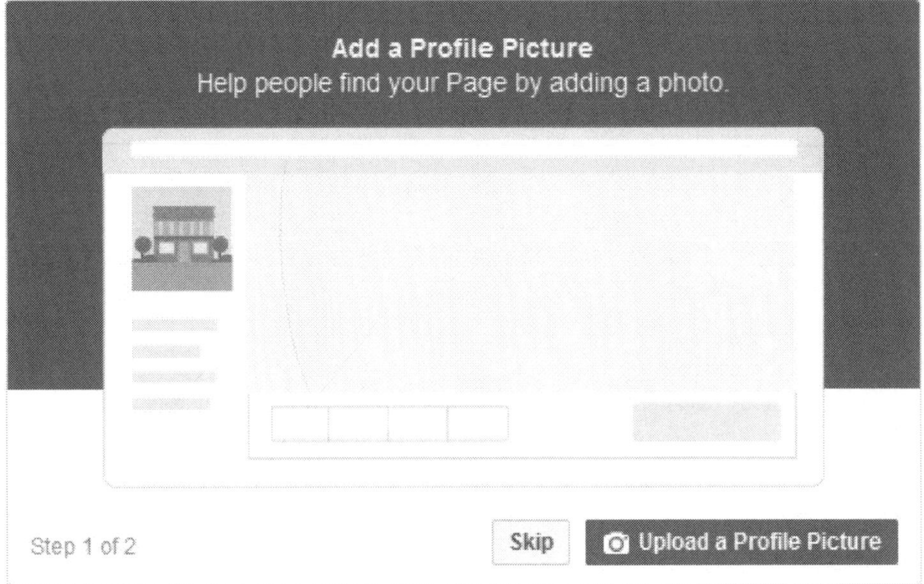

An attractive image can draw attention to your page. Consider using a product photo. For instance, if you're running a restaurant, adding a delicious looking dish from your menu may be a good idea. If you're promoting a beauty salon, try using a fabulous hairstyle. Another idea is to use your business logo or any image that customers can easily associate with the business like a storefront or street sign.

The same applies for the cover photo. It has to represent the business but also be of great quality, as well as, visually appealing. To look the best, it has to be 828 by 315 pixels. Canva is one of the resources you can use for this. It allows you to create a quality image with the right dimensions. When choosing the image either for your profile picture or the cover photo, you should keep the following rules in mind.

- Pick something visually appealing.
- It should represent your business.
- It must be a high-resolution image. A profile photo should be at least 170 by 170 pixels. A cover photo should be at least 828 by 315 pixels.

Don't skimp on the images. If you have the budget, hire a photographer for product shots. You can outsource the job on websites like Fiverr or Upwork.

4. Complete your business details.

When you're done with all the steps above, Facebook will offer you tips on how to maximize the potential of newly created business page. While a visually appealing profile picture and cover photo can paint a thousand words, it is still essential that you complete the details and provide as much information as possible in order to bring life to your page.

Short Description - Tell your target audience what you are all about. This is your opportunity to humanize your brand or business. Write a quality description with smart use of keywords relevant to your industry/niche.

Keep it short and concise. As much as possible, do not exceed one to two sentences. You can describe your page's or business' focus.

Business Hours - Let your potential customers know your store opening hours.

Username – Your chosen username will be attached to your Facebook URL (facebook.com/username). Because of this, you should choose an easy and memorable one. This will help people find your page effortlessly.

Website Link – If you have one, do not forget to add your website URL. Get attention from potential customers through Facebook and drive them to your website.

Create a Group – This is definitely something you should consider. Create a section for your audience to connect with each other. It will give them a chance to talk about your business, your products and services. We will talk about this further in the next section.

5. Add call to action buttons.

If you look at the upper right hand corner of the Page, you will find the option to Add a Button. Take advantage of the traffic you're getting to prompt visitors into taking action and get the results you hope to achieve e.g. visit your website, visit your online e-commerce store etc.

Book Service - There are two options for buttons here. *Book Now* is ideal for traveling agencies, hotel or B&B's. The second button is *Start Order* which is appropriate for businesses in the food industry or any business offering products.

Get In Touch - The following five button options will direct them to various points of contact you make available.

Call Now - Let people call you without memorizing a number.

Sign Up or **Contact Us** - These buttons will direct users to your website and a form for their details. It's best for subscription capture and lead generation.

Send Message - This allows users to send you a private message through your page.

Send Email - For lengthy messages, customers can use this button to use email from the Page itself.

Learn More - Use this button to provide more information about an offer, a product or service or anything about your brand or business. There's also an option to Watch Video for people who want to see a full video post on Facebook itself or viewed from your website.

Make a Purchase or Donation - You can use this button to take them to your product page. Link it to your website. One click can take them where they need to be and purchase products or avail themselves of your services.

Download App or Game - This is best used if you're promoting or using an app to improve user experience. The Play Game button can also make your Page more interactive.

You have several options. Feel free to explore them all before you decide which is best for your business.

6. Adjust privacy and security settings.

Whether or not you're getting help in managing your business page, it's incredibly important to ensure the security of your Page. We'll look into the different settings you can customize.

General Settings

This is where you control your page. You can access the General Settings page by clicking on *Settings* located at the top right corner above the Page cover picture and next to *Help*. It should contain the below information:

Shortcuts	Page is pinned to shortcut	Edit
Page Visibility	Page Published	Edit
Visitor Posts	Anyone can publish to the page	Edit
News Feed Audience and Visibility for Posts	The ability to narrow the potential audience for News Feed and limit visibility on your posts is turned off	Edit
Messages	People can contact my Page privately	Edit

Tagging People	Only people who help manage my page can tab photos posted on it	Edit
Others Tagging this Page	People and other Pages can tag my Page	Edit

There are a couple of essential things you must do on this page and they include the following.

Shortcuts

This is about saving time by pinning your page to shortcuts section. One click from your personal profile will take you directly to the business page.

Visitor Posts

In this section, you can allow your visitors to post, add photos or publish videos to the page. At the same time, you can review the content first to make sure no inappropriate content goes through. To do this, tick the box for reviewing the posts made by others. This will give you a chance to either approve or disapprove posts before they get published.

Messages

You have to make sure that visitors are allowed to send you messages through Messenger. In fact, you should encourage them to. You can get started by checking the box for Messages.

Others Tagging This Page

Allowing individuals and businesses to share and tag the page can further expand your audience. Tick the box to allow it.

Age Restriction

If you're selling or promoting age-sensitive products like tobacco and alcohol, it is necessary to prevent minors from accessing your page.

Page Moderation and Profanity Filter

If it's important for you to keep things clean, it would be wise to edit these settings. Blocking comments containing words you may consider offensive or inappropriate will help you control published content. Do this by adding words on the prohibited section.

Similar Page Suggestions

By ticking this box, you allow the system to include your page in results of relevant searches. For instance, if you have a pet grooming business and a user searches for pet products, your page will appear as a relevant search.

Page Updates

Whenever you change or update any information from your page like a phone number or description, the system can send out notifications. It's also possible to stop Facebook from publishing those updates.

Post in Multiple Languages

If you're catering to non-English speaking audiences, you can make your page multi-lingual. This will make your page and posts appear to visitors in their local language.

Comment Ranking

Comments can be ranked so that the most recent ones or the most relevant ones appear at the top. Use this setting to indicate your preference according to what will be more beneficial to your business or brand.

Content Distribution

Your page's followers can download published videos. You can allow it or restrict it by editing this section.

Messaging Settings

When traffic volume on your page increases, it can become more challenging to manage. This is the best time to start thinking about automation.

A Response Assistant is useful in delivering automated responses to queries or any messages you receive through your page at least until you are able to respond to them. You can even customize the response to mention the name of the user who sent the message. With auto-response, you can let the sender know that the message has been received and you'll be responding yourself soon.

Page Settings

Even though Facebook Pages come with a set of tabs in default order, you can actually customize it. Pay particular attention to the tabs under the profile photo. Open to edit the settings and customize the order by clicking and dragging the tabs in the sequence you prefer. For instance, if you want to focus your strategy on videos, put that tab first.

Notification Settings

You get notified every time an activity occurs on the page. You can adjust the notification settings so you can receive them as they happen or schedule them every day. Moreover, you can choose the type of activities you want to be notified. For instance, would you like to be informed whenever your followers share your post, when you receive a comment or when someone mentions your page? You can also set to receive information through text or email or both.

Page Role Settings

This is essential if you're working with a team. Each role is assigned access to specific areas of the page. This helps clear up communication channels and delegate responsibilities among your team members.

People and Other Pages Settings

The people and pages that clicked the Like button on your page will appear here. If you ever want to ban anyone, this is where to do that.

Preferred Page Audience Settings

This is where you can specify your target audience so that the right people see your page. You can also edit this setting so they can access your posts.

7. Finalize the details.

Whenever you can, take advantage of opportunities that allow you to bring granular information pertaining to the brand or the business. Here are a few additional things you should not forget when polishing the details on your page.

- Add your other Social Media account information under Contact Info.
- To build a stronger brand and make it more personal, you may also want to consider connecting your team by linking their profiles to each other.
- Add product descriptions.
- You may also add menu.
- If you've won awards, let the public know.

After completing your page profile, save your changes and you're ready to go live and start connecting with your target audience.

Creating a Facebook Group

If you want to grow your brand or business, you would need the support of the online community. An online presence can help you stay in touch with your target audience, collect useful insights, spread the word about your business and build customer loyalty. A Facebook page will help you achieve all these. However, a group creates a more intimate and exclusive setting for your target audience to discuss among themselves and connect with each other.

What can you achieve with a Facebook Group?

- Provide ongoing updates, support and promotion to your audience who are already interested in your business and the products or services that you offer.
- Convert casual visitors to fans and then to paying customers.
- Make sure you keep your current customers happy, maintain their business and encourage loyalty.
- Always stay in touch with your business' or brand's customer base.

How to create a Facebook Group?

While you're on your way to creating your own Facebook Group, do not forget to check out existing ones. There are a couple of industry-focused groups you can learn from. They gather professionals within the industry to exchange experiences, ideas and talk about trend. They can inspire your posts that can ultimately help your business grow.

To start creating your group, follow these steps.

1. Go to your Page.

Log in to your Facebook Page, click the Create tab at the top menu bar and choose Group. This will bring up a new window where you will be asked to enter your Group details.

- Create a name for your Group. As much as possible, keep the name relevant and close to your Page's name.
- Add people to the Group.

- Include a personal note with your invite.
- Set your Group's privacy settings: closed or public.
- Pin your Group to shortcuts for easy access.

Complete the details and make all the necessary changes on your settings, then click Create.

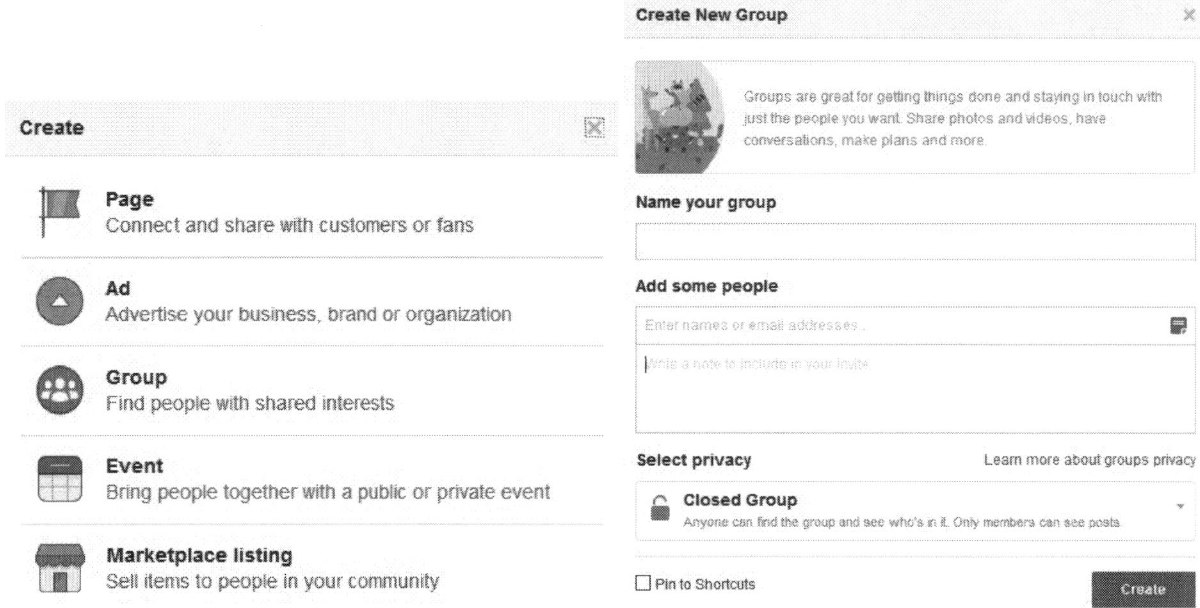

2. Assign roles.

Your Facebook Page can be the automatic admin for the group. However, you may also want to use your personal profile as a backup admin. This will allow you to manage the Group using both your profile and your page. To do this, go to the Member's tab and click the dots that show beside your name. From the dropdown menu, choose Make Admin.

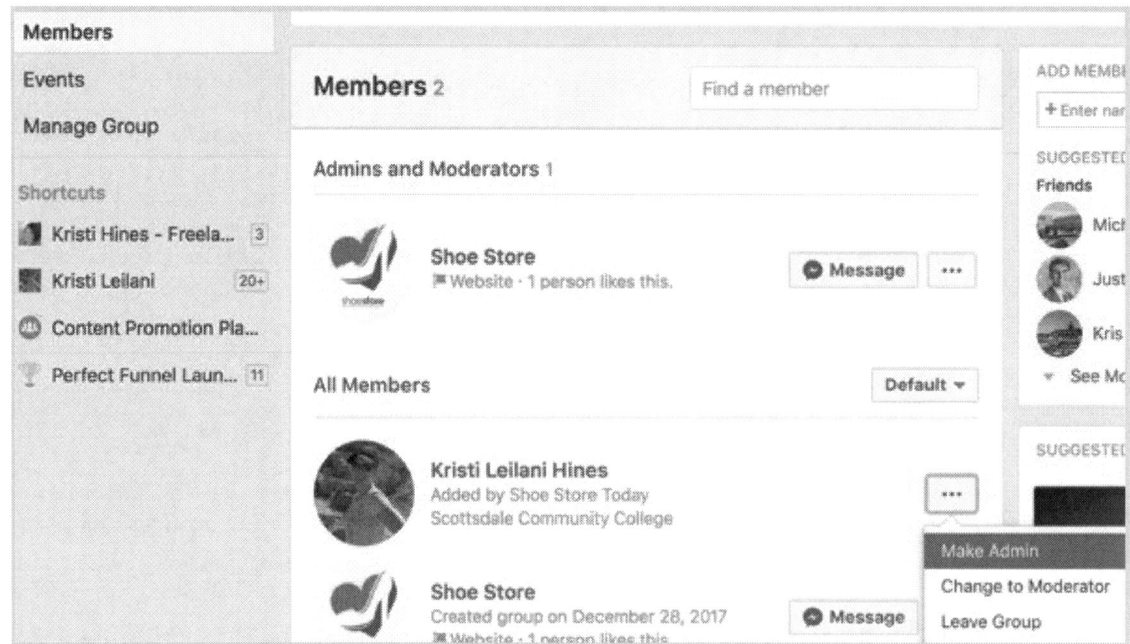

3. Add a cover photo.

Images make everything much more interesting. Personalize your Facebook Group by uploading a cover photo that best represents the group's personality.

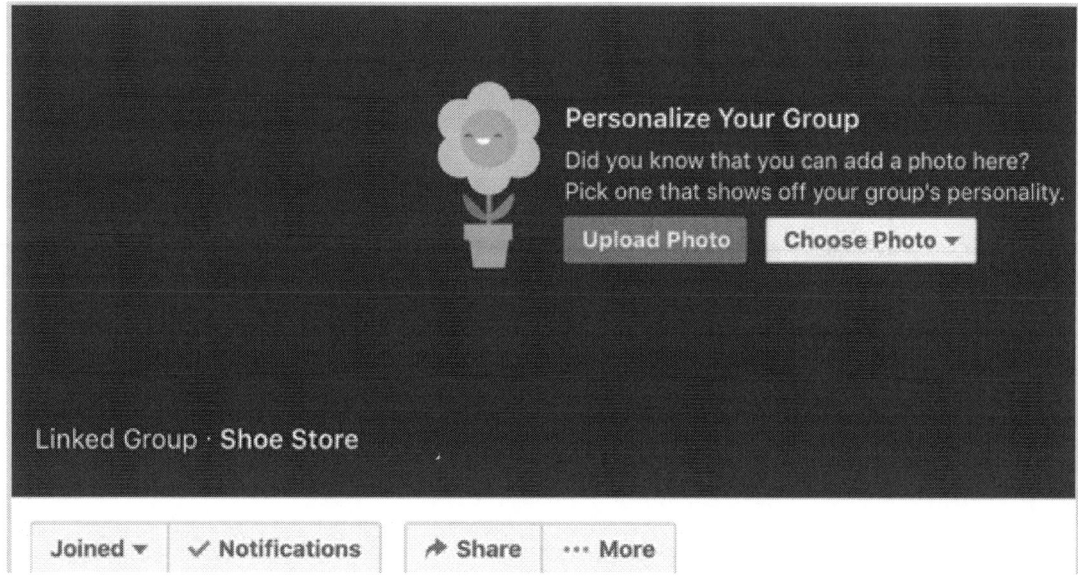

4. Edit your Group Settings.

Complete your Group's profile by adding a category, including a description, some tags, locations, and other important details.

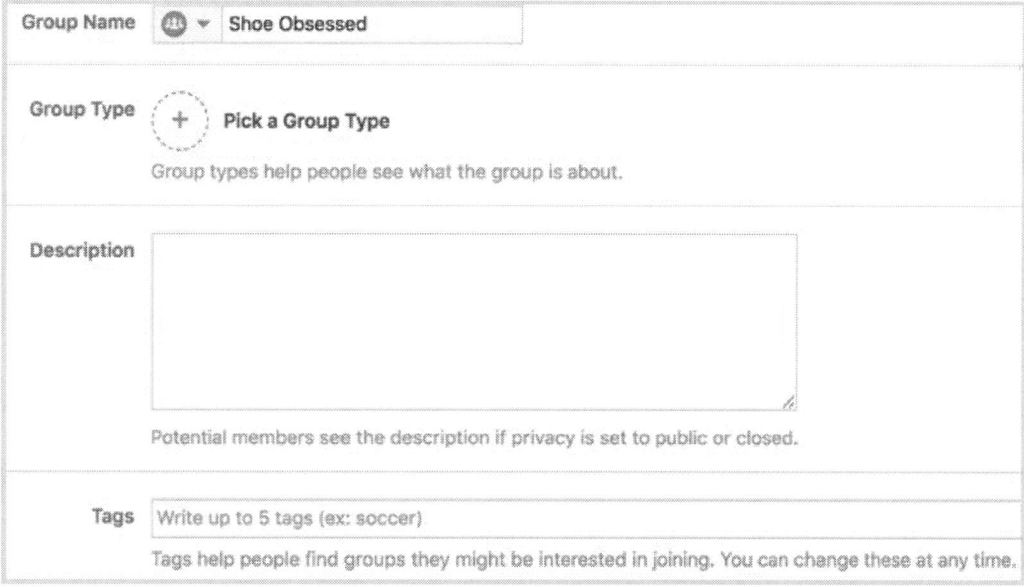

5. Promote your Group.

After making sure that your group profile is open and inviting, you have to start working on promoting it. To grow your community, the following strategies will help.

- Add your group's link in your correspondences with your current customers.

- Create a post about your group in all your social media accounts. Pin the post to the top of your Page so it's the first thing your visitors see. You can also tweet about it to get the word out.
- Consider boosting posts about your group.
- Invite more people who are possibly interested in the group. Make sure you customize the message of the invite.

6. Check out Group Insights.

You can learn much from Group Insights. This can be accessed from your Page. Click on Insights and Groups from the left sidebar. This will show you analytics data about your members, their demographics, comments, posts and reactions. Note however, that Group Insights only become available when you reach over 250 members so keep growing your numbers.

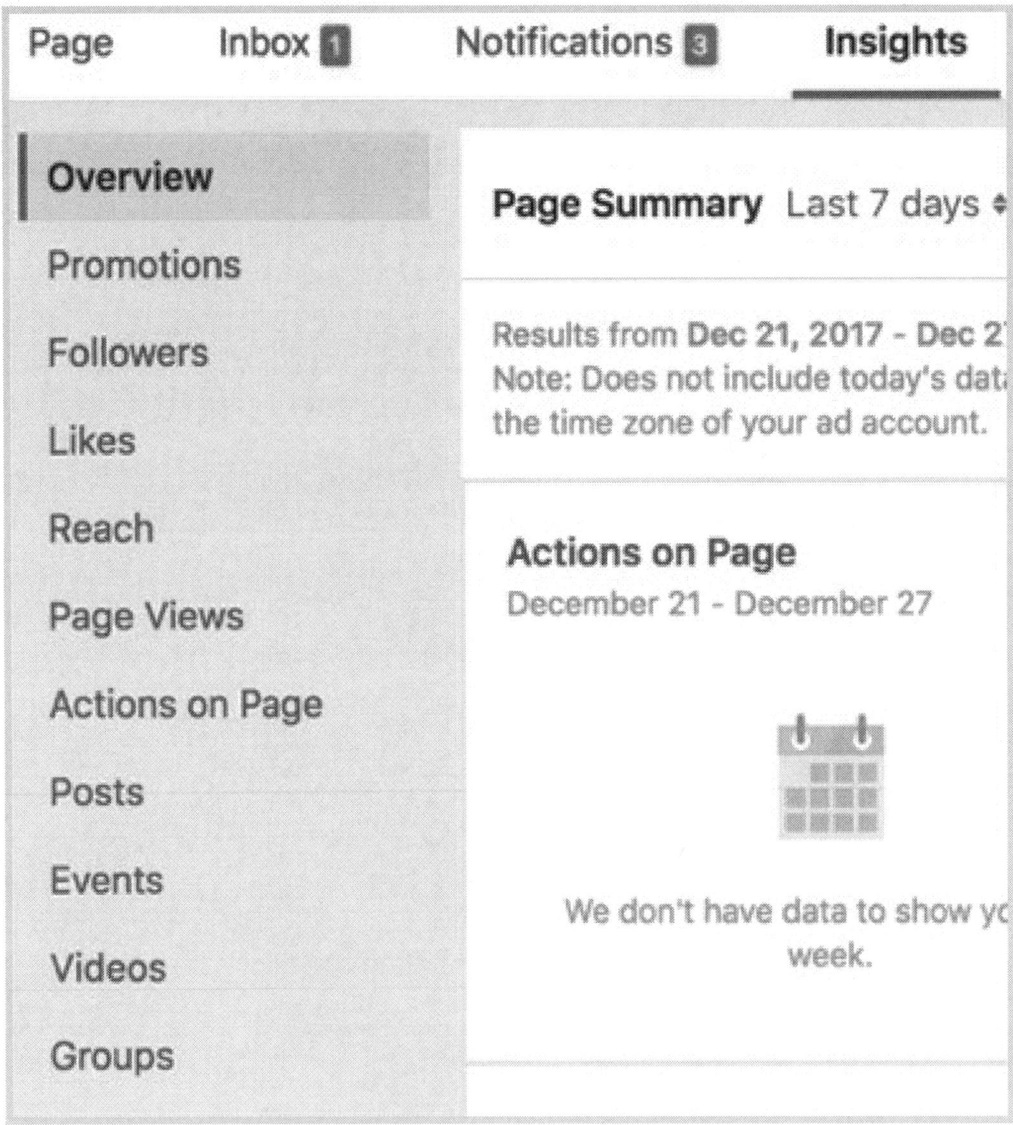

This is not just about collecting members for your group. It is extremely important that you keep them interested, engaged and active. Here are a few things you can do.

Regularly update your posts.

Continue generating new content that your members can discuss among themselves. Keep updating yourself about the hottest topics within your industry. Your members will appreciate your effort to keep them informed. Engage them by posting questions, surveys etc. Encourage them to add comments.

Share other content.

Don't be too self-centered. You will probably find other relevant articles worth sharing. Do not hesitate to do so. Stop selling and promoting all the time. Take a break from the sales pitch and become a genuine source of valuable information.

Explore other Facebook features.

You may also want to consider putting a face on the brand. And one of the best ways you can do this is through Facebook Live. Take the opportunity to showcase your products. You can also do Q&A or simply offer them an exclusive insight to any aspect of your business.

Keep trying different things. Through experience, you will be able to figure out what strategies work best for you. Test the waters and don't hold back. You may even want to use paid ads in order to grow your fan base.

What are Boosted Posts and Why You Should Take Advantage of Them

Facebook boosted post is one of the options you have to increase your organic reach. This feature is available to you as long as you have a business page. Taking advantage of this feature means you can get more people to see your post. However, boosted posts cost money.

If you are to spend money on anything, it is essential that you make sure the tool is worth it. Let's talk about the top benefits of boosting your posts.

- **Reach a wider and more targeted audience.**

You may be happy with the number of your page subscribers but its possible you can reach more. With boosted posts, you can reach people outside your subscriber list. You can also choose the parameters and the specific types of people you want to target. For instance, you can choose a specific demographic like a certain age group, ethnicity, education, religion etc.

- **They're quite easy to use.**

After clicking Boost Post and once Facebook has reviewed and approved the content, it will go live immediately. You can boost any type of post containing website links, videos, images or even short messages.

- **You have full control.**

When you choose to boost a post, you're not locked in. If you're not getting the results you were aiming for, you have the option to stop the boost or boost another in its place.

- **Evaluate the boosted post's performance.**

You have analytics tool at your disposal. Facebook Insights offer you a detailed summary of performance. You will be able to assess your boosted post according to the number of clicks and shares it's receiving, the extent of its reach, the quality of comments and reactions. If the boosted post is doing well and meeting your goals, you can apply the same tactic to other posts in your page.

What can you include in a Facebook boosted post?

The type of content you choose to boost is entirely up to you. You can boost a call to action, a promotion or an announcement. However, there are 3 major factors you have to consider when choosing the boosting feature.

1. Who is your audience?

Start with demographics when defining your target audience. How old are they? Where are they located? Are you targeting male or female audience or both? What are their interests?

Creating custom audiences based on your current contacts is also an option. You can create lookalike audiences that are based on the contacts who have already shown interest in your Page and posts.

2. What is your budget?

Your goals will dictate your budget. You have the freedom to spend as little or as much as you can to meet these goals. Your daily budget can be set to as low as $1. When setting low budgets, you need to adjust your expectations. If you do it properly, you can maximize your low budget. In which case, you need to plan accordingly and be as strategic as possible.

3. How long will you run it?

You can set a specific period when to run your boosted posts. You can run it for a day, a week etc. You can also turn it off manually.

How much does a boosted post actually cost?

Let's face it, there's only so much you can do for free. Especially when it comes to social media marketing, promotions cost money. How much should you expect to spend?

Unlike other social media ads, you're free to set your own budget with a boosted post. The bare minimum you can expect to spend is $1 a day. If we base it on the minimum, a boosted post with a $7 ad budget can run for as little as 7 days. Will you be able to get the results you're aiming for with this budget? The harsh truth is the more you pay the more people you can reach. The Facebook team will give you an idea about your estimated reach for any given budget.

Let's say your target audience are people above 18 years-old who are living in the United States. A $2 daily budget will allow you to reach anywhere between 163 to 872 people. If you increase it to about $5, you will probably be able to reach between 432 and 2,070 individuals. If you increase it further to $15, your estimated reach is 1,506 to about 6,834 people. The number is not set in stone. Demographics also affect the numbers.

You are encouraged to experiment with variables in order to get a better idea about your expected cost and the corresponding estimated reach. Once you get this information and the full price estimation, you can then make a final decision about your budget.

Creating a Facebook Boosted Post

Now that you have some basic info about boosted post, let's learn how to make them.

1. Choose which post to boost.

You can boost an existing post or create a new one. If you're in the process of creating a post, look for the Boost Post button found in the lower-right corner like in the image below.

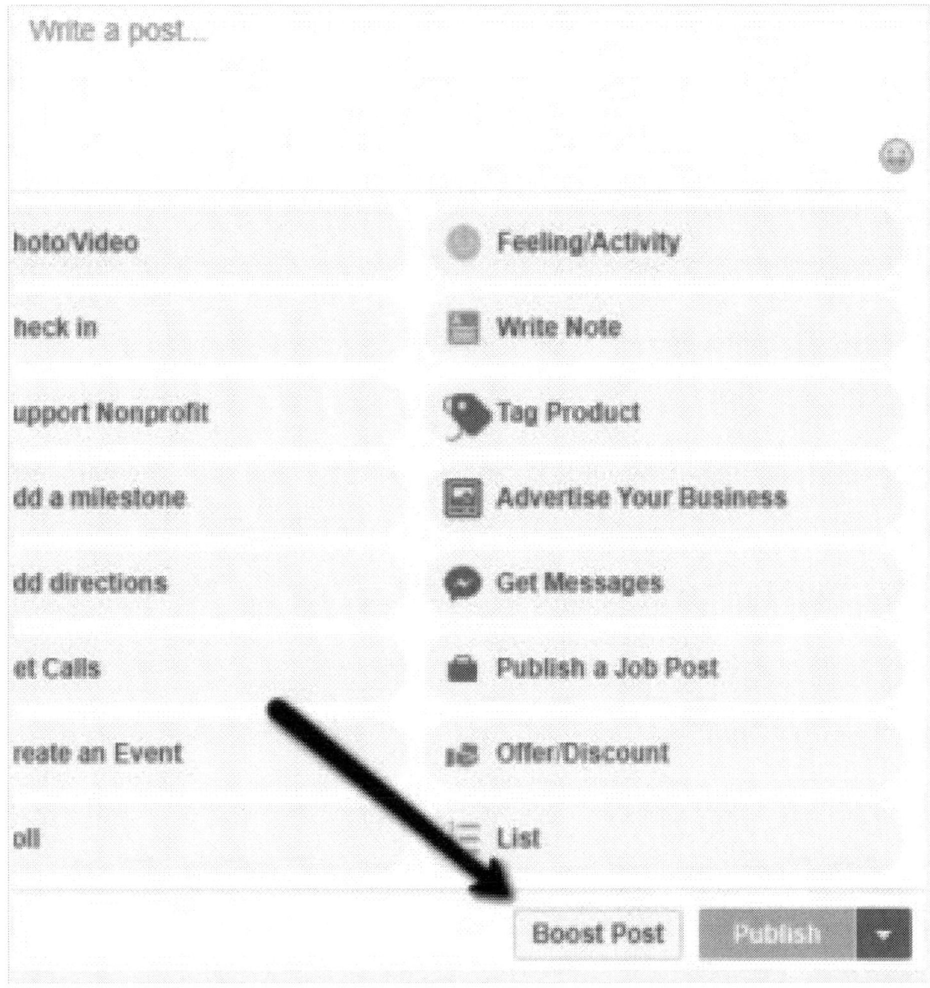

You can also go through all your previous posts and proceed to the Insights tab where you will see all of them. Each of the post will appear with a Boost Post option next to it.

2. Decide on your targeting options.

After selecting a post to boost, you will see a menu of targeting options. The default setting targets the people who are already following your Page. It may also include their friends and followers. You can be a little more specific by setting demographics for your target audience. You can create one or multiple custom audiences to target. To do this, start by clicking the option to **Create New Audience**.

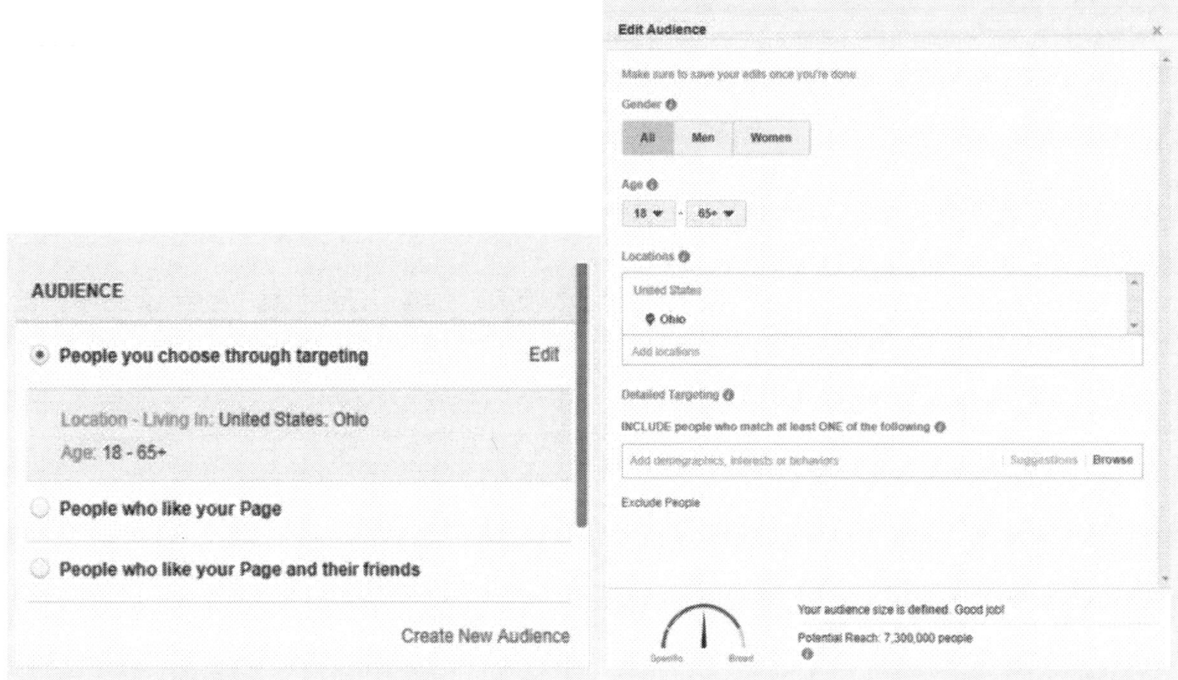

You will find several options that allow you to define your target audience further like setting the age range, adding, or deleting locations or including people interested in topics related to your Page or your posts.

3. Choose your budget.

The next step is to set your campaign budget. With your target audience defined, you will have a realistic estimated reach. You can adjust the reach according to how much money you're willing to spend or base your decision on how far you want to go with reach. As we mentioned before, the lowest you can set is $1 a day. You can choose to spread your budget by choosing the duration as well.

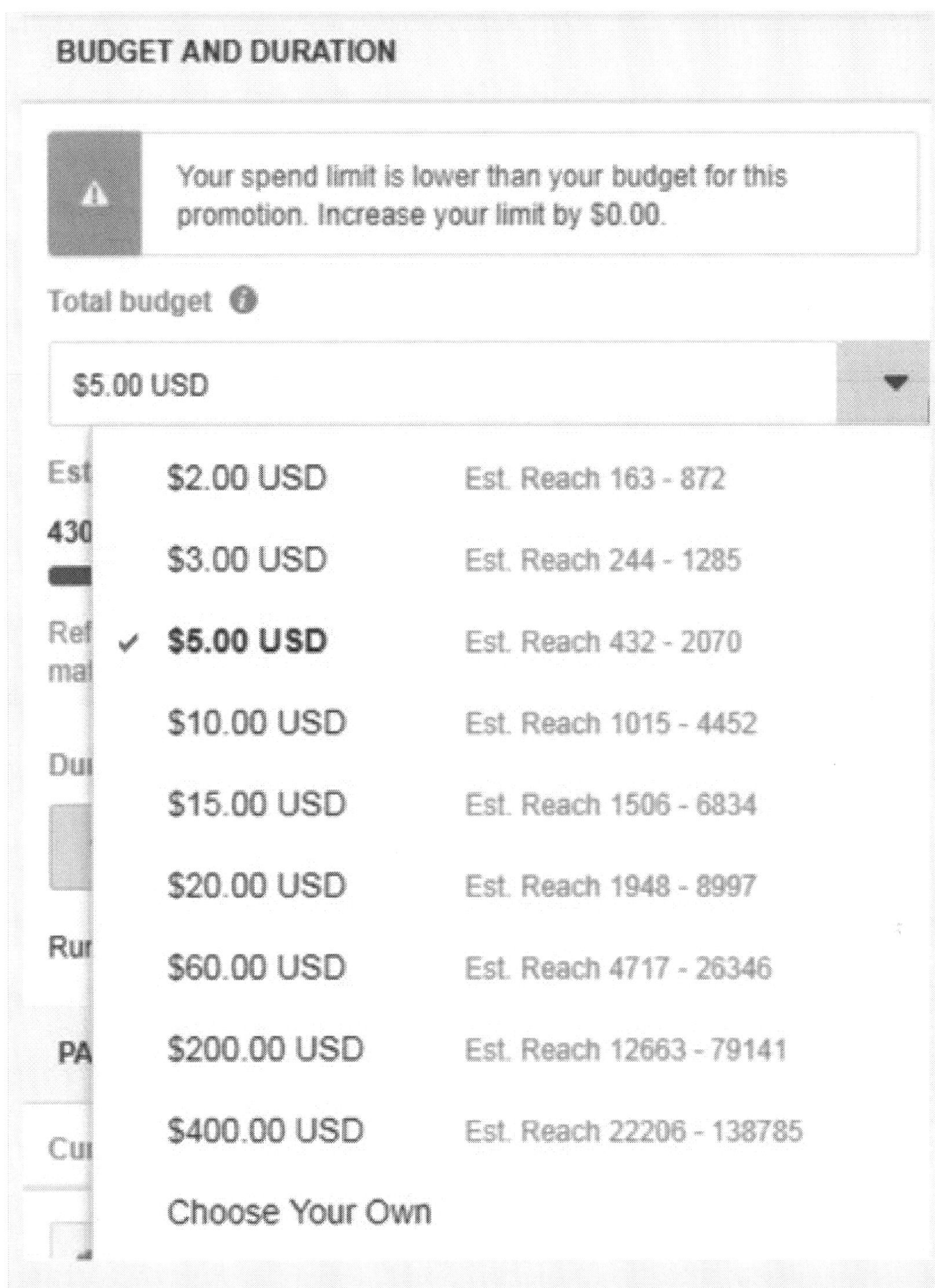

4. Set the duration.

You can choose from the default options: 1 day, 7 days or 14 days. At the bottom, you can also set the date if you have a specific one in mind. You have full control with regards to how long you want your boosted post to run.

5. Preview

After putting in the details of your campaign, it is important that you preview your post. Check the copy to make sure it looks the way you want it to. You're going to be spending money on it so it is important that it's error-free. Review the visual elements and check the links. Make sure they're working. You can still make changes at this point so go through it carefully.

6. Choose your payment option.

When you're satisfied with everything, you will be taken to a page where you select your preferred payment method. Here's how the section looks like.

Your post is ready for a boost! It will go through the review process. Once approved, Facebook will publish it. The process may take some time. You can review the status by checking it out in the Ads Manager. You will find the information in the Delivery column.

Chapter 2 Quiz

Please refer to the Answer Booklet for the solution to this quiz

1. What are 3 major factors you have to consider when choosing the boosting feature?

   A) Audience
   B) Duration
   C) Budget
   D) Social Media Accounts

2. This will show you analytics data about your group members, their demographics, comments, posts, and reactions.

   A) Audience Insights
   B) Members Insights
   C) Group Insights
   D) Group Data

3. Which of the following can help you promote your Group?

   A) Add your group's link in your correspondences with your current customers.
   B) Create a post about your group in all your social media accounts. Pin the post to the top of your Page so it's the first thing your visitors see. You can also tweet about it to get the word out.
   C) Consider boosting posts about your group
   D) Invite more people who are possibly interested in the group. Make sure you customize the message of the invite.

4. What are the benefits of having a Facebook Group?

   A) Provide ongoing updates, support and promotion to your audience who are already interested in your business and the products or services that you offer.
   B) Convert casual visitors to fans and/or paying customers
   C) Make sure you keep your current customers happy, maintain their business and encourage loyalty
   D) Always stay in touch with your business' or brand's customer base

5. You can use this section to either allow or restrict your page's followers to download your published videos.

   A) Content Distribution
   B) Video Distribution
   C) Member Distribution
   D) Exclusive Access

6. Comments can appear with the most recent ones first or the most relevant ones at the top. Use this setting to indicate your preference according to what will be more beneficial to your business or brand.

A) Post Ranking
B) Comment Ranking
C) Post Pinning
D) Comment Priority

7. By ticking this box, you allow Facebook to include your page in results of relevant searches. For instance, if you have a pet grooming business and a user searches for pet products, your page will appear as a relevant search.

    A) Same Page Result
    B) Similar Page Result
    C) Same Page Suggestions
    D) Similar Page Suggestions

8. If it's important for you to keep things clean, it would be wise to edit these settings. You can block certain comments that include words that you may consider offensive or inappropriate.

    A) Page Moderation
    B) Profanity Filter
    C) Age Restriction
    D) Page Updates

9. If you're selling or promoting age-sensitive products like tobacco and alcohol, it is necessary to prevent minors from accessing your page. Use this setting to restrict minor access to your page and posts.

    A) Page Moderation
    B) Profanity Filter
    C) Age Restriction
    D) Page Updates

10. In this section, you can set and choose to let visitors post, add photos and videos to the page. At the same time, you can review the content first to make sure no inappropriate content goes through.

    A) Guest Post
    B) Visitor Post
    C) Member Post
    D) Messages/Posts

Did You Know?

Fifty-eight percent of social media users said they follow brands through social media (MarketingSherpa):

- 95 percent aged 18-34 (Millennials) follow brands through social media .
- 92 percent of adults aged 34-44
- More women (61 percent) follow brands on social media than men (55 percent)

Chapter 3

Facebook Business Manager

Facebook business manager sounds fancy, but do you really need one? First of all, it is a free account. Its main objective is to help businesses, companies, or individuals in managing and organizing their Facebook Pages and other advertising accounts. It's an alternative to tying all of these work stuff to your personal Facebook account.

Remember we talked about using your personal profile log in to create your Facebook business page earlier? That in itself is an okay option. However, if you have several Pages under your name and you simply prefer not to connect your business Pages with all your friends, family, or co-workers on Facebook, you can use this free tool instead. Before we get into detail about creating one, let's take a look at the benefits, drawbacks, and some issues you should know.

Advantages of Having a Facebook Business Manager Account

Business Manager offers a solution to many pain points for businesses. Having one for yourself will allow you to reap the following benefits.

1. It helps prevent the mixing of your personal and professional profile.

A lot of people take advantage of their personal connections to get the word out about their business or brand. However, there are times when this can be an issue. Let's say you posted something on your page which you want to be strictly professional. In this case, you hope that it will be published on behalf of your business persona. However, it also gets displayed in your personal profile where it can be viewed by all your personal contacts.

If you use a Business Manager, on the other hand, you can make sure that a mix up like this never occurs between your personal and professional life. After creating a business manager account, you will see a visible grey at the upper portion of your page. This lets you know that you are currently working, posting, and acting on your professional profile.

2. It makes managing multiple accounts easier.

If you have several user accounts to manage, it is your best interest to create a business manager account. This will allow you to synchronize and manage your multiple accounts from one central place. It is also ideal if you're working with a team. It will allow you to assign different roles and responsibilities to each member. You can assign usage rights on the Page of the account.

3. It makes business interaction more professional.

Because you avoid any chance of mix up, you can maintain a professional image and limit adding accounts to those relevant to your business or brand. Through this, you can add and manage your business assets as well as communicate with other business entities. You can include your ad accounts, apps and product catalog pages and display them according to your target audience. If you’re in the advertising business with several clients, you can also add their Facebook pages and have full control over what they can and cannot access.

4. You can access additional functions.

There are simply more tools and functions that become available to you with a business manager account. For instance, if you have an app, you can add it to the developer's section. Your business manager account also includes one-pixel code. This will allow you to customize the settings according to the requirements of each ad accounts. Managing your product catalogs, linking other sources, adding product feeds, adding people and other business tasks become much simpler. Essentially, it makes your job easier.

To sum it up, here are the things you can do with a Facebook Business Manager account.

- Access Pages and ad accounts without sharing everything with your personal connections.
- Limit access to clients' Pages, ad accounts and other Facebook assets.
- Avoid sharing logins and prevents the need to change passwords for security purposes.
- Add or remove agencies and employees to the account with ease.
- Grant varying permission levels according to your business objectives.
- Manage several Pages and multiple ad accounts using a single Business Manager.
- Organize your Pages and accounts by grouping them into projects.
- Allows a more collaborative opportunity among team members.

Overall, it leads to a better and more efficient management of all your Pages and ad accounts.

Disadvantages of a Facebook Business Manager Account

We can't deny the many opportunities a business manager account opens up. However, the platform is not perfect. There are downsides to using one as well. Among them are the following.

1. There is a risk of bugs.

It doesn't happen all the time but it has happened before and you should prepare yourself to the risk of a bug incident happening. In the past, people reported bugs (or malfunction) and in the worst cases, have lost their accounts. There have also been reports and complaints about their admin rights changing without prior information. If this happens to you, you could lose pertinent business information.

It is worth mentioning that most of these incidences occurred at the early phases of introduction i.e. the beta testing phase. Facebook has probably made necessary changes to prevent such cases from happening in the future. Be that as it may, it is still a risk for your business and is something worth considering and preparing for.

2. It takes time to get used to the platform.

Migrating from a personal account to a business manager account is a big change. There is a huge difference in the process which means it will take some time to learn. One of the major differences is that unlike a personal account where you can schedule posts before your preferred launch date, a business manager account does not offer the same option. Things have to be done in real-time which may result in extra manual work for you especially if you're handling multiple clients.

If you're doing social media marketing, chances are you're not only using Facebook. You probably have several social media handles. Managing them all can be quite challenging. On Facebook, you are allowed to publish them on your multiple pages. However, you may not be able to publish them on selective groups.

This may mean you will have to incorporate various tools in your media strategy combining the use of Facebook business manager, page posts and power editor. It's not an impossible feat but it is a complex process that increases the risk of making mistakes.

3. Information is limited.

One of the best reasons why a lot of people have had success with Facebook marketing is that they can laser target consumers from different categories. They can group their target audience according to demographics, educational level, purchasing power, etc. Whether or not the same option is available for Business manager account holders is unclear.

4. It doesn't operate like a personal profile.

If you're used to using your personal profile for your business, you may find moving to a business manager account beneficial but also limiting. There are a lot of tasks and tools that may not be available to marketers such as scheduling posts.

Is a Facebook Business Manager account necessary?

With all these said, it is still important to note that each personal user account is only allowed to link to one advertising account. A business manager account eliminates that problem which is a significant advantage. Not only will you be able to link multiple accounts, you are also able to link to different time zones and corresponding currencies. There is a limit to the number of accounts but with Facebook's permission, the limit may be increased.

If you are handling multiple ad accounts anyway, it may be a better option to set up a business manager account. Having one will allow you to work more efficiently.

What do you need to set up a Business Manager account?

One of the prerequisites of a Business Manager account is a page. The Facebook page should be about the business you are promoting. In addition, you need to link it to your FB account. Facebook uses it as reference for verification purposes and for security reasons.

Two Layer Permission

The Business Manager account does offer more security for businesses. It offers a two-layer permission model which allows you to securely maintain and manage your Pages, ad accounts and catalogs.

The first layer of security allows you to add people to the account either as admins or employees. Team member who are assigned as admins have full control of all the aspects of the account. This means they can modify the business or delete it. They can also remove people who are in the employee list. On the other hand, business employees may be able to view business data settings. However, they are not able to make changes unless they are given the role of Finance Editor.

The second layer of security grants agencies or partners the ability to manage your business assets including business accounts and Pages. The Page and ad account can only be handled by one Business Manager at a time. However, there can be multiple individual accounts and partners who can post, manage, and access ads on its behalf. The shared permission may be changed at any time.

There are various things you can do in a Business Manager account. Such tasks and privileges include the following.

1. Assign roles to people.

Different roles with varying degrees can be assigned to partners, agencies or employees. For security reasons, you are strongly advised to limit access. As much as possible, keep access to a minimum while allowing them to fulfill their roles.

Admins versus Employees

There are two roles available in the account for businesses. These are admins and employees. Let's look at what each can do.

Admins can...

- Add or delete employees or partners
- View the settings and change them
- Manage permissions given to employees
- Add ad accounts, Pages and assets
- Handle ad accounts, Pages and assets assigned to them

Employees can...

- View business settings
- Handle ad accounts, Pages and assets assigned to them by admins
- Can apply changes to business settings ONLY when admins assign them as Finance Editor

Admin versus Advertiser versus Analyst

There are 3 roles to assign for ad accounts. Their roles, responsibilities and access are as follows.

Admin can...

- Manage the settings on ad account
- Add people and delegate ad account roles to them
- Create ads and edit them
- Edit the source of funding
- View the adds
- Access reports

Advertiser can...

- Create ads and edit them

- View the adds
- Access reports

Analyst can...

- View the adds
- Access reports

Admin versus Editor versus Moderator versus Advertiser versus Analyst

There are several roles that are available for Pages.

Admin can...

- Manage and control roles and settings
- Edit Page
- Add apps
- Create and remove posts
- Send messages in behalf of the Page
- Respond to and remove comments
- Delete and ban users from the Page
- Create Page ads
- View Insights

Editor can...

- Edit Page
- Add apps
- Create and remove posts
- Send messages in behalf of the Page
- Respond to and remove comments
- Delete and ban users from the Page
- Create Page ads
- View Insights

Moderator can...

- Send messages in behalf of the Page
- Respond to and remove comments
- Delete and ban users from the Page
- Create Page ads
- View Insights

Advertiser can...

- Create Page ads

- View Insights

Analyst can...

- View Insights

Catalog Admin versus Catalog Advertiser

These are the two roles that can be assigned for catalogs in a Business Manager account. Each role's responsibilities include the following.

Catalog admin can...

- Add people and give them catalog roles
- Share the catalog with agencies and partners
- Choose a product set or catalog to create an ad for
- Preview the ads for a product set
- View and choose catalogs, catalog settings, events in the Catalog Manager section
- View and remove data feeds and product sets in the Catalog Manager section
- Link a pixel or an app to a specific catalog

Catalog advertiser can...

- Choose a product set or catalog to create an ad for
- Preview the ads for a product set
- View data feeds
- View and choose catalogs, catalog settings and events
- View and remove product sets in the Catalog Manager section

Finance Editor versus Finance Analyst

For finance management, these are the two roles available. While a Finance analyst can only view details, the Finance Analyst can both view and edit the following.

- Credit card information
- Contact information and financial details
- Invoices or transaction information
- Invoice Groups
- Details about account spending
- Payment methods

2. Manage people, ad accounts, assets, settings, apps and video.

In a single account, you can organize everything your business requires on Facebook. This is why the Business Manager is referred to as the best management tool on the platform. You can edit, control and manage all these things under the Accounts section of your Business Manager.

People

You can add, remove and assign roles to people using the account. Here are some of the things you can do as far as people are concerned.

- **Add individuals.**

Note that you can definitely add an agency or a partner. But in order to add individuals you can go to the Business settings, choose People and click the option to Add. Use the email address of the people you want to add to the account and choose the role to assign them. They will get an email about the invite. As soon as they accept the invite, you can assign them roles to ad accounts, Pages and other assets or even to the Creative Hub project.

- **Add an agency or a partner.**

You will find the option to add a Partner from the Business Settings. After selecting the business role and access to the Partner, Facebook will automatically generate a link and send it to the partner. This link must be opened within 30 days. Otherwise, it will expire.

- **Accept invitation for Business Manager.**

Facebook sends the invite. When you receive it, you must sign in with your personal account. This is for identity verification. Facebook will match your FB identity with your work email address. To accept or decline the request, you can go to Business Setting and choose Request.

- **Delete people from the account.**

With a business manager account, you can also remove people that you have previously added. This is useful when someone leaves the team whether an admin or an employee, you can immediately take action and remove their access.

- **Assign assets to people.**

To assign people to assets, you can go to Business Settings and click People under the Users section. Choose the person you want to assign to the asset and click on Assign Assets. You can assign them roles in the Catalogs, Ad accounts or Pages.

- **Make changes to people's roles.**

Aside from assigning roles, you also have the freedom to edit those assignments. Select the name of the person and choose Update Person.

- **Remove yourself from the account.**

Not only will you be able to add and remove people or update their roles, you can also remove yourself from the business. To do this, proceed to the Business Settings section and choose Business Info. If you scroll down, you will find My Info and the option to Leave Business.

Ad Accounts

A newly opened business account is allowed to create one ad account. Upon activation of the ad account through active spending, a business will be able to host as many as 5 separate ad accounts. As of yet, this is the limit that Facebook sets. There are three ways to create an ad account under Business Manager.

Once added, the account will be permanently under Business Manager. You won't be able to transfer it to an individual owner. Here's how it's done.

- Proceed to Business Settings.
- Next, choose Accounts and click Ad Accounts.
- Select Add and choose any of the following options: Create a new Ad Account, Add Ad Account or Request Access to an Ad Account.
- Create new ad account when you're starting from scratch.
- Add an ad account when you have an existing ad account and want to move it to Business Manager. To be able to do this, you must meet the following requirements: be the owner of the account and be the admin in Business Manager. As with creating a new ad account, the existing account will permanently belong to Business Manager once moved.
  After successfully adding it, all management actions will be made within the Business Manager profile. You will not be able to add an account that is owned by another person or another Business Manager. However, if you need access to work on the account, you can choose the third option.
- Request access to an ad account when the account is not under your name and you are not an admin to the Business Manager. When the request is granted however, the admin can grant you access or permission to do work on the said account.

The current limit is 5 ad accounts for every Business Manager. There is no option yet to delete an existing ad account. Deactivating it is an option. However, you will not be able to add a new one in place of the deactivated account. It will still be counted as one of the 5 ad accounts you're allowed to create.

To add an existing ad account or request access to one belonging to another Business Manager, you can simply enter the account ID. Facebook will generate it for you.

Why can't I add an ad account?

There may be some instances when you are unable to add one. It could happen because of any of the following reasons:

- The ad account may already be under another business listing. It can only be owned by a single Business Manager.
- A personal ad account has already been added to Business Manager.
- Only one ad account from your personal FB account can be moved to Business Manager.
- You have already reached the limit for adding new accounts to the business although it may be possible for you to adjust the limit if your advertising spending is increased.

If you are unable to add an account you still need to work on, keep in mind that you have 2 other options which are to request access to the existing account or create a new one except when the limit has already been reached.

Delete an account audience.

You may not be able to delete the ad account itself. However, you can remove the ad account audience. If you want to do this, follow the below steps.

- Go to Business Settings.
- Choose Audiences.
- Pick the audience you want to edit.
- Go to Actions.
- Click on the Delete option.
- Choose Delete Audience for permanent removal.

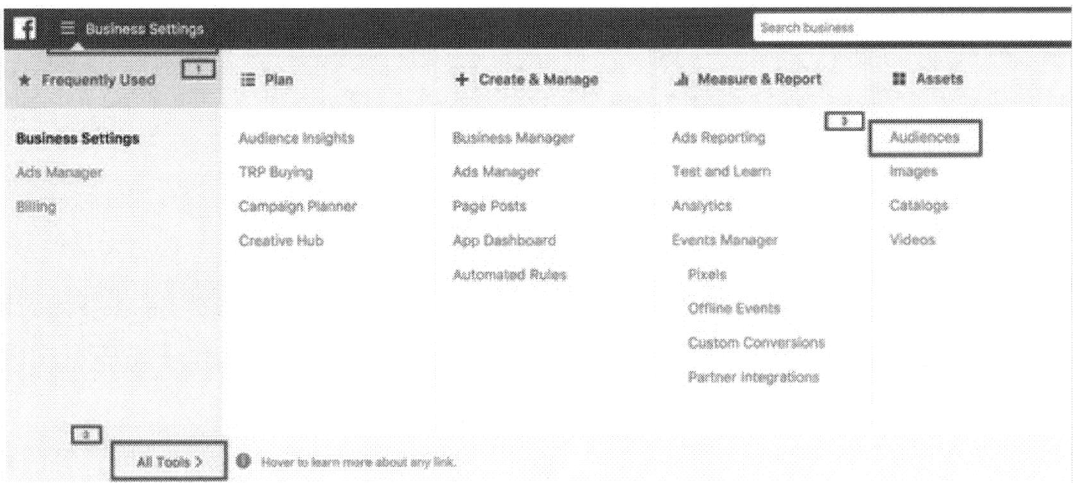

Deactivate an ad account.

Again, you can only deactivate an account not delete them in Business Manager. To do this, proceed to Business Settings and choose Ad Accounts. Pick the ad account you want to edit and click the option to Deactivate.

Control Settings

There are four major things you can do in the Settings page and they are as follows:

- **Change the primary Page.**

You can set the primary Page and edit it at a later time. To start with, proceed to Business Settings. Go to Business Info and choose the option to Edit. Pick a page and Save.

- **Locate a Business ID.**

This is one of the important pieces of information you should know how to access. To find your ID number, Choose Business Info in the Business Settings section. You will find your ID under Business Manager Info.

- **Update your work email address or edit name in Business Manager**

To make changes to your information, access the Business Info section. From there, select the Edit option which you can find under My Info section. Change what you need to update and Save the changes. Facebook will automatically send you an email about the requested change. You will need to verify that the actions were initiated by yourself. Choose Verify Now in the confirmation email to proceed.

- **Adjust the Notifications.**

From Business Settings, go to the Notifications section. There you will find a list of options from the dropdown menu. Adjust it as you prefer.

Apps

In addition to adding ad accounts, you can also add apps to Business Manager. To do this, go to Accounts under Business Settings. Choose Apps. You will find an option to Add New App in this section. You will be given two options. One is to add a completely new one and the other is to request access to an already existing app. In the second option, locate the app by entering the Facebook App ID. If Facebook doesn't allow you to add it, it's likely it has already been added by a Business Manager.

Videos

You can control videos, access to it and actions done by other people.

- **Allow crossposting of videos.**

Remember what we emphasized earlier about the downside of Business Manager? Ads won't be able to run or get boosted unless you publish it manually from your Page settings. To do it the Business Manager way, you can follow the below steps.

  - Access the Page to be published.
  - Choose the Settings Tab.
  - Click on General.
  - Choose Edit from Page Visibility.
  - Select Page Published.

You can save it after making your desired changes.

- **Crosspost videos from a Page that isn't owned by Business Manager.**

Pages that are not under your Business Manager can also be granted permission to crosspost your videos. Before this is possible however, both parties are required to give permission. Follow these steps.

  - Proceed to your Page.
  - Access Settings tab.
  - Select Crossposting.
  - Find the Page by typing the name in the search field or enter the URL corresponding to the Page.
  - Select the Page to add it. The Page you're trying to add also needs to take similar steps. To make the process easier, include your Page to their settings. Choose Link and a dialog box will appear

containing a URL. Copy and share it with the admins of the other Page. This way, the Page admins can access the link which will automatically take them to their Crossposted Videos settings.

After permission from both parties are secured, you can choose specific videos for crossposting. The selected videos will appear in the Page's Video Library and listed in the **Videos You Can Crosspost** section.

- **View Insights.**

In Business Manager, you can also access the Insights for your videos which are crossposted. To access this info, choose Publishing Tools from your business Page. Go to Video Library. Select from the list of videos and you will be able to access the data you're seeking.

System Users

It is important to note that access to System Users is not available for all businesses. For others, this option may not be available. To add a new one, you can start with the following steps.

- Access Business Settings.
- Click on Systems Users.
- Select the option to Add New System User.
- Name the user and choose Create System User.
- Assign assets and corresponding roles to the new system user.
- Generate a new token. One token will be assigned to every new system user so you will have to generate a new one every time you add a new user. You will find the option from the right side of your Page. Copy and save the info.

Instagram

You don't really need a Business Manager account to run Instagram ads. You can do it on a business page. What makes a business manager account great for Instagram ads is that it allows you to review, as well as, answer to comments on the ads. Like we mentioned before, engagement with the audience is crucial in making social media advertising work.

If you have an existing Instagram account, you can link it to your ad account through Business Manager. For this to be possible, you must have both the ad account and Instagram account under the *same* Business Manager to associate the two. Unlike with pages, you can't request access to an Instagram handle that belongs to another Business Manager. It has to be your own. Follow the below steps to link your accounts.

- Access your Business Manager and go to Settings.

- Choose Instagram Accounts and select the one you want to connect to an ad account.
- Choose the option to Assign Ad Accounts.
- You can also grant authorization to multiple ad accounts to access and use the Instagram account. To do this, check the box beside the ad accounts before clicking on Save Changes.

Projects

Another way of organizing your Pages and ad accounts is through Projects. With this option, you can assign ad accounts and Pages to your team. If for instance, your business operates and is organized through various locations, you will find it easier to group and assign your team using Projects. To access this feature, you can follow these steps.

- Go to Business Settings.
- Look for Projects. This will be found in Accounts section.
- Create New Project.
- Name it. Click on Next.
- Check on the Pages you want to include in this newly created project and choose Next.
- Check on the ad accounts you want to include in the project and choose Next.
- Click on Save Changes.

3. Manage Your Data Sources

These include: Catalogs, Pixels, Event Source Groups, Offline Event Sets, Custom Conversions and Shared Audiences

Under the Data Sources of your Business Settings, you will find all these options. You can set them up according to your brand or business needs. Let's go over them one by one and look into how they can be useful.

Catalogs

Organization is key in managing a business. In this section, you can add a new product catalogue, add an existing catalog to your product feed or request access to another catalog.

How to add a new product catalog?

- Go to Business Settings.
- From Data Sources, go to Catalogs.
- Click on the option to **Add New Catalog** and **Create a New Product Catalog**
- Name it. Choose which products to include. Click on **Create Catalog**.
- Choose people to manage the catalog. Click on Save Changes.

You also have the option to assign management roles to your team. You can skip this step if you prefer not to add anyone else.

In addition, you can also link apps and any pixels to your product catalog. All you need to do is tick the boxes next to available apps and pixels. If you don't have any yet, you may add them later and Skip the step in the meantime.

How to add an existing catalog to product feed?

- Select the catalog and click on the option to Add Product feed.
- Enter your name and select the corresponding currency.
- Pick an upload type for the feed.

You can set it up for either Single Upload or Schedule Recurring Uploads.

Single Upload - You will have to manually do the uploading. Every time you make changes to the file, a manual one-time upload will be necessary.

Schedule Recurring Uploads - You can select your preferred intervals for automatic uploading.

After making your choice, proceed to creating the feed by completing the required information. File uploads have to follow the instructions so they can be uploaded correctly.

Column Name	Instructions
id	Type in a unique ID for each item. Note that this will show as "retailer_id" after the product is imported.
availability	Mark if the item's in stock. You can type: "in stock", "available for order", "preorder", "out of stock", or "discontinued". Max 100 characters.
condition	You can type "new", "refurbished", or "used".
description	A short paragraph describing the item. Max 5000 characters.
image_link	Link to item image used in ad. See image resolution guidelines.
link	Link to merchant's site where you can buy the item.
title	Item title. Max 100 characters.
price	Item cost and currency using ISO 4217 currency codes. Ex: 9.99 USD.
sale_price	Discounted price if the item is on sale. Currency should be specified as the ISO 4217 currency code. Required for creative overlays. Ex. 4.99 USD.
sale_price_effective_date	Start and end date and time for the sale, separated by a slash. Required for creative overlays. Ex: 2017-11-01T12:00-0300/2017-12-01T00:00-0300.
gtin, mpn, or brand	GTIN: Global Trade Item Number (UPC, EAN, JAN,ISBN). Mpn - A unique number that identifies a product to its manufacturer. Brand: brand name. Max 70 characters.

- Your file must be saved using a TSV or CSV format. Using 3rd party feed provider is also allowed. In which case, you can use the following file formats: RSS XML, ATOM XML, compressed zip, gzip or bz2 file.

- Choose Next and complete your catalog.

How to request access to a catalog?
- Go to Business Settings.
- Go to Catalogs which you will find under the Data Sources section.
- Choose the option to Add New Catalog.
- Click Request Access to a Catalog.

Pixels

You need to know whether your advertising efforts are effective or not. Facebook has an analytics tool that measures the effectiveness of your ads. It's called the Pixel. With this tool, you will be able to understand how people respond to your ads and posts through their actions on your website. We'll discuss this in more detail in the coming chapter about Events Manager.

Once you have a pixel set up, you can manage and share it in your Business Manager. An admin can grant access to other team members by adding them. People can also be added through a specific ad account.

Unless a person is a Business Manager Admin, team members will have to be added manually to be able to access pixel. A person who is part of the business with no access to any of the ad accounts in the business will have to be added. Otherwise, that person may have access to ad account but none to the pixels associated with the ad account. Only a Business Manager admin can both view and edit a Facebook pixel. Access to a specific pixel associated to an ad account can be granted by requesting access to the account itself.

How to add people to your Facebook Pixel?

To add an individual or a specific ad account to your Facebook Pixel, you can follow these steps.

- Access Business Settings.
- Go to **People and Assets** section.
- Click on **Pixels**.
- Select one to assign someone to.
- Choose **Add People** to assign a person to a specific pixel or **Assign Ad Accounts** if you want to assign all the people who has access to an ad account to the pixel.
- Select the preferred access.

  Add People - You can choose the people and assign them roles which you will find in the dropdown menu.

  Assign Ad Accounts - You have to select the account to be assigned to your pixel.

- If you have completed the necessary changes, click on Save Changes.

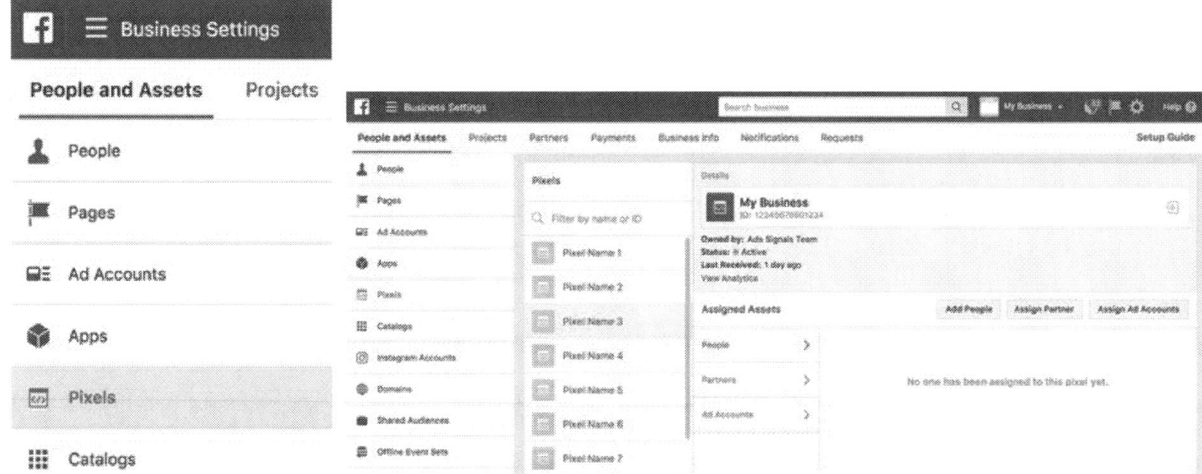

What roles can you assign to people on your Facebook Pixel?

As a Business Manager Admin, you can specify roles and select people for them. When another admin from a different Business Manager gives you access to their pixel, they can also choose to assign you roles. There are two roles available: Pixel Editor and Pixel Analyst.

Pixel Editor - This person will be able to view pixel information and apply changes as well. Editors are also able to create audiences. In addition, they can use the pixel to create conversion ads. In other words, editors can do as much as admins can except the latter is the only one who can add and remove people from pixel or change their previously assigned roles.

Pixel Analyst - This person will have access to the Facebook Pixel but only for viewing purposes. Unlike admins and editors, analysts won't be able to edit the pixel. They are also unable to create conversion ads or audiences.

Event Source Groups

Every action that are taken by people on your website are recorded as an event in Facebook Analytics. All information is received in the event source. A combination of these is referred to as ESG or Event Source Groups. Through Business Manager and by being an admin, you can create and manage your ESG.

How to create an Event Source Group?

- Proceed to Business Settings.
- Go to **Data Sources** and choose **Event Source Groups**.
- Click on the option **Create Event Source Groups**.
- Enter a name for the group.
- Pick out the data sources to include in the group. Among the choices are **Offline Data Set, Facebook Pixel** and **Mobile App**.
- Wait for the confirmation and click Close.

How to remove event source groups?

- Access Business Manager Settings.
- Choose any of the following: **Pages, Pixels** or **Apps**.
- Select the event source you want to remove and click on the X mark at the right side section.
- Choose the option to Remove and confirm the action to delete the event source.

You can also edit permissions to grant access to other Analytics users in the team. They can view the event source group. You can also assign different roles to people. The roles available are Analyst and Limited Analyst.

An Analyst can...

- View and explore event source group data except monetary data
- View as well as explore ESG monetary data
- Create charts and dashboards and save changes

Limited Analyst can...

- View and explore event source group data except monetary data

How to assign roles to people?

- Access Business Settings.
- Go to **Event Source Groups** and choose the one you want to assign people to.
- Click on the option to **Add People**.
- Choose the users from the team you want to assign to the ESG and specify their roles.
- Save the changes.

When users are assigned to an event source group, they will be able to access the data within the event sources. Admins automatically get access to the ESG as Analysts. As an admin yourself, you can change this default setting.

Offline Event Sets

We've talked about how actions taken on a website are tracked and recorded. To make your online ad efforts more inclusive as far as results are concerned, Facebook also allows you to monitor and measure actions taken offline in response to your Facebook ad campaign.

By default, an event set may be automatically created as well as assigned to an ad account. You can access details about it in Events Manager. We'll go into more detail about creating and uploading offline event sets in the coming chapters.

In your Business Manager, you can manage permissions for your existing sets. Data about an offline event can be uploaded by specific users only. This privilege is limited to the following roles.

- Admins of the Business Manager
- Employees who are assigned as Offline Event Set admins
- Business Manager system user

*Offline event set admin roles can be edited or assigned in the Business Settings.

How to add admin to an event set or share it to another business?

- Access Business Settings.
- Go to **Offline Event Sets**
- Choose the set and click on **Add People** if you intend on assigning an admin role to one of your team members.
- Click on **Assign Partner** if you want to share access to an event set with another business. And enter the corresponding **Business ID**

Custom Conversions

Instead of adding conversion pixels to your individual success pages, you can track as well as optimize conversions by using Custom Conversions. In other words, Custom Conversions can make tasks simpler. It can eliminate the need for manually adding codes to your site.

You can create Custom Conversions by accessing Ads manager. You can also edit or remove Custom Conversions through your Business Manager.

How to edit details on your custom conversions in Business Manager?

You can change the name, description as well as the conversion value of custom conversions. To change any of these, you can follow these steps.

- Access your Business Manager.
- Go to the main dropdown which can be found in the upper left section.
- From the **Measure & Report** option, click on **Custom Conversions**.
- Choose which one you want to edit.
- From the dropdown menu, choose **Actions**.
- Click on the option to **Edit Custom Conversion**.
- Apply your changes and choose **Done**.

How to remove your custom conversions?

Before deleting your custom conversions, you can avoid issues with your custom conversion event by changing the way the ad sets are optimized first.

- Access your Business Manager.
- Go to **Custom Conversions** which you will find under the **Measure & Report** section.
- Choose which one you want to delete.
- Click on **Actions**.
- Choose the option to **Delete Custom Conversion**.
- Confirm the action by clicking on **Delete**.

Shared Audiences

After creating audiences for your ads, you can grant access to it to other people. This is called Shared Audiences. It is possible to bulk share Lookalike and Custom Audiences between ad accounts as well as between media agencies provided that the one sharing and receiving are both associated to the same Business Manager. As long as the sharer allows it, the receiver can access insights and use it for targeting strategies and creative planning.

There are a couple of limitations including the following.

- Shared Audiences cannot be used for creating Lookalike Audiences.
- When you're utilizing a particular shared audience for one of your ad sets and the one who owns the audience deletes it, the ad set that you own will become inactive.
You will have to set a target audience for your ad set.
- Saved Audiences cannot be shared.
- Audiences cannot be sold to other businesses.

How to share an audience?

You can share your audiences with your team or other businesses but you can also choose to prevent other people from accessing Insights about these shared audiences. Choose the levels of permissions to assign to people you're sharing your audiences with.

Access can be granted either for **Targeting Only** or for both **Targeting** and **Insights**.

- Access **Audiences**.
- Click on the boxes for the audiences you intend on sharing.
- Go to the dropdown menu for **Actions**.
- Choose Share.
- Choose or enter the names or ad account IDs you want to share your audiences with.

- From the Permission dropdown menu, decide whether you want to share the audience with either **Targeting Only** or **Targeting and Insights** access.
- Choose Share.

How to view all shared audiences across your business?

- Access **Business Manager**
- Go to **Business Settings**
- Choose **Shared Audiences**

Brand Safety Domains and Block Lists

To preserve content integrity and ensure that only the verified owners are allowed to edit their content and the way it is presented, Facebook has created domain verification. Verified domain owners can overwrite link metadata as an added functionality when they create link page posts. This is an essential free feature that business owners and marketers can take advantage of in order to ensure content security.

What exactly is Domain Verification?

This is among the many features of Business Manager. It provides businesses with a simple way of showing domain ownership without making it necessary for them to edit Open Graph markup tags. Through Business Manager, you can also assign verified domains to your Pages or share your domains with partners. In other words, domain verification allows you to safeguard the integrity of your content and prevent misrepresentation of your brand.

When you verify your domain, you are staking claim to your links and contents. This way, you remain in control and on top of every post, ad or any type of content you put in Facebook.

How to verify domain in Business Manager?

There are two verification methods available in Business Manager. These are DNS TXT record and HTML file upload. You can use either of these methods as part of a streamlined approach. By using these methods, you won't have to manually edit your website's HTML metadata.

What if domain has not been verified?

In an effort to ensure that rightful parties only have the privilege of editing link previews associated to content and reduce the risk of misrepresentation, Facebook encourages businesses and marketers to use domain verification. And as of May 2018, only verified domains are allowed to edit their organic Page post links as well as their unpublished Page post links. If your domain has not been verified yet, you won't have access to this editing privilege.

In addition to domain verification, Facebook also offers other brand safety tools. These tools will allow you to block your content from running with certain kinds of content found within **In-Stream Video, Audience Network** and **Instant Articles** placements.

These brand safety tools include the following.

1. Placement Opt-Out - With this safety tool you can choose to opt-out and prevent your ads from showing in **In-Stream Video, Audience Network** and **Instant Articles** placements.

You can do this by removing these placements in the **ad create flow** under **Edit Placement** section.

2. Category blocking - This is another way of protecting your ads by preventing them from showing side by side with content of certain categories. There is an option in Ads Manager that will allow you to Exclude Categories. You will also find this in the Edit Placements section.

3. Block lists - With this tool, you can prevent your ads from showing on certain apps or websites within the placements.

When you use any of these placement opt-out options, your ads and campaign delivery options become limited. This means fewer people may see your ad. However, it also ensures brand safety, content integrity and prevent any brand misrepresentation.

Integrations Lead Access

Lead generation campaigns for both Instagram and Facebook can best run through lead ads. Lead ads are a way of allowing people to show interest in a certain product or service with the use of a form within an ad that they can fill out with their details. This will allow businesses and marketers to follow up with these leads.

By default, Page admins can access lead information. Also by default, Page roles including analyst and advertiser are allowed to view insights and run lead ads but they are unable to download leads. The settings for lead access can be changed in your Business Manager. Without a Business Manager account, there is no other way to change the settings.

How to control access to your leads?

There is a tool in Business Manager called Lead Access manager that allow admins to customize the level of access for people in the team, partner agency or business and CRM. They may or may not be granted rights to download leads. With this tool, you can grant people with Page roles to download leads. The Lead Access manager is an advanced tool. It must be activated and customized. Otherwise, only Page admins will have the right to access your lead information.

How to enable Leads Access Manager?

A Business Manager admin can activate Leads Access manager. To enable this tool, you can follow these steps.

- Access **Business Manager** settings.
- At the bottom of the page, click on the **Lead Access** icon.
- A message will appear, choose **Customize Access.**

By taking these actions, you will automatically prompt the system to assign permission access to current CRMs and Page admins. Further action is required to customize lead access.

How to assign/ remove leads access?

Go to the **Assigned People and Partner** section found in the middle panel. This will show a list of people, agencies, partners or CRMs who have access to your leads.

From this section, you can edit the settings for any of the following: **People Partner and CRMs.**

How to restore permissions to default settings?

After customizing leads access, you can go back to the default settings at any time. Restoring to default access will remove any changes you've made before.

- Access **Business Manager Settings**.
- Go to the icon list and click on the **Lead Access** icon.
- Choose the page to manage your leads access.
- At the top right corner, choose the option to **Restore Default Access**.
- Confirm the action by clicking on **Restore Default**.

Payment Methods on Business Manager

In order to edit Business Manager payment methods, you must be either a Finance Editor or an admin. All billing details can be managed in Business Manager. After adding a payment method in the account, the same method can be added to an ad account associated with the Business Manager. It can then be set as primary method for all your ads.

How to add a payment method to Business Manager?

- Access Business Manager settings.
- Go to Payments.
- Choose the option to Add Payment Method.
- Click on Continue.

From here, you can follow the indicated instructions for adding your preferred payment method. This will be saved to your Business Manager account.

How to connect a Business Manager payment method to an ad account?

- Access Business Manager.
- Go to Billing.
- Choose the ad account.
- Select Payment Settings.
- Choose the option to Add Payment Method under the Payment Method section.
- Pick your preferred payment method in Business Manager.
- Follow the instructions and save the changes.

If you want to use the method to pay for your ads, you can set it as the primary method for the ad account.

Chapter 3 Quiz

Please refer to the Answer Booklet for the solution to this quiz

1. What can a Business Manager admin do that an employee can't?

   A) View business settings
   B) Handle ad accounts, pages and assets
   C) Add or delete employees or partners
   D) Manage permissions

2. What are the roles that can be assigned to ad accounts?

   A) Admin
   B) Advertiser
   C) Analyst
   D) Editor

3. What is the maximum number of ad accounts that a Business Manager can have?

   A) 3
   B) 4
   C) 5
   D) 6

4. What are the different ways to add an ad account in Business Manager?

   A) Add Ad Account
   B) Request Access to an Ad Account
   C) Create a new ad account
   D) Choose an admin

5. Which of the following cannot be done in Business Manager?

   A) Deactivate an ad account
   B) Delete an ad account audience
   C) Delete people from the account
   D) Delete an ad account

6. How many ad accounts does Facebook allow for new Business Manager?

   A) 3
   B) 4

C) 5
D) 6

7. Which of the following statements is not true?

A) You can cross-post videos with other Pages not in Business Manager.
B) You and the admins of the other Page need to give cross-posting permission
C) All businesses have access to System Users.
D) You can assign assets and roles to users.

8. When do you need a new token?

A) When you lose the other one.
B) When you get permission from admins.
C) Every time you cross-post
D) Every time you create a new System User.

9. Which tool in Business Manager allows admins to customize the level of access for people in the team, partner agency or business and CRM?

A) Lead access manager
B) Business manager admin
C) Brand Safety tools
D) Category Blocking

10. Who can edit Business Manager payment methods?

A) Finance editor
B) Analyst
C) Partners
D) Business Manager Admin

Did You Know?

Eighty-seven percent of active Facebook users access the platform via mobile. (Hootsuite)

Chapter 4

Facebook Ads Manager

The starting point of ads and the overall command center for your ad campaign is the Facebook Ads Manager. All the tools you need in order to create and manage your ads, any relevant settings, where and when they run, as well as, monitoring your campaign performance can be found here. At its core, this powerful management tool is designed to assist advertisers no matter their experience level.

Opening the Ads Manager tool will display four sections in the interface. Each tab contains a different set of information that can help you in evaluating the Facebook ads you create.

Account Overview Tab

This section offers a glance on the performance of your Facebook ads. Campaigns can also be filtered and you can switch your view from your active ads to a completely different timeframe.

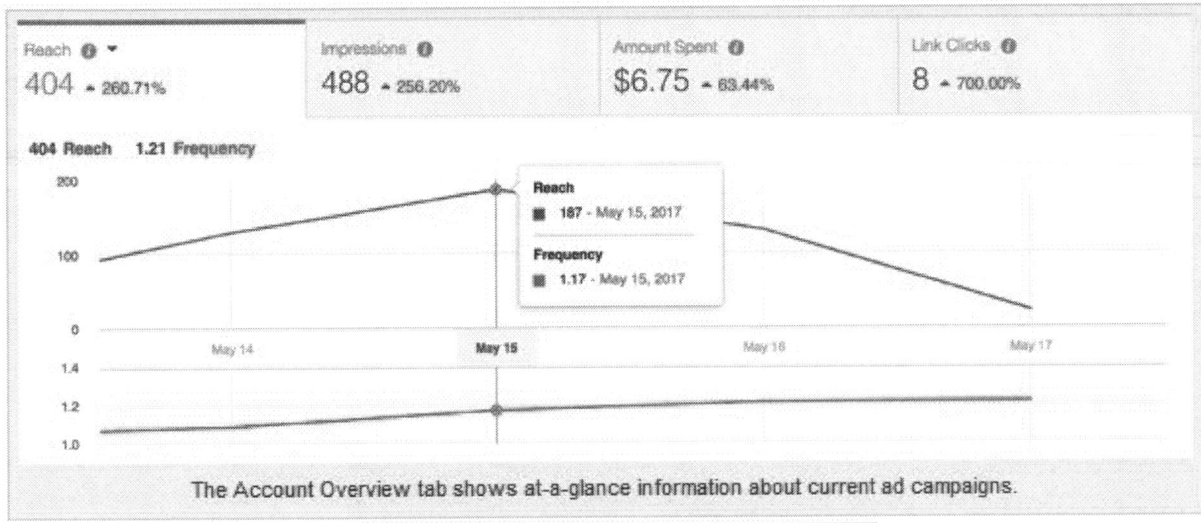

The Account Overview tab shows at-a-glance information about current ad campaigns.

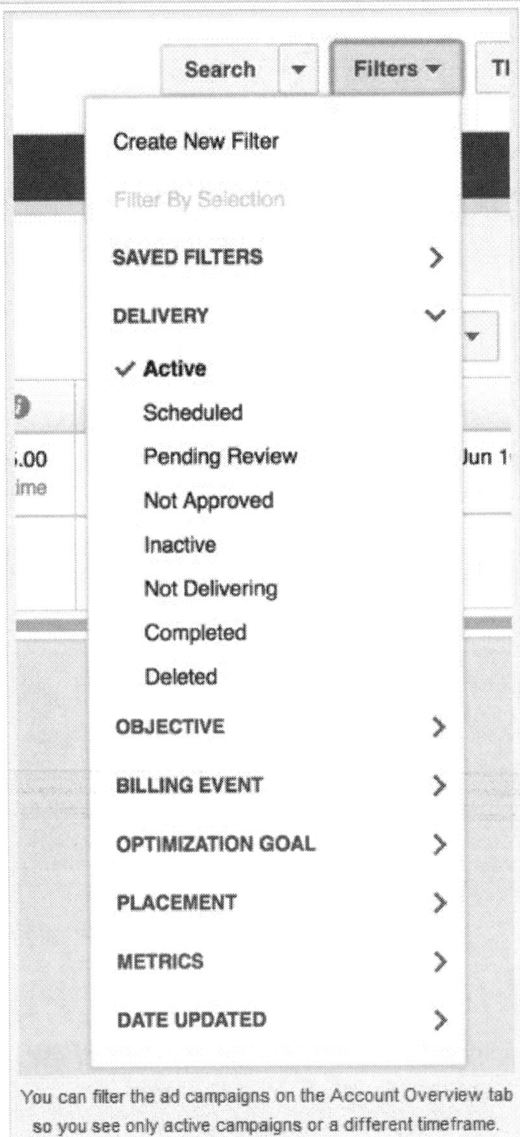

You can filter the ad campaigns on the Account Overview tab so you see only active campaigns or a different timeframe.

Campaigns, Ads and Ad Sets

Coming up with a strategy to guide the creation of ads can take some time. That being said, understanding how your ad is performing is crucial. It is very important to familiarize yourself with the important metrics and get data for **click-through rates (CTR)** and **cost per conversion (CPC).**

The section dedicated for Campaigns, Ads and Ad Sets is a way for you to analyze your ads. You can choose the tab for the specific grouping you want to analyze. You can also use the **Breakdown and Performance columns** for more details.

Opening the Performance column will display a couple more options. From here, you can access specific aspects of the campaign. You can simply click one of the options to view related metrics.

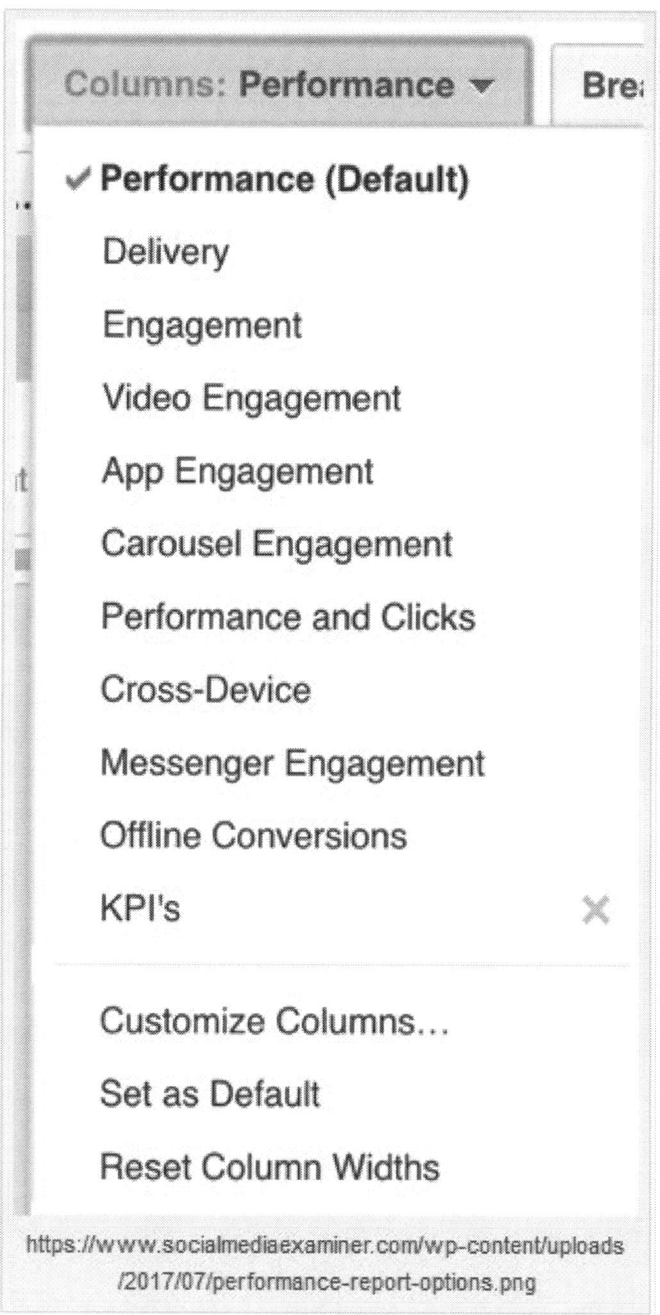

https://www.socialmediaexaminer.com/wp-content/uploads/2017/07/performance-report-options.png

Breakdown column opens up to more data. It can offer you specifics. For instance, if you want to know the specific days when conversions occurred or the device used by people when they clicked on your ad, this is the section that will display the information.

The columns can be further customized to come up with unique reports which you can share with your team. You can use it to analyze the performance and success of key metrics. For instance, when you care about knowing whether or not your ads perform 5% or above on click-through rate, you can set the columns so it shows the higher metrics at the top. After customizing your report, you can save it and use it for future reference. You can click on Save Report, name the report and complete the action by clicking Save in the dialog box.

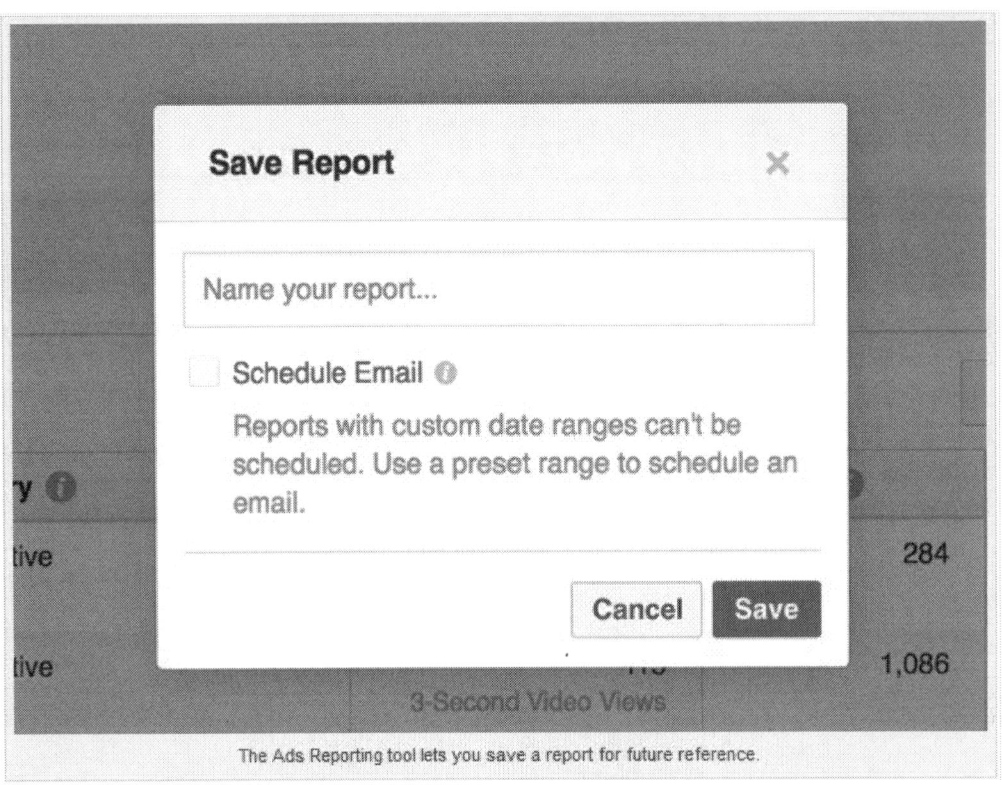

The Ads Reporting tool lets you save a report for future reference.

How to create ads?

Facebook Ads Manager offers two workflows that you can use for creating and managing your ads. You can choose between **Guided Creation** and **Quick Creation**.

Guided Creation

This is a complete walkthrough in the process of creation up to completion of your campaign. It's the perfect workflow for advertisers who are completely new to Facebook ads. The step-by-step instructions are quite easy to follow.

Quick Creation

With this option, you can set your campaign up and proceed to the creation of ads and ad sets at a later time. This workflow is ideal for advertisers who possess a more advances skill set. It will work perfectly with a knowledge of Power Editor workflow.

Your initial choice of workflow will become the default. Every time you click on the button to Create Ad, this option will be set. If you want to change or switch in between the workflows, you can do so by simply clicking on the Switch button which you will find at the top of the section for creation flow.

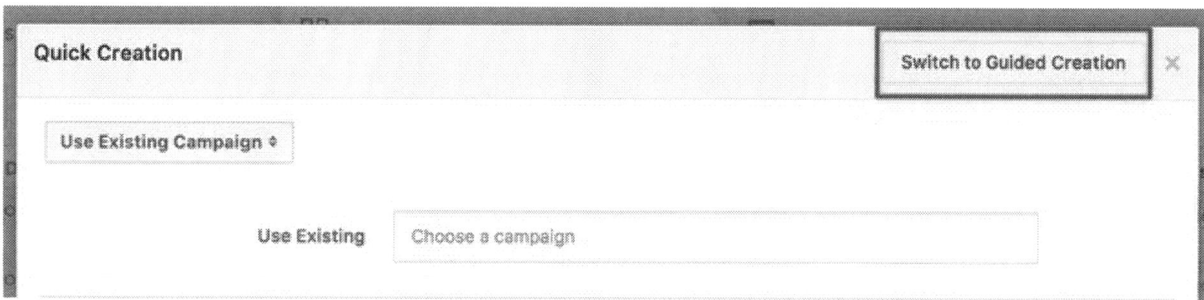

How to edit ads?

The updated interface of Ads Manager allows you to edit your ads and publish them immediately. You can also make the changes and save the ad for later publishing.

To edit and publish the ads right away, you can follow these steps.

- Choose the **Campaigns, Ads and Ad Sets** you like to edit.
- Click on the **Edit** icon which will open to a side panel.
- Apply the changes you want to make.
- Click on the option to Publish.

If you want to edit but save it for later publishing, you can follow the initial steps above. However, instead of clicking on Publish, click Close.

- Choose the **Campaigns, Ads and Ad Sets** you like to edit.
- Click on the **Edit** icon which will open to a side panel.
- Apply the changes you want to make.
- Click on the option to **Close**.
- To publish the edited ad, access the **Review and Publish section**.
- Select from the list of pending edits and confirm the changes.

How to create and find reports?

You will find the reports in the **Ads Reporting section** which you can access from the **Ads Manager Main Menu**. You can go to the same section to create your reports. You can follow these steps for creating your reports.

- Access the **Ads Reporting section**.
- Choose the option to **Create Report**.
- Select from Account, Campaign, Ad Set or Ad whichever you want to get a report on.
- Click **Apply** after making the choice.
- Save your report by clicking on **Save Changes**.
- Enter the name for the report and Save.

From accessing Ads Manager and exploring the report section, you will come across a couple of ad terms. Below are some of the terms.

Reach

This counts the number of people who have seen your ad at least once.

How it's used - The number of people that are exposed to your ad from your campaign is measured through reach. Although not all of these people may click on the ad itself, reach gives you an idea on how many people have seen your message. And they are more than likely to engage with your brand or business after being exposed to your message. Reach can be affected by several factors including budget, bid and audience targeting.

How it's calculated - Reach is estimated and calculated based on sampled data.

Impressions

Impressions denote how many times your ads were viewed. In contrast to reach that counts how many people are exposed to the ad at least once, impressions may include more than one view of the ads by the same people.

How it's used - This is one of the most common metrics relied upon by advertisers in online marketing. Impressions counts the viewing frequency of your ads or how many times your target audience viewed your ads on screen.

How it's calculated – Impressions counts how many times your ad is on the screen for the first time. In which case, when a person scrolls down and sees your ad and scrolls up again to view the ad, impression counts this as 1. On the other hand, if someone is exposed to the ad twice at different times during the day, this is equivalent to 2 impressions.

Impressions are counted in the same way for all types of ads whether the ads contain videos or images. In which case, a video ad is not required to play before it gets counted as 1 impression. It may not be the most accurate way but this calculation allows for consistency in the reporting of impressions across all ad campaigns that contain images and videos.

In cases of mobile phones where it cannot be determined if the ad is on screen, the impression is counted at the instance the ad is delivered to the device. Invalid traffic such as those that come from non-human sources like detected bots are not counted in the calculation of impressions.

Cost Per Result (CPR)

Result is defined as the number of times an ad was able to achieve the desired outcome depending on the selected settings and objectives. Cost per Result is simply the average of cost for every achieved result from the ads.

How it's used - This metric determines the cost efficiency of your ads. It is indicative of how efficient you were in achieving your ad campaign objectives. The data can be very useful in comparing the performances of your ad campaigns. It can help you in identifying areas of opportunity you can exploit and apply in your future bids for your upcoming ad sets. Cost per result is affected by several factors including target audience, auction bid, ad creative and messaging, schedule and optimization type.

How it's calculated - Cost per result is calculated based on the total of amount spent divided by the total number of results.

Link Clicks

This metric counts how many clicks there were on links within your ad which directed people to experiences or destinations within or outside of Facebook. Link clicks on ads that promote Instagram profile views include the clicks on comments or ad headers leading to the advertiser's profile.

How it's used - Link clicks indicate the interest generated by your ad among your target audience. The most effective way to use link click data is to use it in conjunction with other metrics.

How it's calculated - Clicking on any part of the ad that links to another experience or destination counts. This means a click on a call to action button within an ad or a click on an image within the ad counts equally. Destination and experiences can be in or out of the Facebook platform. Ad links may include any of the following.

- App Stores or App Deep Links
- Click to Message
- Click to Call
- Facebook Marketplace
- Facebook Lead Forms
- Facebook Canvas
- Maps/Directions
- Videos hosted by another website
- Videos launching the Watch & Browse experience
- Websites

Link Clicks For Instagram Profile Visits

Counting link clicks for Instagram ads with a Visit Instagram Profile button is a little different. To be counted, people must click the profile name either in comments or in the header because these will lead them to the same destination as they will be taken to when they click on the **Visit Instagram Profile** button.

Relevance Score

This is a rating of 1 to 10 estimating how well the audience responds to your ad. The relevance score is displayed when the ad has over 500 impressions but this only applies to ads and not to campaigns and ad sets.

How it's used - It lets you know how well your message resonated with your target audience. A higher score is an indication of your ad's performance. An estimated relevance score of 1 means your ad may not be as relevant to your target as you may think and it calls for some changes.

How it's calculated – It's based on numerous factors including the following.

- Positive feedback i.e., clicks, app installs and video views
- Negative feedback i.e., when a person clicks "I don't want to see this" on an ad
- How well your ad performs

Cost Per Click (CPC)

A click can come from various types of interactions. It can include the following.

- Clicks for actions identified as one of your campaign objective i.e., Like to your Page
- Clicks for expanding media to full screen i.e., images
- Clicks for associated business profile picture or Page profile
- Comments or shares
- Link clicks
- Post reactions i.e., likes or loves

Cost Per Click calculates the average cost for each click from multiple types as mentioned above. It is calculated by dividing the total amount spent with the number of clicks.

Post Reactions

This is the total number of reactions received by your ads. Upon viewing your ad, people can use various reaction buttons including Wow, Haha, Angry, Sad, Like or Love.

How it's used - Post reactions are a way for you to tell how relevant your ads are for your target audience, relevant enough for them to post a reaction. You can use this data to make your ads perform much better. You would want people to react to your post because this will move them to start following other reactions and comments. It allows further engagement and encourages ongoing conversation within your business Page. Knowing how the ads help in influencing such reactions is extremely important.

How it's calculated - All reactions whether negative or positive are counted as long as it is in response to your ads as they run.

Click Through Rate (CTR)

This metric counts the number of unique clicks received by your campaign and ads divided by impressions or how many times they're shown.

How it's used - This metric is an indication on how well your ads and keywords are performing. When you're paying your ads through CPM or oCPM, getting a high score for CTR is ideal. It will only mean your ads or campaign are receiving a greater number of clicks for much less money. For instance, when you're getting 1,000 impressions for 1 dollar, you would want to get as many clicks as you can from those impressions because what it costs you won't change whether 1 or 1000 people click.

How it's calculated - CTR is calculated by dividing the total number of clicks with the number of impressions. For instance, if you get 5 clicks and 50 impressions, your CTR is 10%.

Facebook Analytics

Facebook allows business owners and marketers with a variety of actionable data. One of the powerful tools you can take advantage of is Facebook Analytics. It offers a way for you to explore more user interactions with sales funnels and goal paths.

This tool is free and it is designed to be compatible with Facebook Ads. Granted Facebook ads do cost money. However, given the many updates and valuable data you can gather using the tool, it's hard to pass up on. Since the big update, many features and functions were added including the following:

- **Create Event Source Groups** from dashboard, retarget and segment people who took action following specific event path from your page
- Build your **Custom Audience** according to **Omni-channel Insights**.

How to access Facebook Analytics?

For the **Facebook Analytics Dashboard** to work, you must install pixel and allow it to run. After giving it time, it will eventually become populated with data.

- Open the dashboard to get an overview of the data.
- Click on Dashboards from the left sidebar. This will display **Omni-channel and Custom dashboards**.
- Choose Activity to explore data specific to funnels, purchases and active users among others.
- Add relevant charts and move them to your custom dashboard for a much easier access.

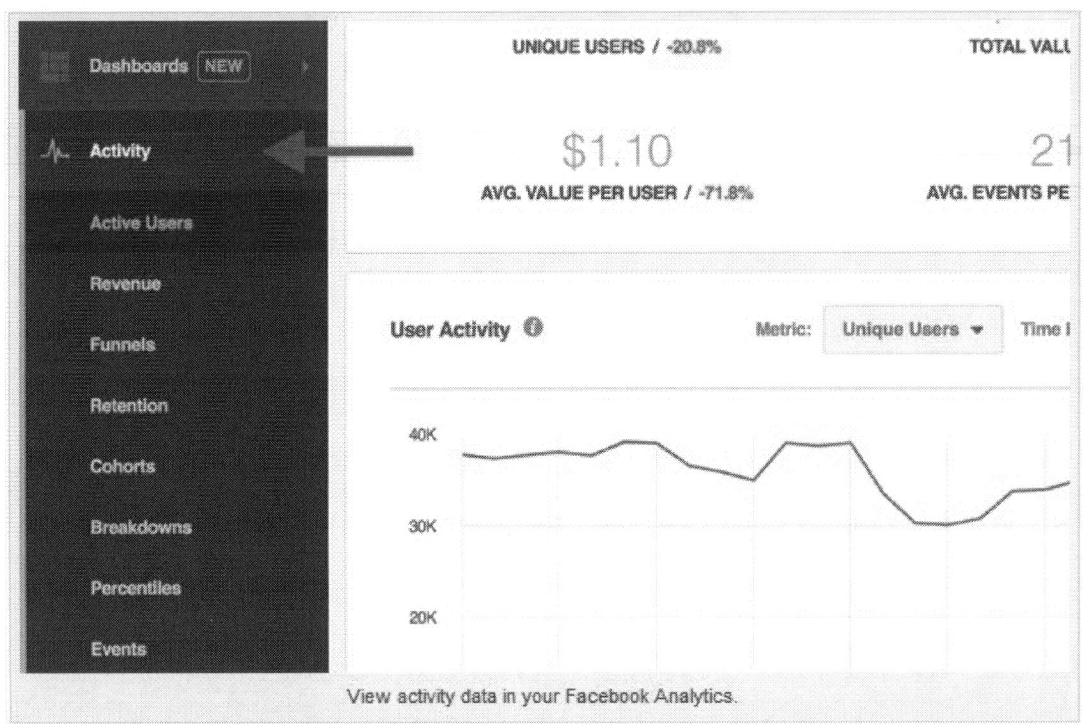

View activity data in your Facebook Analytics.

Here's how to add/ move relevant chart to your custom dashboard.

- Click on the icon for **Pin to a new dashboard**
- Choose the option to **Create a new dashboard** from the pop-up box
- Or pick from an existing dashboard.
- Add a name for the chart.
- Click on **Add to dashboard**.

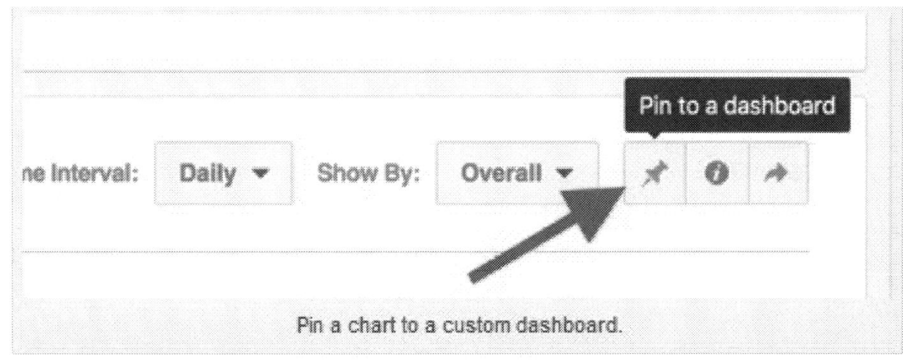

Pin a chart to a custom dashboard.

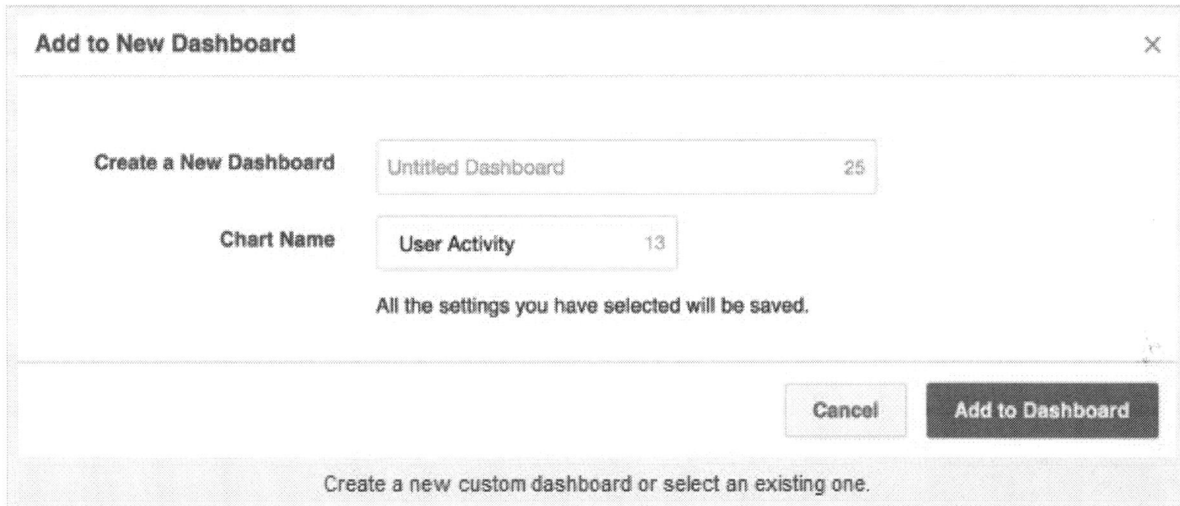

Create a new custom dashboard or select an existing one.

How to review Activity Reports?

Reports are crucial in understanding data. With this data, you are able to make informed decisions according to your specific needs. The good news is that the updated version of Facebook analytics dashboard offers a much more extensive reporting capabilities. It allows you to dig deeper into the available data. You can view micro-conversions combined with events and demographics.

For instance, if you're running an online store and you want to know which of your customers have the best conversion rate from Facebook, you can click on Activity and choose Revenue. This will display purchase-related data.

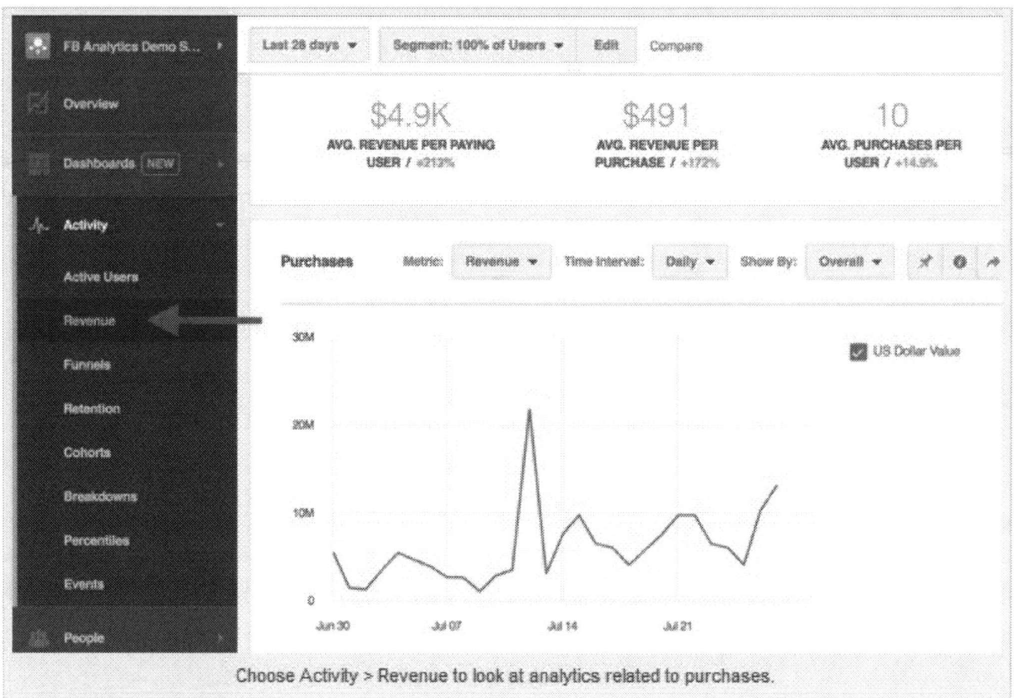

Choose Activity > Revenue to look at analytics related to purchases.

From here, you can narrow down the data even further by picking an option from the drop-down menu.

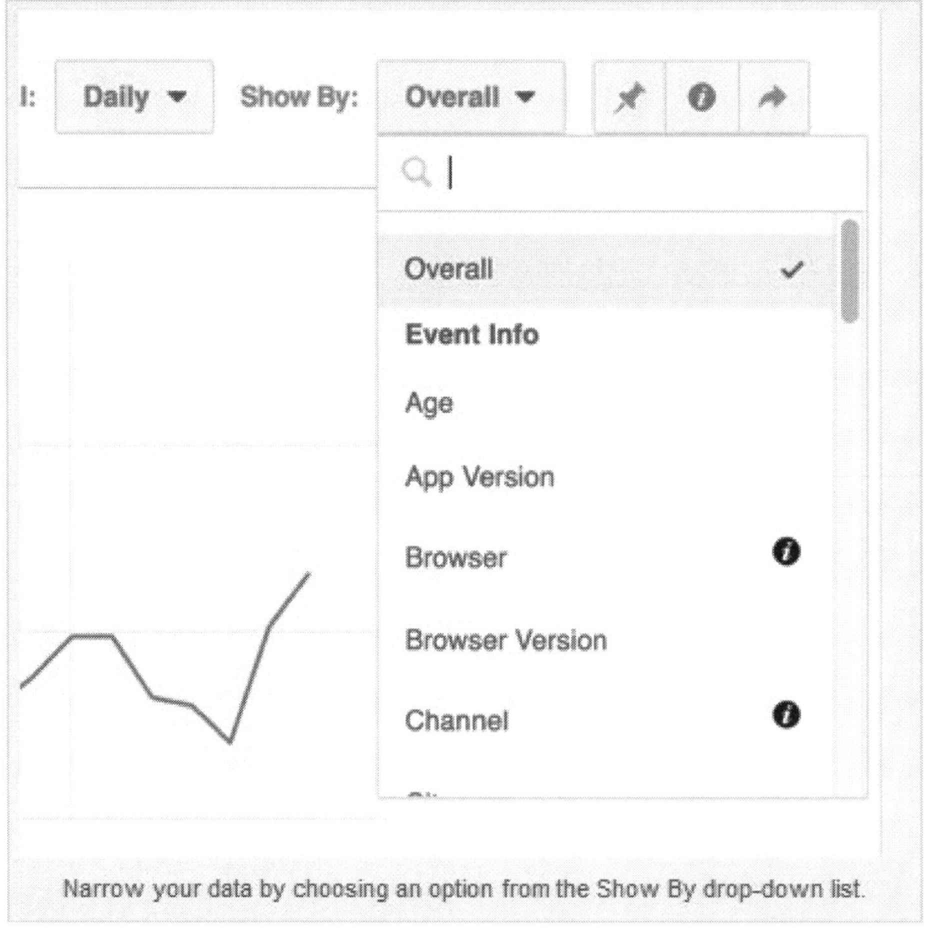

Narrow your data by choosing an option from the Show By drop-down list.

For example, if you want to see conversions according to the source of all the traffic, choose **Traffic Source**

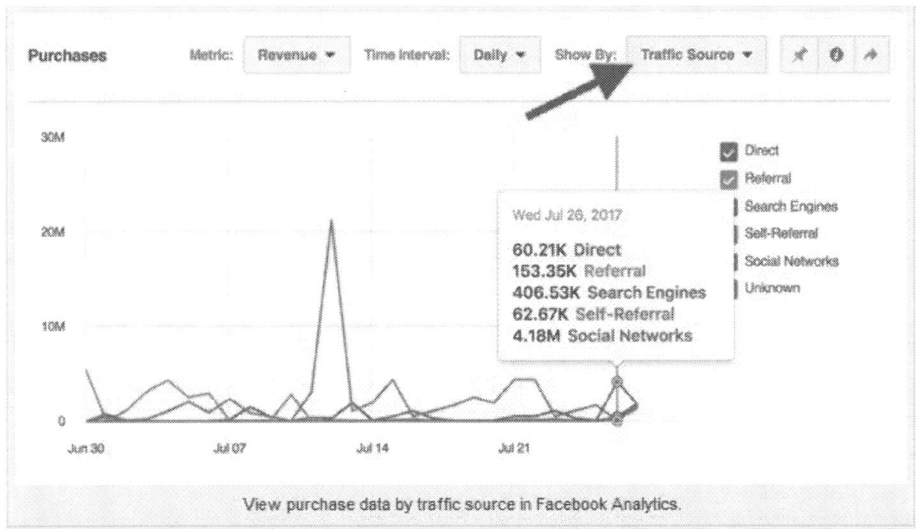

View purchase data by traffic source in Facebook Analytics.

You also have an option for creating cross-channel funnels. Doing so will allow you to test the different interaction paths and find out which ones offer the highest conversion rates.

Here's how to create funnel.

- Access Activity.
- Click on Funnels.
- Choose the option to Create Funnel from the upper-right corner.

Your funnels can be as detailed as you make them to be. Here are a couple of examples.

- Users who sent a message on your Facebook page and purchased from your website
- Users who went for app installation and purchased on your website
- Users who posted a reaction and purchased
- Users who posted a comment on one of your posts and purchased

How to use data from Facebook Analytics?

Facebook Analytics becomes very valuable when you are able to use the data to inform your campaigns. One of the best ways to maximize its use is to pay attention to the funnels that have the best conversion rates and push it further to get more customers from those funnels.

For instance, if the data shows you that people are converting after sending a message, you can take full advantage of this by engaging with people who *Like* your page with the use of Messenger chatbots. On the other hand, if people are converting much better after posting a comment, you should encourage more comments by including questions in your posts.

The bottom line is, if you are able to use the analytics data properly, you can make better decisions for your business and find out the best audience to target, the best placement for your ads, the best channels for driving traffic and the right kind of content to post.

Chapter 4 Quiz

Please refer to the Answer Booklet for the solution to this quiz

1. This section of Ads Manager offers a glance on the performance of your Facebook ads.

    A) Account Overview
    B) Ads
    C) Ad Sets
    D) Campaigns

2. What are the workflows offered in Facebook Ads Manager for creating and managing your ads?

    A) Assisted Creation
    B) Guided Creation
    C) Instant Creation
    D) Quick Creation

3. This workflow is ideal for advertisers who possess a more advances skill set. It will work perfectly with knowledge of Power Editor workflow.

    A) Assisted Creation
    B) Guided Creation
    C) Instant Creation
    D) Quick Creation

4. Which section do you need to go to in order to publish one of your edited ads?

    A) Edit
    B) Publish
    C) Review and Publish
    D) Edit and Publish

5. Where do you need to go to access reports from the Ads manager main menu?

    A) Access Report
    B) Campaign Report
    C) Ad Findings
    D) Ads Reporting

6. This counts the number of people who have seen your ad at least once.

A) Reach
B) Impressions
C) Target
D) Results

7. This metric counts how many clicks there were on links within your ad which directed people to experiences or destinations within or outside of Facebook.

A) Reach
B) Impressions
C) Link Clicks
D) Cost Per Result

8. This metric counts how many clicks there were on links within your ad which directed people to experiences or destinations within or outside of Facebook.

A) Reach
B) Impressions
C) Link Clicks
D) Cost Per Result

9. What are the things you can do with the updated Facebook Analytics?

A) Create event source groups from dashboard
B) Build your custom audiences you can base on omni-channel insights
C) Omni-channel analytics
D) Advanced machine learning/Artificial Intelligence capabilities

10. What do you need first before the Facebook Analytics dashboard can work?

A) Customize your dashboard
B) Install Facebook Pixel
C) Access Reports
D) Explore Activity

Did You Know?

The best days to post on Instagram are Monday and Thursday. The best times to post are 2 a.m., 8-9 a.m., and 5 p.m. (CoSchedule)

Chapter 5

Facebook Events Manager

Every click counts as an event as much as engagement and conversions do. And Facebook allows advertisers to measure all these online and offline events.

Events Manager is a feature of Business Manager. In this unified interface, advertisers are provided with an avenue for managing customer data sources both online and offline in a single place. Customer data sources can come from email, Point of Sale (POS), Customer Relationship Management (CRM), apps and websites among other online and offline sources. Access to these data sources can be done under the **Measure and Report Tab**

With Events Manager, you can simplify all tasks related to customer data source handling such as troubleshooting, management, setup and customer data discovery. There are five major aspects of Events Manager and they include the following.

App Events

This is helpful in managing app customer data in Facebook. It comes with a diagnostic tool for standardized custom events from apps and events and they can be used for reporting, audience creation and ad optimization.

Partner Integrations

This is a feature which can be used to connect to other platforms especially those used for customer management, interaction and purchases. Data can be pulled from these platforms into Events Manager. Among the platforms that are integrated into the Facebook events manager system include Shopify, Wix, Magento and Big Commerce.

Custom Conversions Enhancements

This tool paves the way to a much improved rule creation process. It allows businesses and marketers to share their custom conversions between different ad accounts. The enhancement also features an increase in the number of allowed custom conversions for every ad account up to a hundred.

Facebook Pixel Enhancements

The enhancements for Events Manager features a diagnostic tab that offers diagnostics about event errors, location link errors and the corresponding recommended troubleshooting steps.

Offline Events Enhancements

We've briefly mentioned offline events in the previous chapter. This includes events in your business' physical location. In Events Manager, the offline events enhancements now have a more efficient upload functionality. It includes automatic data mapping.

The importance of data sources in Facebook advertising cannot be emphasized enough. With data sources, advertisers can target customers more effectively and efficiently. With the Events Manager, data management has become much simpler. By allowing the tracking of events, measuring the effectiveness of Facebook ads and the value they bring to in-store sales, Facebook significantly increases the chance of success for businesses and marketers.

Facebook Pixel

You need to know whether your advertising efforts are effective or not. Facebook has an analytics tool that measures the effectiveness of your ads. It's called the Pixel. With this tool, you will be able to understand how people respond to your ads and posts through their actions on your website. With a better understanding of their behavior, you are more likely to effectively and efficiently reach a bigger audience.

There are three major ways where Pixel can be really helpful and such include the following:

- Ensure that ads are reaching the right people
- Grow your audiences
- Discover more Facebook advertising tools that can help grow your brand or business

The Facebook Pixel can be incorporated into your website by placing the code in your website's header. When a user pays a visit to your website and takes action during the visit, the pixel is triggered. It will then report the action to you. Not only will you be able to know when someone takes action, you will also be able to connect or reach the same customer in the future using Facebook ads (i.e. retargeting). An action can vary from making a purchase, doing a search or clicking buttons to get more information about a certain product.

What are the perks of using Facebook Pixel?

With the data collected by Pixel, you can refine your marketing strategy. By using this analytics tool effectively, you can reap the following benefits:

Target and reach the right audience

With the Pixel, you can find more customers. It will also allow you to find previous visitors who took the desired action on the website. You can even duplicate your best customers by creating Lookalike Audiences.

Increase your sales

Create automatic bidding so you can target users who are likely to take the desired action on your website. Through Pixel, you can figure out best ways for optimizing your ads for conversions.

Measure the effectiveness of ads

There's no more guess work. Pixel will let you know the direct result of putting out an ad. Useful data such as sales and conversions are accessible.

How to create a Facebook pixel?

Before you can create one, you must have a business website and you should be able to update the code for that website. To proceed, you can follow the below steps.

- Access Events Manager.
- Go to Pixels and click on the option to **Create a Pixel**.
- From the box, click on Create to finish the pixel creation.
- Copy your **Pixel ID or code**.

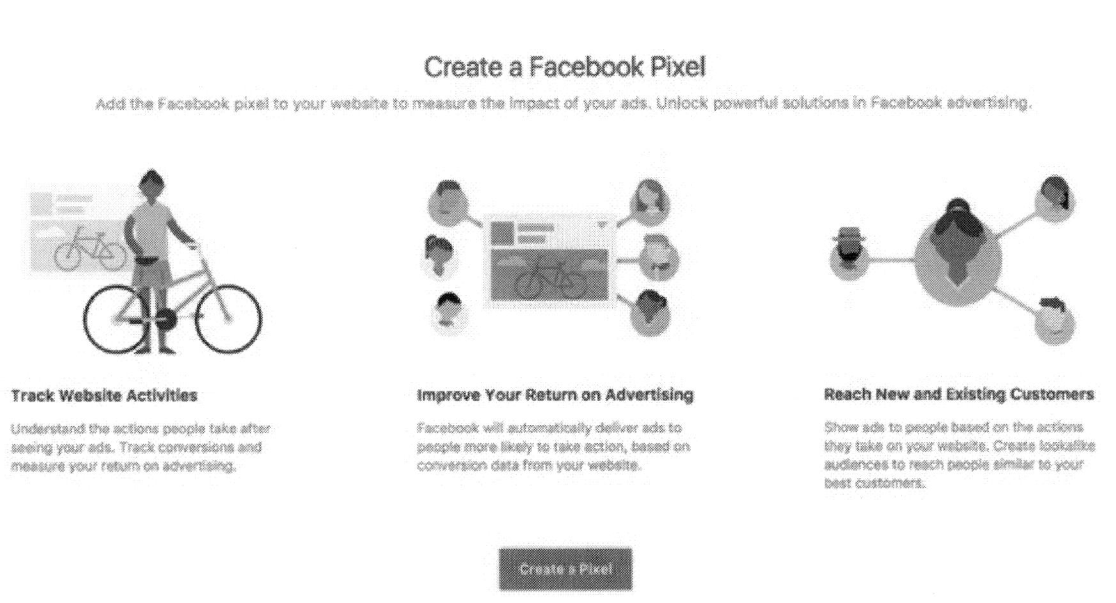

After creating pixel, you can proceed to place the code on your business website. The steps vary according to your specific situation.

How to add Facebook pixel when another person makes changes to your website?

If another person takes care of updating your website's code, you can use the steps here to send them an email of instructions for setting up the pixel on the site.

- Access **Ads Manager**.
- Go to **Facebook Pixels Tab**.
- Choose the option to **Set up pixel**.
- Click on **Email Instructions to a Developer**.
- Add the email address and click on Send.

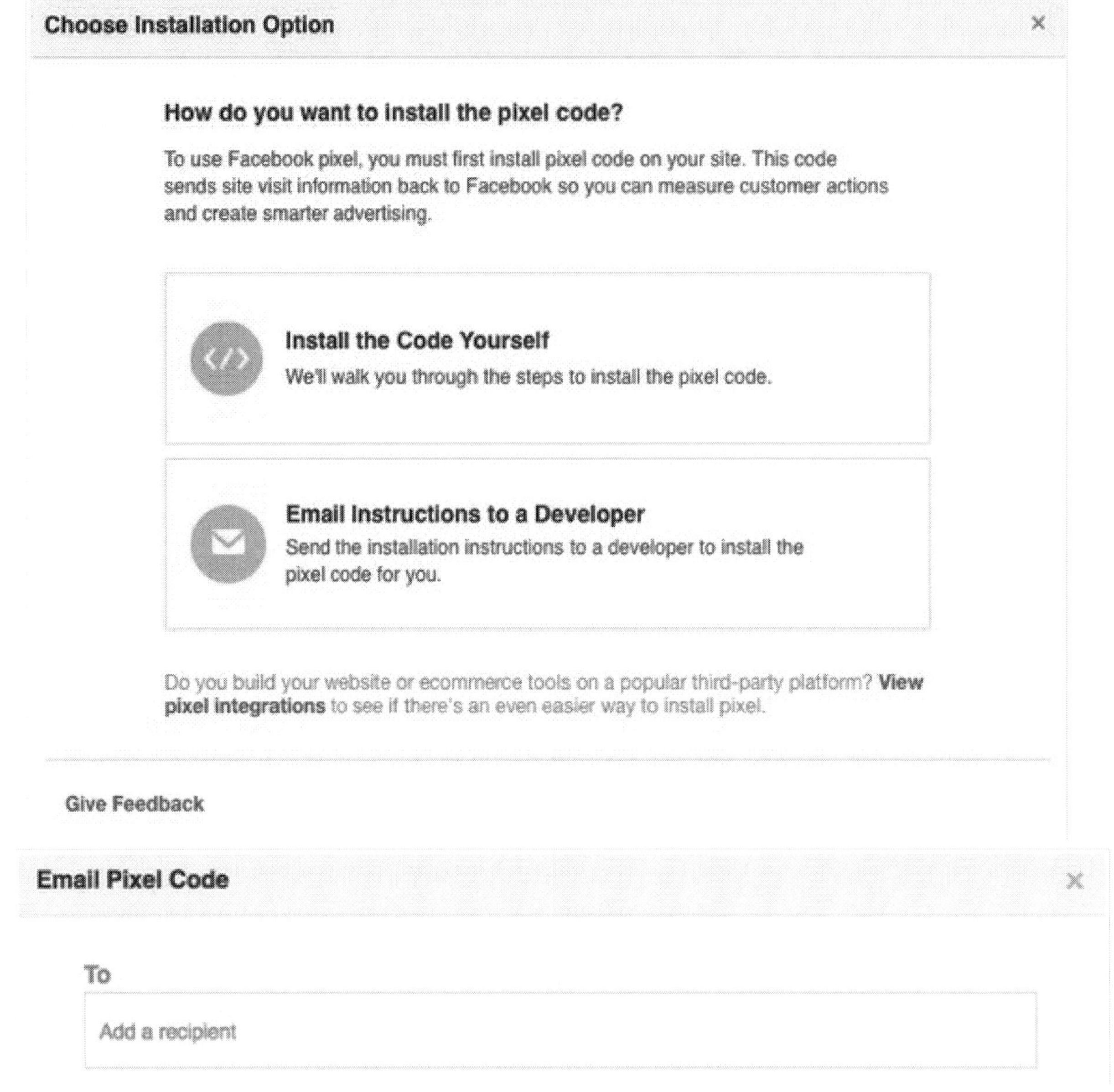

How to update the website code yourself?

If you are updating the code for your website by yourself, you can follow these steps.

- Access the website's code and look for the header.

Find the **<head> </head> tags** in your webpage code, or locate the **header template** in your CMS or web platform. **Learn where to find this template or code** in different web management systems.

```
<!-- Example -->
!DOCTYPE html>
<html lang="en">
  <head>
    <script>...</script>
    insert_pixel_code_here
  </head>
```

- Copy and paste the entire code. Add it in the website's header by pasting it at the very bottom of the header right on top of the closing head tag.
- Make sure the code is working correctly by sending a test. Click on the option to **Send Test Traffic** after successfully adding the code to the website.
- Updating can take a couple of minutes. When the status shows Active, it means you have successfully installed the base code.

USE ADVANCED MATCHING

```
<!-- Facebook Pixel Code -->
<script>
  !function(f,b,e,v,n,t,s)
  {if(f.fbq)return;n=f.fbq=function(){n.callMethod?
  n.callMethod.apply(n,arguments):n.queue.push(arguments)};
  if(!f._fbq)f._fbq=n;n.push=n;n.loaded=!0;n.version='2.0';
  n.queue=[];t=b.createElement(e);t.async=!0;
  t.src=v;s=b.getElementsByTagName(e)[0];
  s.parentNode.insertBefore(t,s)}(window,
  document,'script','https://connect.facebook.net/en_US/
  fbevents.js');

  fbq('init', '1234567890');
  fbq('track', 'PageView');
</script>
<noscript>
  <img height="1" width="1" style="display:none"
  src="https://www.facebook.com/tr?id=1234567890&
  ev=PageView&noscript=1"/>
</noscript>
<!-- End Facebook Pixel Code -->
```

No Activity Yet

Last Received: Never

www.mysite.com

Send Test Traffic

If you're using a tag manager like Adobe, Google Tag Manager, Segment and Tealium or your website is hosted on a web platform like Weebly, Shopify, Wix or Magento, the instructions on adding the pixel code is specific to the tag manager or web platform in use. Other web platforms supported include WooCommerce, Squarespace and BigCommerce.

How to track actions that matter?

After completing the step of placing the pixel on your website, you will have to add events that will allow you to monitor specific actions taken by people on your website. As we mentioned before, events are any actions that occur on your website. You can follow these steps to add events on the site.

- Access your **Events Manager**.
- Go to **Pixels Tab**.
- Proceed to **Set up pixel**.
- Choose the option to **Manually Install the Code Yourself** and Continue.

Install Your Pixel Code ×

To use Facebook pixel, you must first install pixel code on your website. This code sends site visit information back to Facebook so you can measure customer actions and create smarter advertising.

Choose an option to install the pixel code. You can change this choice later.

Use an Integration or Tag Manager

Facebook pixel currently integrates with **BigCommerce, Google Tag Manager, Magento, Segment, Shopify, Squarespace, Wix, WooCommerce** and many more. Learn about platform integrations.

Manually Install the Code Yourself

We'll walk you through the steps to install the pixel code.

Email Instructions to a Developer

Send the installation instructions to a developer to install the pixel code for you.

- Select the option to **Install Events**.
- Click on the toggle icon beside the event you want to track.

Purchase

Lead

Complete Registration

Add Payment Info

Initiate Checkout

Add to Cart

Add to Wishlist

Search

View Content

- Choose either of these options: Track Event on Page Load or Track Event on Inline Action

Track Event on Page Load

This option is ideal if you care about an action which is traceable when a user lands on a specific page on your website. A good example is a user reaching the confirmation page after a purchase has been completed.

Track Event on Inline Action

This option is best if you care about tracking an action which requires a user to click on something. For instance, if you want to trace clicks on Add to Cart or clicks on Purchase Button, you should choose this option.

- Add your event parameters such as Currency or Conversion Value. This is a recommended step and will allow you to measure any additional information pertaining to your event.

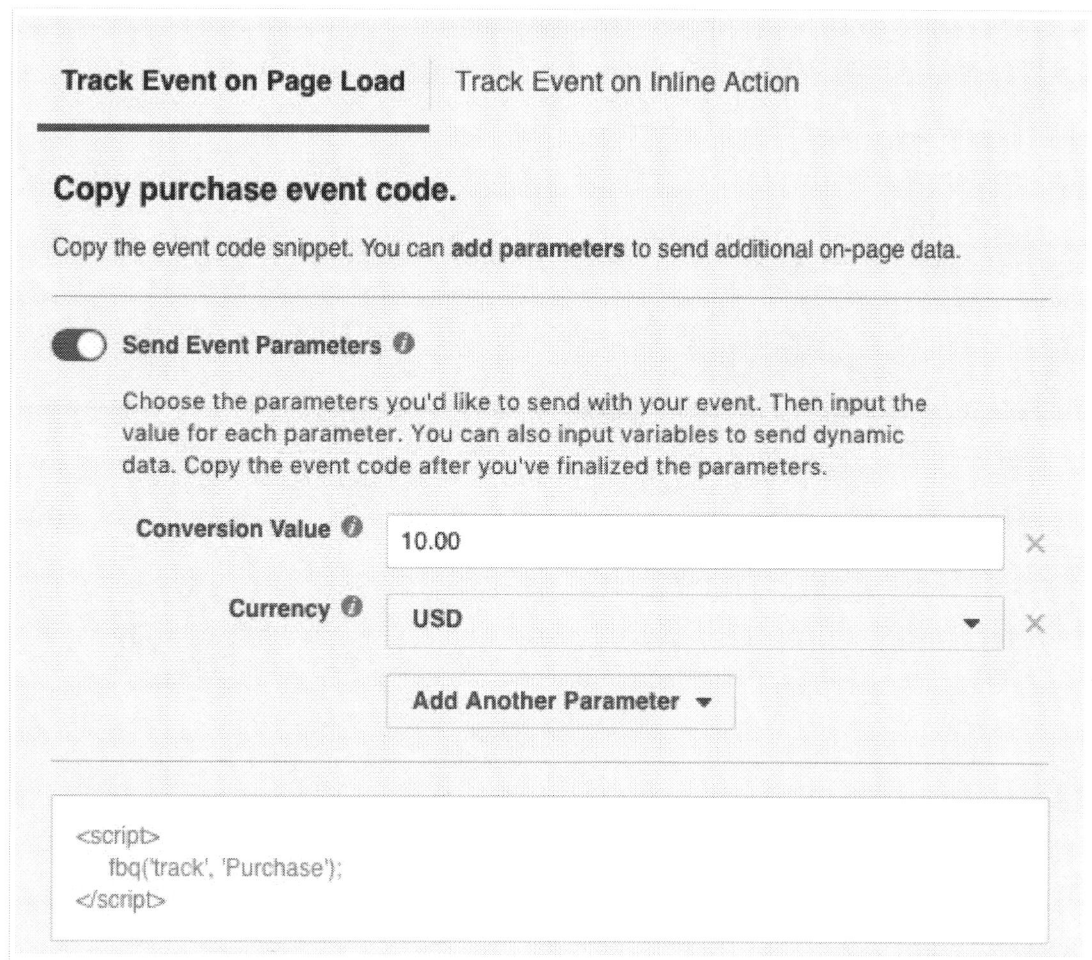

- Copy the event code and add it to your website's relevant page. Do not modify the pixel code that's already in the site's header. The placement of the pixel code shall vary between page load events and inline action events.

Page Load Events

The event code should be placed below the page's closing header section. For most sites, this is the spot after the opening <body> tag.

Inline Action Events

The event code should be placed between the script tags beside the action that you prefer to track. For instance, if you care about tracking a click on the Like button, the event code should be right next to it.

Event codes should be updated if you want to link an event to a specific action. These steps should be repeated for any additional listed events you want to track.

How to check if your pixel is up and running?

To make sure that the pixel you just added is working correctly, you can use a troubleshooting tool called **Facebook Pixel Helper**.

This is a Chrome plugin which you can use to check if the pixel is properly installed on your website. It can also be used to further understand information gathered from pixel as well as check for errors. Here's how to install the tool.

- Access the Chrome web store.
- Search for **Facebook Pixel Helper**.
- Click on **Add to Chrome**.
- Choose the option to **Add extension**.

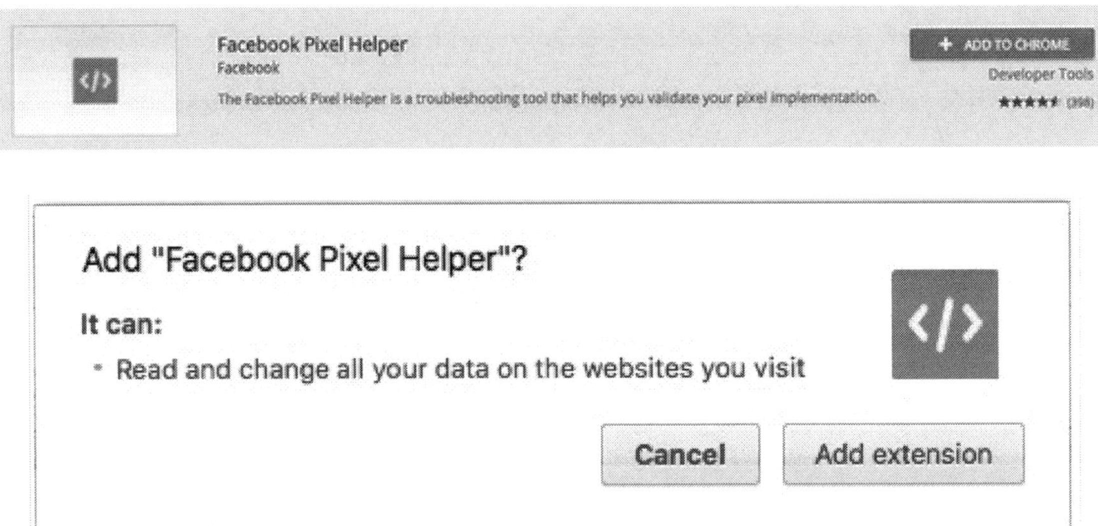

After successfully installing the extension, you will receive a notification indicating the addition of the plugin to Chrome. Also, you will see a small icon in the address bar.

- Click on the icon for Pixel Helper found in the address bar.
- A popup will appear showing the pixels found on the page. It will let you know whether or not the pixel setup was successful.

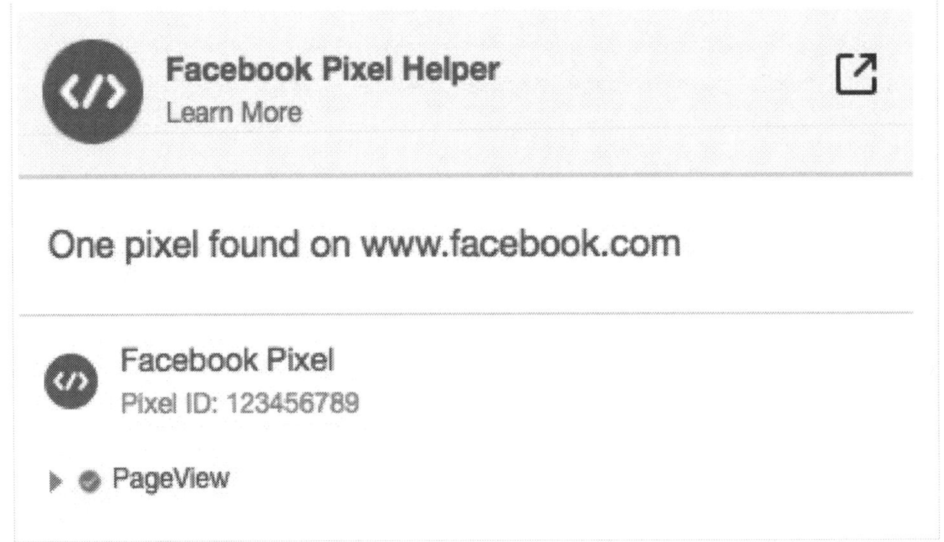

When the Facebook Pixel Helper is able to locate the pixel on your website and you receive no errors, you can commence creating your ads with the pixel.

What to do if you run into troubleshooting Pixel errors?

If Facebook Pixel Helper detects an error after installing the pixel on your site, you can also use the tool to troubleshoot and fix the issue to get the pixel up and running. There are five common errors that you may run into. These errors include the following.

- No Pixel Found
- Pixel Did Not Load
- Not a Standard Event
- Pixel Activated Multiple Times
- Invalid Pixel ID

Here are a couple of suggestions for fixing these common errors.

No Pixel Found

If you see this error message, the pixel code must be placed on your website. It may not have been added correctly. In this case, go back to setting up the pixel and make sure the steps are done properly.

Pixel Did Not Load

With this error, the Pixel Helper may have found the pixel in the site. However, it may not be able to pass the back data from your website. There are two possible causes for this error. One, this may appear as a result of firing up the pixel for a dynamic event. To fix it, you can try clicking on the button where the code is attached and clicking back on the Pixel Helper. Two, the error may appear as a result of a discrepancy on the pixel base code. You can attempt to remove the code from the site and trying to add it back again.

Not a Standard Event

In this case, Pixel Helper may have found the event code. However, it may not be a match to any of the standard events. It may be caused by a simple typo error. For instance, the event name may have been entered as Purchased instead of Purchase. Check back on the standard event names and make sure that the exact event code is entered correctly.

Pixel Activated Multiple Times

To fix the error, make sure that the pixel code is only used once. Do not place the same event code more than once on a single page to avoid this error.

Invalid Pixel ID

This error means that the pixel base code is not recognizable by Facebook. You can try replacing the pixel ID in the pixel base code with the one assigned to one of your active ad accounts.

Understanding the Pixel Event Data in Your Events Manager

Through Facebook pixel, advertisers can understand the actions taken by people on their website as a response to their Facebook ads. Event data is accessible on Pixel page. Now the next concern is how to understand the data. Here are a couple of factors you need to pay attention to.

High Level Event Metrics

From the Data Sources section, you will find information that allows you to measure and optimize ad campaigns that leverage pixel event data. On this page, you're able to view basic information about the pixel including last activity and status. If you're using multiple pixels, you can simply choose the pixel you want to access. These are a few sections you must get acquainted with.

Events Received

This section tells you the total number of events your pixel was able to receive.

Top Events

This is where you find out how well matched your data is to Facebook users.

Activity

This is a graph showing the number of events that are measured daily for the past 7 days that can be linked to people who viewed the ads. It is a valuable section that allows you to understand the behavior of the most recent visitors to your website. This also helps you identify any issues that may affect your events.

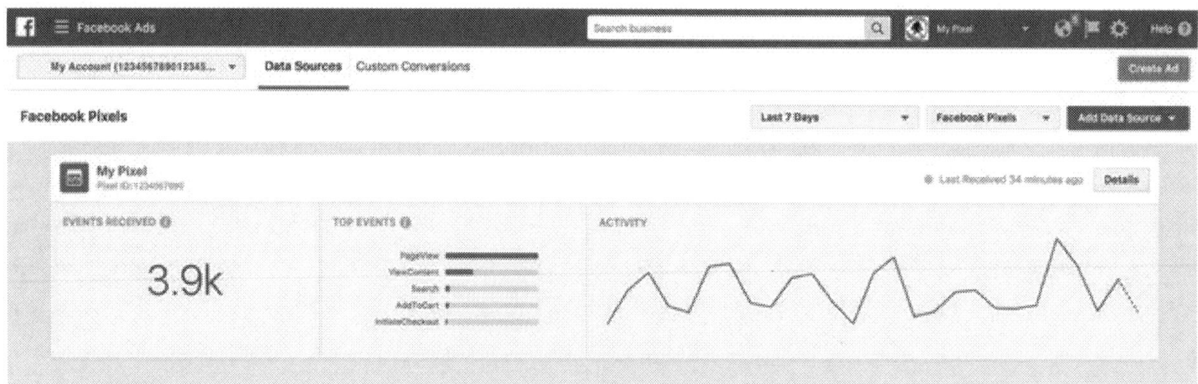

Events

From the summary page of Facebook Pixels, either choose the pixel you want to get information about or click on Details to access detailed insights about the performance of your Facebook ad. Among the key elements in the detail page are the following.

- **Time Frame** - You can use this section to make adjustments to the data's time frame. You can do this by clicking the corresponding button. Choose one of the options from the list in the dropdown menu.
- **Events Tab Graph** - This will display the number as well as the value of the received events, the matched and the attributed events. From here, you will know the amount of traffic received on your website. You can

hover over different points in the graph for a view of the metrics breakdown. You can review the table in this section. If you see a dotted line, it only means the data on that section has not been updated for the day yet. You should remember that raw pixel fires are counted. Know the difference between page loads and browser sessions.

- **Events Tab Table** - This is another section that shows a table where you can find out the number and value for received events, matched and attributed events.

There are various reporting metrics and they include the following.

- **Events Received** - This is the total number of events that your pixel received.
- **Total Value** - This is the total value of all of the events within a selected time frame. The value is based on monetary value specific to the uploaded events.
- **Matched Events** - From the total number of events received, matched events is the number of events matched to Facebook users.
- **Matched Value** - This denotes the total value of matched events within a selected time frame.
- **Attributed Value** - From the total number of matched events, attribute events are the number of events that can be attributed to users who either viewed or clicked the ads across all your ad accounts associated to the event set. Events can be attributed with a maximum of 28 days after the occurrence of a click or an impression.
- **Attributed Events** - This counts the total of attributed events within a selected time frame.

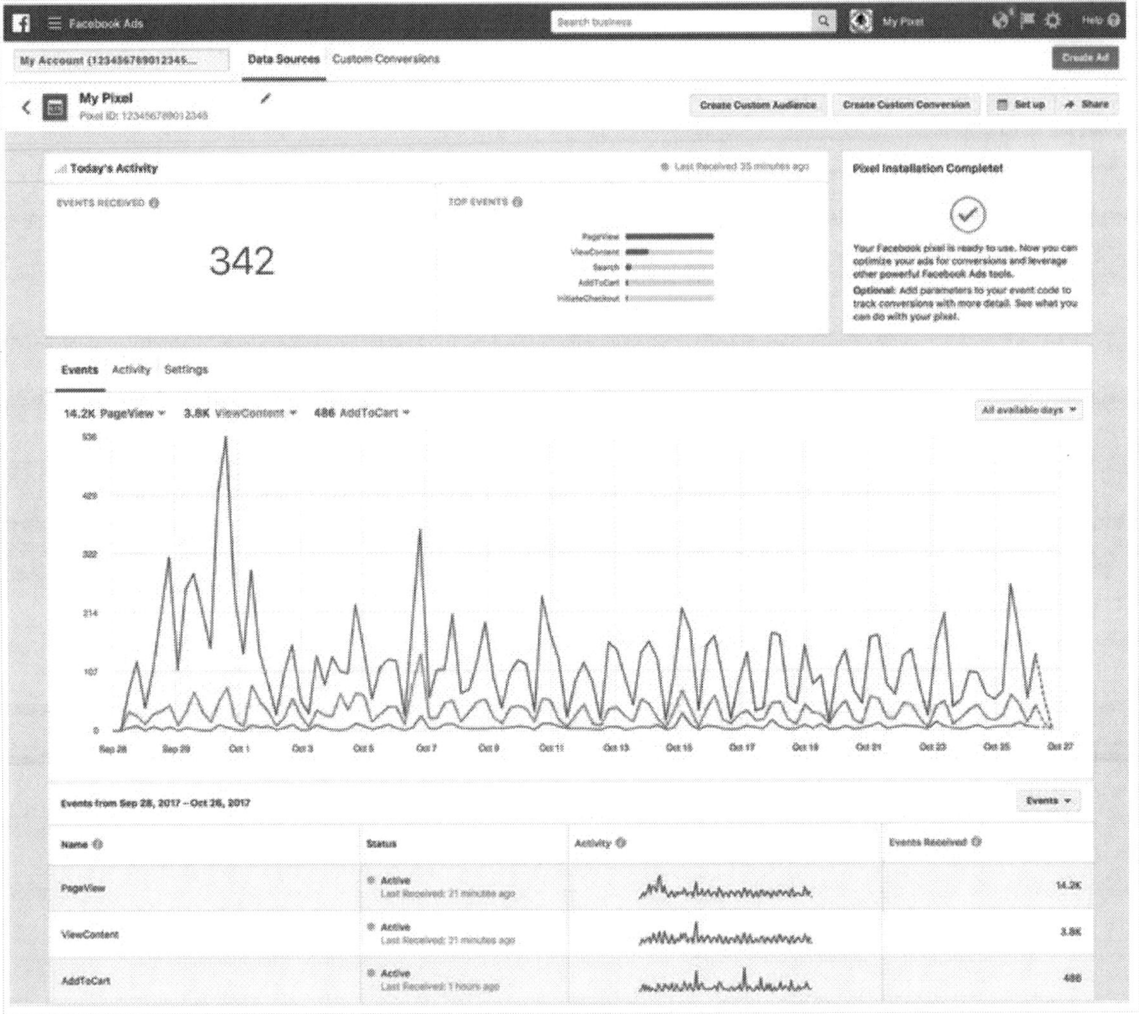

Activity

You refer to this section when you want to access a list of actions people have taken on your site. Choose the event you want to see and the most recent 100 events will be displayed.

You can review the columns and breakdown the information by...

- Event Category
- Event Time
- Device
- Referring URL
- Parameters such as currency or value

You will know the amount of traffic received for each of the metrics. You can also use the Activity page if your event setup requires some troubleshooting. It is also useful for making sure the website's event code is working properly.

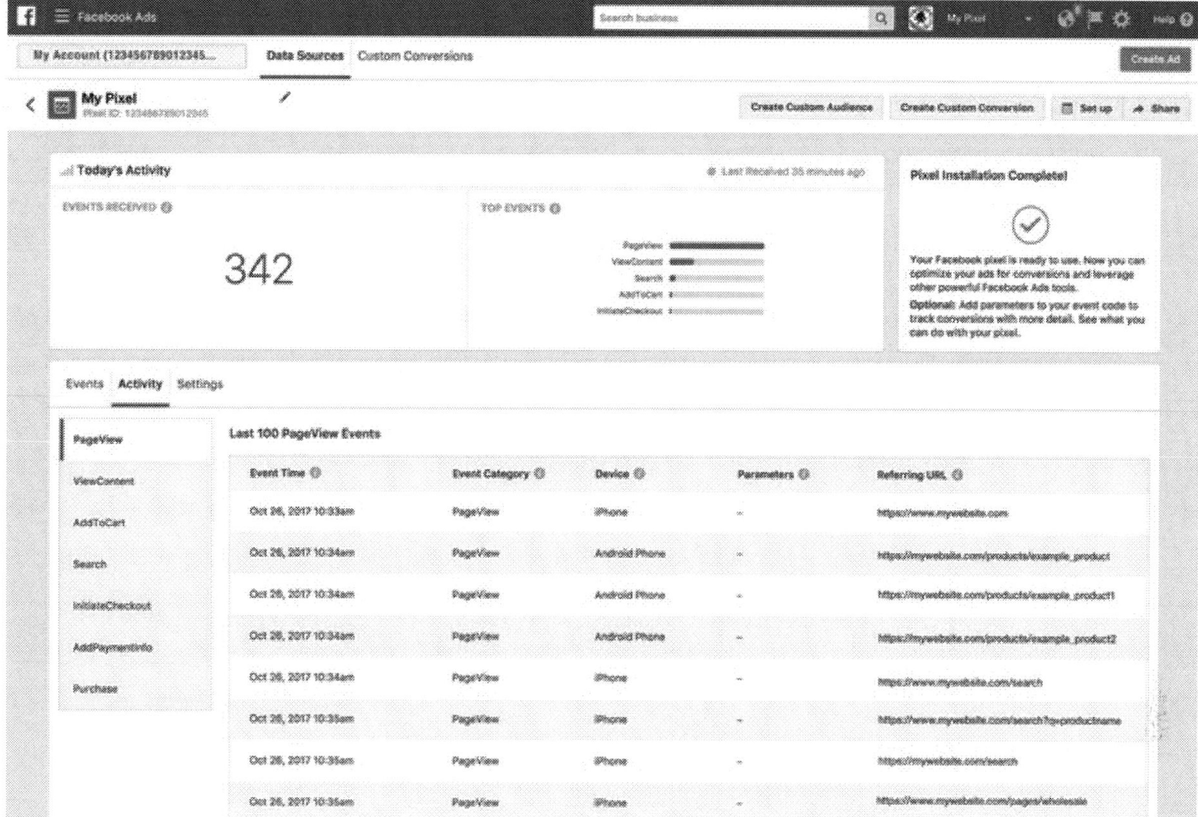

Settings

This section gives you access to the custom conversions and custom audiences associated to your Facebook pixels. This page will show you how they are performing. In addition, you will be able to view and create custom conversions and audiences by volume on this page.

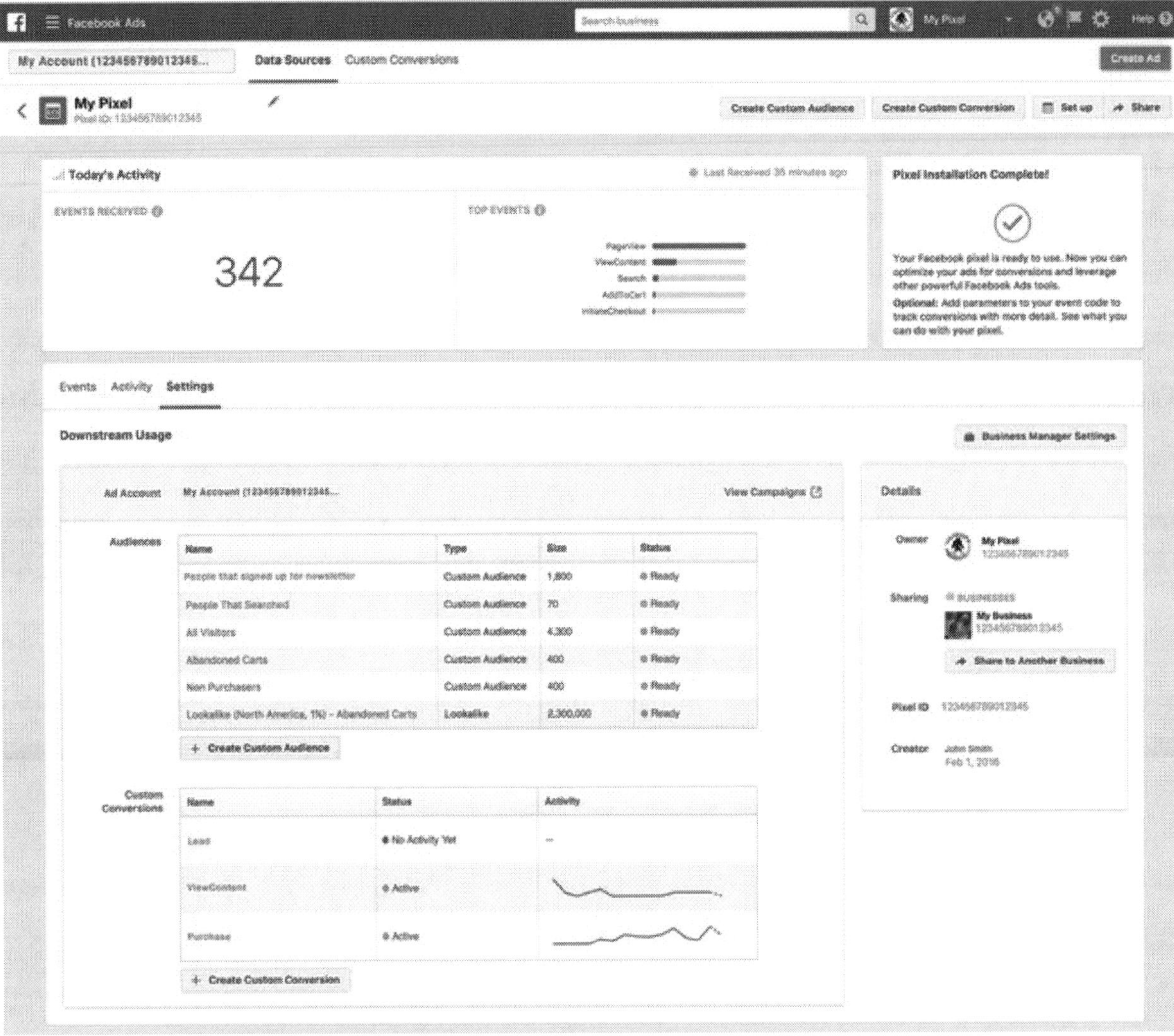

Standard Events versus Custom Conversions

You can use both standard events and custom conversions to track actions and optimize your ads. The major difference between the two is that standard events provide more features. While custom conversions may have less features, it proves to be much simpler to set up. If you do the editing yourself on your website, you may find it easier to use custom conversions. If you want more features, the ability to add parameters and you feel comfortable editing your site's code, then you should consider standard events.

To get a better idea of the differences between the two, refer to the list below.

Standard Events	Custom Conversions
You create it by adding to the pixel base code	You create it in Ads manager with the use of URL rules and there is no need for additional code
You can customize it with parameters	You can customize it using granular URL rules
You get aggregated reporting	You get separate reporting
Compatibility with dynamic product ads	You can't use it with dynamic product ads

How to create custom conversions?

- Access the section for **Custom Conversions**.
- Click on the option to **Create Custom Conversions**.
- Enter the URL or at least a portion of the URL representing the custom conversion. For instance, if you want a thank-you page when a purchase is completed, you can use a URL containing **/thankyou.php**.
- The equivalent of this URL in standard event is **Make Purchase**.

When you use URL Equals, you must include the domain "www" without either "http" or "https." Below are a few examples so you can get a better idea.

URL Option	How you'd set your rule	Equivalent Standard Event
URL Equals	www.mywebsiteurl.com/thankyou.php	Purchase
URL Contains	/thankyou.php	Purchase

Note: When you have other analytics tools, you can make it simpler by copying and pasting the URL from the page views list. This will help you ensure that mistakes and inaccurate numbers are avoided.

- Choose the category and click on Next.

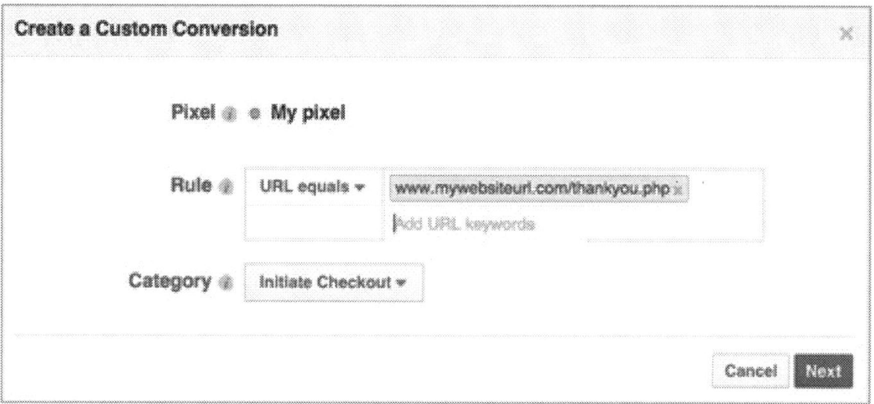

- Enter the name for your custom conversion and add a description.
- Include a conversion value if it applies in the situation. For instance, when you are selling $15 worth of tickets, you must enter "10" as the value. Conversion values are only whole numbers. Additional characters like dollar signs are not accepted. When you include a conversion value, you'll be able to see the report with the return on your ad spend.
- Click on Create and click on Done on the next pop up.

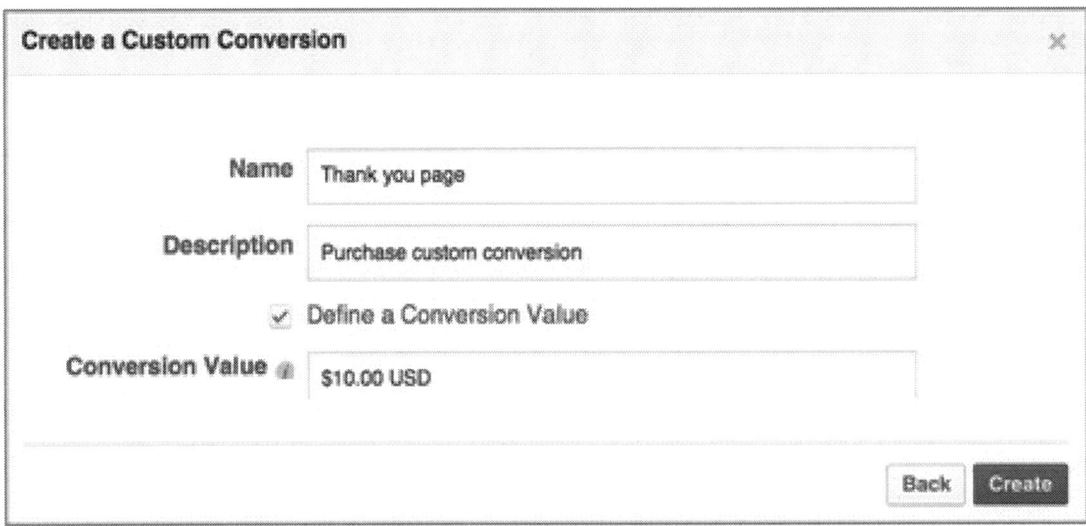

- After completing these steps, you'll be able to create an ad according to your site's conversion objective. Choose the custom conversion to track and optimize for.

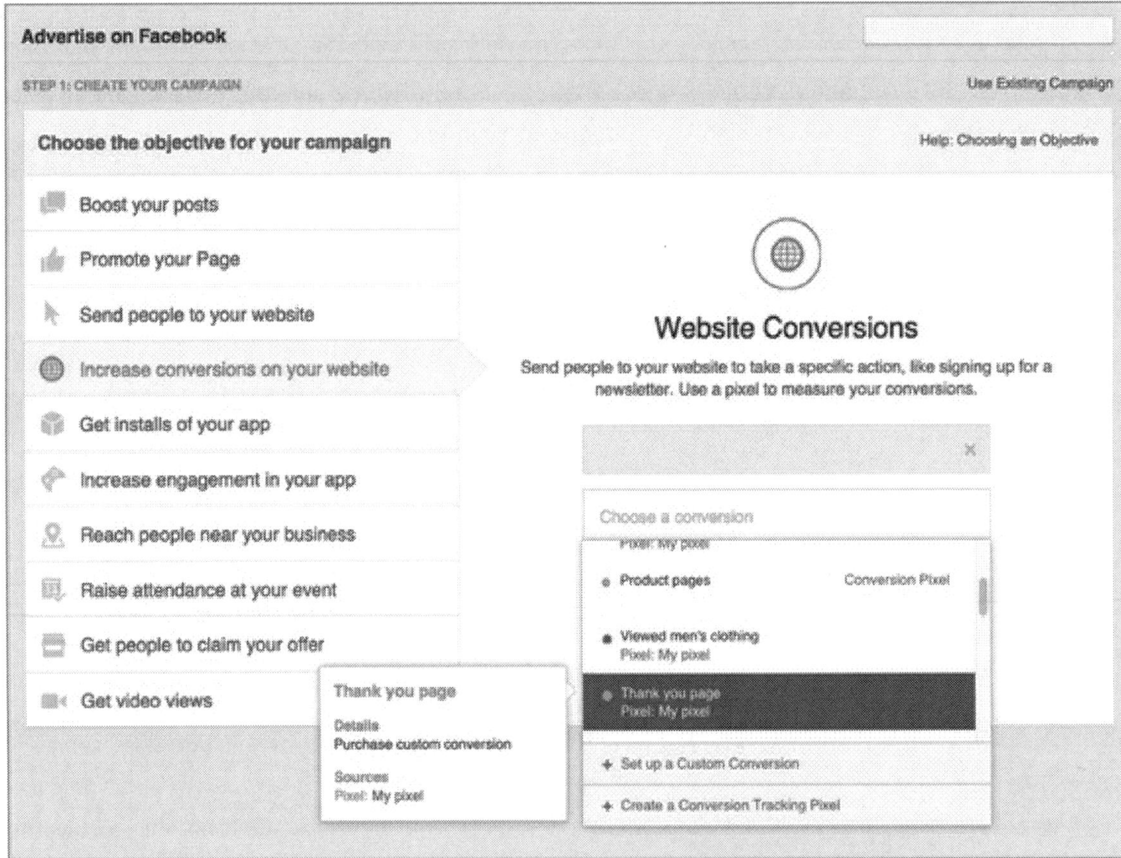

How to use custom conversions for splitting standard events?

After you've started utilizing standard events and found that you require more customization, you can add custom conversions in the mix. For instance, if you're selling ready to wear clothes and been relying on **ViewContent standard events** across all product lines but prefer to optimize them for separate categories, you can do this using custom conversions.

This can be achieved by creating the conversions based on the URL rules for different categories. Here's an example of applying the URL rule to optimize only for those that view clothing for men.

Create a Custom Conversion

Pixel: My pixel
Pixel ID: 786008474824985

Rule: URL contains /products/clothing/men

Category: View Content

Cancel | Next

Remember, you are allowed a maximum of 100 custom conversions. You are also allowed to delete previously created ones to make room for new conversions.

Retargeting

Most of the people who would visit your website may not be ready to buy yet. They may drop by, wander around but eventually leave. This does not necessarily mean they are completely uninterested. As a matter of fact, they probably are interested but something came up or got in the way. It's your job to get them back and complete the action that you want them to finish.

Simply put, retargeting is about bringing your previous visitors back to your website. This form of online advertising works by using a cookie. When someone visits your ecommerce site for instance, a cookie is put in the browser. Through this cookie, you will be able to recognize and follow your visitors as they drop by other websites. With this information, you will be able to reach them effectively and efficiently with ads.

Facebook is an excellent tool for retargeting. There is a good chance that the visitors you want to reach again are part of the 2 billion active Facebook users.

To use retargeting effectively and maximize its full potential, your timing is incredibly important. Retargeting is most effective when implemented within 2 weeks of their visit. Here are a couple of tips on how to use retargeting effectively.

Remind them to complete the action.

In most cases, these visitors aren't just highly motivated to buy. Because of this, they need that little push to complete the action you want them to take. Sending them reminders will be of great help in this regard.

Reach them in places where they are most likely to make that purchase.

Here's an interesting finding. Most people use their mobile phones to browse but aren't exactly comfortable making the purchase on mobile. In which case, you may want to consider displaying retargeting ads exclusively for desktop. This is not a hard and fast rule however. Analyze your data and find out whether desktop users outperform mobile visitors or the other way around.

Capture their attention. Remind them of the items they're interested in.

One of the best ways to catch these visitors' attention is through the use of dynamic retargeting ads. This type of ad can be used to automatically show them the products they viewed previously. It is more likely to work because the ad is highly relevant.

Offer them a compelling reason to return and complete their purchase.

A great number of customers click Add to Cart but never get to checkout simply because they're looking to see if there are better options. The great number of cart abandoners can be attributed to a simple change of mind. However, you can change their mind back into completing their purchases by offering them a great deal. One of the best examples is to use a free shipping offer. A freebie or a discount can also work. Explore your options and offer them a little extra.

Consider providing customer service.

According to statistics, 83% of online shoppers require support in order to complete their purchases. The absence of customer support to help them along the way and answer their questions is one of the biggest reasons why add to cart actions do not translate to sales.

Although email and phone support are good, they are not as proactive as some shoppers need it to be. One solution that comes to mind is the use of **Facebook Messenger Destination Ads.**

These are simply ads that encourage customers to get in touch with the website. The ads can also direct them to Facebook Messenger. Through this, a one on one conversation is initiated with the hesitant customer. It's an excellent way to keep them interested and eventually complete the sale.

Stay in touch with them.

The longer you wait to close the sale the harder it gets to actually complete it. However, you can still benefit from staying in touch with them even after 14 days from their first visit. Just because they did not complete their purchase does not necessarily mean they are uninterested. While you have to think about immediate purchases, you also have to consider building long term relationships.

Through **Facebook Lead Ads**, you can entice them to subscribe and be part of your email list so when a great deal comes along, they'd be among the first to know. Simple things like this can help you convert more potential customers to paying customers.

Chapter 5 Quiz

Please refer to the Answer Booklet for the solution to this quiz

1. Which of the following is a feature which can be used to connect to other platforms especially those used for customer management, interaction and purchases?

   A) App Events
   B) Partner Integrations
   C) Custom Conversions
   D) Offline Events

2. Which of the following is helpful in managing app customer data in Facebook and comes with a diagnostic tool for standardized custom events from apps and events and they can be used for reporting, audience creation and ad optimization.

   A) App Events
   B) Partner Integrations
   C) Custom Conversions
   D) Offline Events

3. What are the benefits of using Facebook Pixel?

   A) Target and reach the right audience
   B) Increase your sales
   C) Measure the effectiveness of your ads
   D) Allow partners and agencies to share audiences

4. Which of the following are standard events?

   A) Purchase
   B) Lead
   C) Complete Registration
   D) Add to Cart

5. What is the troubleshooting tool you can use to check if the pixel is working correctly?

   A) Facebook Pixel Assistant
   B) Facebook Pixel Agent
   C) Facebook Pixel Help
   D) Facebook Pixel Helper

6. Which of these errors will appear when a pixel is found but unable to pass the back data from your website?

A) Pixel Did Not Load
B) Invalid Pixel ID
C) Not a Standard Event
D) Pixel Activated Multiple Times

7. Which of these reporting metrics pertain to the number of events that can be attributed to users who either viewed or clicked the ads across all your ad accounts associated to the event set?

A) Events received
B) Matched events
C) Attributed events
D) Attributed value

8. Which of the following statements is false?

A) You create Standard events by adding to the pixel base code
B) You don't need an additional code for Custom Conversions
C) You can customize conversions using parameters
D) Standard events are compatible with dynamic product ads and custom conversions are not

9. What is the limit of custom conversions you are allowed to have at a time?

A) 25
B) 50
C) 90
D) 100

10. Which strategies could work in retargeting audiences?

A) Reach your audience where they are most likely to buy
B) Remind them of the items they are interested in
C) Offer them a compelling reason to complete their purchase
D) Leave them alone

Did You Know?

Customers spend more money (20-40 percent) on brands who engage directly with them on social media. (Social Media Today)

Chapter 6

Customer Avatar and Facebook Audience

A customer avatar is a fictional identity that you can use to guide your decisions about selecting your target audience. It can help you get a better understanding of your customers. Put simply, an avatar is the archetype of who your ideal customers are. Knowing your target audience better will help you create more relevant content and sell more effectively by reaching the right people.

What are the benefits of a customer avatar?

- It can help you create a better connection with your customers when you understand them well enough.
- It will guide you in the process of producing highly targeted messages that can get you better conversion rates.
- It can inspire your ad and content ideas.
- It can help you in driving more sales and increasing customer retention.
- It will allow you to find the audience your product will most likely appeal to.

What are the essentials of creating a customer avatar?

To be more effective, your customer avatar must not be a typical stereotype. It should reflect the persona of real people. You need to really dig deep and get to what makes these people tick. For this to happen, you need to base the creation of your customer avatar according to real data. With this said, you can use the following information to guide you.

Background – This includes basic details about a person like education, employment type, interests and turn-offs among others.

Demographics - Age range, location, gender, income and other demographical info are also essential in determining who they are and where you might find them.

Characteristics - Identify your customer's interests, influences and hobbies. What is it that defines their character? This information is helpful in finding out what can capture their interest.

Pain Points - What are their concerns, challenges or objections? These pain points are very crucial and will help you zero in on how to connect with them effectively. With this information, you can find better ways to engage them.

Gain - Knowing your customers' desires, their preferred results and outcomes are important in determining the best reason why they will buy. It is very helpful information that you can use to increase conversion.

There are many ways to collect these important pieces of information. To be authentic, you need to create your customer avatar based on real and actual customers.

You can utilize your current base of customers for a survey. An offer can be made to compel them to participate in your little survey. Another way is through interviews which you can do via email, phone or even in person.

An interview or a survey will really allow you to go in-depth. However, it can be challenging to get people to participate. An alternative is to utilize resources already available to you. A good example is using analytics systems such as Google Analytics or Facebook Audience Insight.

Facebook Audience Insight

With Audience Insights, you get access to aggregated information about different groups of people starting with Facebook users to users who have connected to your Page and people that belong in Custom Audience.

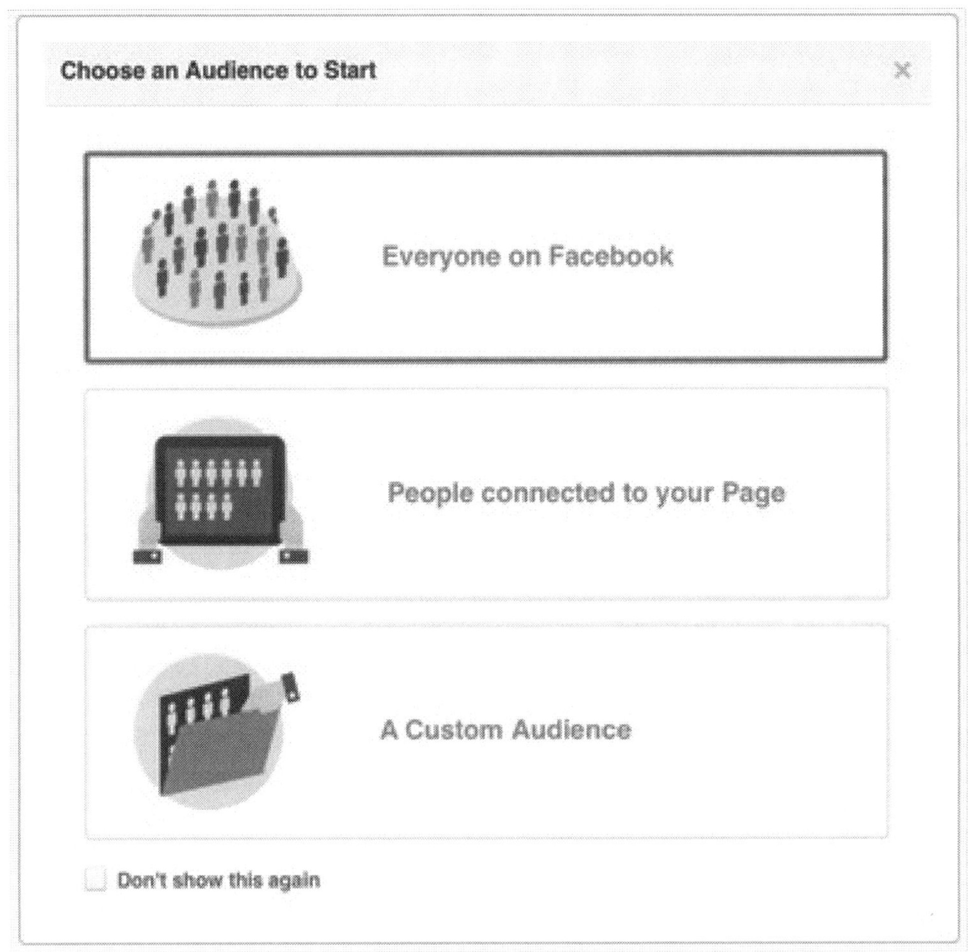

Among the things that you can get from Insights include the following.

Demographics - breakdown of age and gender, job titles, education levels, etc.

Interests and Hobbies - This includes information obtained from third-party giving you an idea about the products your audience may be interested in.

Lifestyles - This is a combination of demographics information and people's interests particularly in your brand or business.

With the options above, you have a good range of audiences to choose from. However, you must be careful about choosing the right one. Accessing data about all users may not necessarily give you a good insight about your target audience while the users connected to your page may not allow you enough room to identify potential niches.

There's also a possibility that some of your followers are not part of your actual customers. To avoid these issues, it will be useful to rely on Audience Insights to determine custom audiences rather than identifying broader audiences.

Custom Audience

From an existing customer list (e.g. email list), a custom audience can be created. And with a custom audience, you can laser focus your Facebook, Instagram and Audience Network Ads to them.

Your hashed customer list can be uploaded, imported or copy and pasted and it will be used to match with Facebook users.

Custom Audiences is an excellent way of reaching customers that you already know using Facebook ads. Your customer list must include contact information such as phone numbers or email addresses. Information you've collected from either an app or your website may also be useful. With this information, Facebook can deliver your ads to the people that match your custom audience from the list.

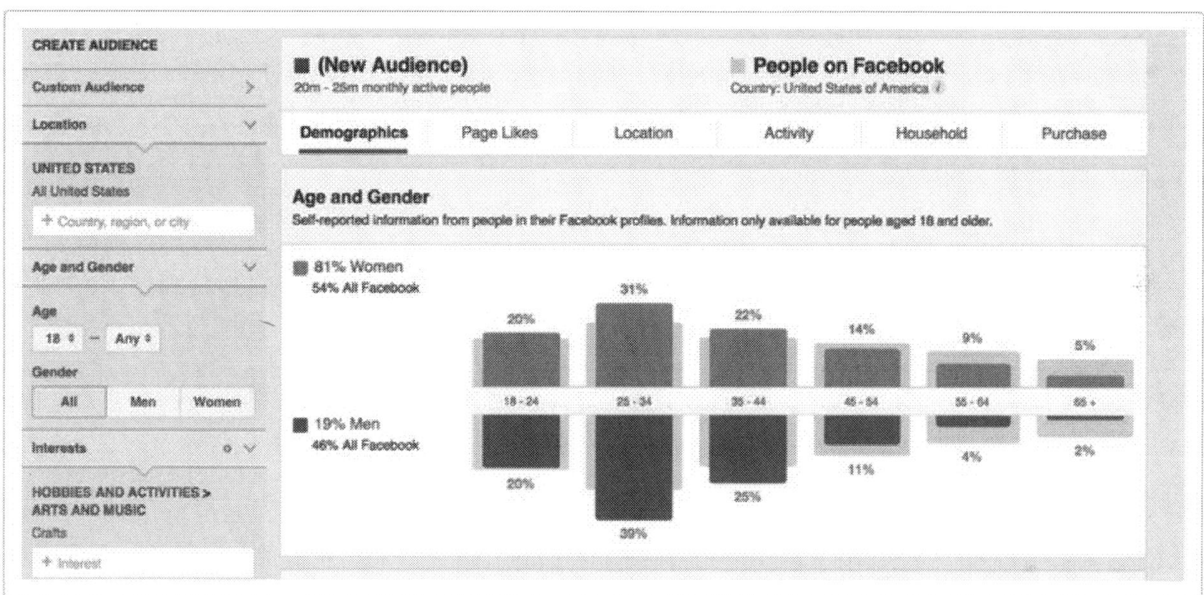

How to create Custom Audience from customer file?

Before you head on to creating a Custom Audience, there are two essential things you have to prepare for. One, you need to get your customer file ready. As you go on creating it, stick to best practices during the process. Two, you have to make sure that you are compliant with the General Data Protection Regulation or GDPR most especially if your customer list includes EU residents. It's an important matter you have to pay attention to. With these two requirements completed, you can follow these steps to start creating your Custom Audience.

- Access **Audiences**.
- With an existing audience, click on the dropdown menu for **Create Audience** and choose **Custom Audience**.
- If you don't have an existing audience, click on the audience creation buttons and choose **Create a Custom Audience**.
- Select the Customer file.
- Choose the option to Add it from your own file.

Adding a Customer File

- Go to the dropdown menu for **Original Data Source**.
- Choose where you want to get the file from. You have an option to either upload it as a .txt or .csv file or copy and paste the information.

- To upload a file, choose the option to **Upload File** and pick the customer file.
- To copy and paste, go to the field that says, **"Paste your content here"**
- Enter a name for your **Custom Audience** and add a description then choose Next.

From the information you obtain about your customers using Custom Audience, you can create a customer avatar that is realistic and truly representative of your target customer. A challenge here is if your Custom Audience is not as large as it should be to get a more comprehensive perspective of your ideal customers.

In this case, you can shift to another group of audience to analyze. You can switch to All Facebook Users and work on segmenting them according to some targeting qualifications. You can segment them based on their interests or any characteristics relevant to your brand or business.

Facebook Live

Facebook Live allows all users including Pages, people and public figures the ability of sharing live video with friends and followers. For businesses and marketers, Facebook live is a way to increase reach and improve audience engagement.

Benefits of Facebook Live

The popularity of social media and online video streaming and the combination of both makes Live a commendable tool. Using Facebook Live for marketing brings a string of benefits.

It can drive engagement.

People are more likely to post a comment on Facebook Live videos. As a matter of fact, Live videos get ten times more comments than regular videos do. People also spend three times longer watching live videos that regular ones.

When you broadcast longer, you present more opportunity for people to share and discover your live video. Facebook allows 90 minutes for Live. By humanizing your brand, you have a bigger opportunity to improve your level of engagement with customers and social followers.

Facebook Live offers a great user experience.

The ability to participate and become involved gives users an exceptional experience. In a world where people are constantly bombarded by ads and announcements, Live video seems like a welcome relief.

Marketers can do a live stream of Q&A sessions, sneak peaks for new products, news sharing or even a behind-the-scenes of a live event. Viewers can provide real time feedback, interact with the broadcaster and other viewers. From the marketing perspective, this is an excellent PR opportunity and is absolutely useful as part of brand strategy.

It can help in boosting organic reach.

One of the most excellent ways of boosting your organic reach is through Facebook Live video. It is quite a distinct type of content. And Facebook algorithm distinguishes between native and Live video with the latter being favored. It means Live Videos have a higher chance of appearing at the top of the News Feed during the broadcast. On top of this, the video is still viewable and discoverable after the broadcast.

There is a unique notification system for Facebook live video. Facebook automatically sends a notification to users who have either recently or frequently interact with the page of the profile broadcasting the live video. This gives such videos more prominence helping brands and businesses reach top-of-mind.

It's affordable.

The cost of live streaming is among its biggest advantages. Sophisticated broadcasting equipment is not a requirement. A little investment on cable, microphone, tripod and lighting can go a long way. Even natural lighting works. People seem to connect better with raw live videos because of their authenticity.

It offers subscription to Live notifications.

People are drawn to dynamic content. With the availability of subscription to Live notifications, interest and a sense of urgency is triggered among followers. The prospect of real time interaction is a compelling enough reason for viewers to join the live broadcast.

The Live Video stays on your Feed.

Even after the live broadcast, the video gets shown on your Facebook page which means followers can still discover and watch the content. This is among the many reasons why advertisers are taking advantage of this opportunity to leverage their videos and boost the effectiveness and efficiency of their online marketing campaigns.

Possible Challenges with Facebook Live

Facebook Live video is not without challenges. In a live broadcast, anything can happen and you must prepare yourself for any possible issues.

Technical Issues

Technical glitches such as blurry videos, lagging, slow streaming or warped sounds can be too obtrusive that viewers may lose interest tuning in to the live broadcast.

Censorship

Facebook Live videos must comply with the Community Standards. You may be in control of the content you broadcast but censoring viewer participation is another challenge.

Controversy

There have been many controversial Live videos and they're not exactly the good kind. In any brand or business, image, confidentiality and conduct are crucial. Boosting your organic reach and building customer engagement should not in any way compromise your brand's image.

Accessibility

If your target audience is within the same time zone, accessibility is not a problem at all. However, if you have a wider target audience, timing can be quite a challenge. It is crucial to catch your viewers at the right time. If you're targeting people across the world, consider the possibility of doing multiple live streams.

Facebook Live Features

Facebook Live is rich in useful features that can help you optimize your brand strategy. Such features include the following.

Notifications

With its very own notification system, Facebook Live can be known to followers in real time. Notifications are also set to on by default which means marketers have a great chance of reaching their audience during their broadcasts. Any person who have recently or frequently interacts with their Page can receive the notification. Other users can also opt to subscribe so they will be notified every time a broadcaster goes Live.

Invite Friends

Broadcasters can reach more people through their viewers. Viewers have the option to send an invite to their friends and watch the broadcast with them.

Facebook Live Map

This map is designed to allow users to discover Live videos easily. All Live videos currently broadcasting will be shown on the map as a blue dot. Popular broadcasts are shown in larger dots. Users can access the map on desktop. When they hover over a dot, they will see a preview of the video.

Live Reactions

Live videos get real time reactions. All the Reactions are shown on the video as the audience clicks on one of the six emoji-like Reactions.

Filters

Live videos can also be filtered which is a great feature for broadcasters. To add a filter, you can follow these steps.

- Start the recording of your live broadcast.
- Tap on the icon for the magic wand.
- Scroll your mouse to the left to access the filter options.
- Tap on a filter to use it.

Snapchat-Like Masks

Masks are also available for broadcasters which can make for a more interesting video. To use a mask during a live broadcast, you can follow these steps.

- Start the recording of your live broadcast.
- Tap on the icon for the magic wand.
- Choose the icon mask from the creative tools tray found at the bottom of the page.
- Scroll your mouse through the options and simply tap on any mask to use it.
- To remove a mask, scroll to the left and click on No mask.

Facebook Live API

An existing broadcasting setup can be incorporated into Live using the Facebook Live API. Instead of streaming from mobile devices, broadcasters can use a professional camera or a sophisticated audio setup. There are other features that come with Live API including special effects, on-screen graphics, instant replay and camera switching. Other sources such as screencasts and games can also be streamed through API. Other possibilities with API include continuous live streaming and scheduled live broadcasts.

Continuous Live Streaming

A continuous live feed is possible with API. The setup is definitely more complex than a mobile broadcast but it's a great option for users who may require a continuous streaming.

Scheduled Live Broadcast

Building up the audience is a good strategy to enforce. This can be done through announcements as posts to your News Feed. One-time notification will be sent as a reminder before the live streaming begins but fans can access a pre-broadcast lobby. It's a way for them to connect and interact. Live broadcasts can be scheduled up to 1 week ahead and fans can enter the lobby 3 minutes before the broadcast.

Share in a Group/Event

Facebook Live has various live streaming options. It allows broadcasting from either a profile or a Page. The Facebook Live Video can also be shared directly in a group or an event.

Metrics

There are different metrics used for measuring the performance of live video broadcasts. Metrics for video in Facebook Insights including number of views, top videos, 30-second videos, viewer engagement and demographic breakdown of minutes viewed among others along with 2 Facebook Live video metrics: peak concurrent viewers and viewers during the live broadcast, are used.

Peak Concurrent Viewers - This records the highest number of viewership during the live broadcast.

Viewers During Live Broadcast - It displays the number of viewers in every moment of the broadcast.

How to start broadcasting a Facebook Live video?

A red icon will show in the top left-hand corner of a live broadcast. **Live** will also appear beside the icon, displaying the number of viewers in real time. To start broadcasting, you can follow these steps.

- Click **Update Status**.
- Tap on the **Live Video** icon.
- Enter a description for the video.
- Select the audience to share the video with.
- Go live.

A broadcaster will be able to see the number of current viewers along with the names of friends watching and the comments in real-time. When the live broadcast ends, a post will be saved on Timeline just like any regular video.

Facebook Live Tips

While there are a lot of things you can do right in Facebook Live so many things can also go wrong. You can ensure the success of your Live videos by following these tips.

Plan the broadcast.

Anything can happen during a live broadcast but this doesn't mean you should just leave everything to chance. Stream with a purpose. Have your objective in mind when planning your content.

You have to think about why the message can be best delivered in a Live stream rather than in another content format. Consider the things you want to say and the topic you want to cover during the broadcast. Be clear about the things you want to say and do.

Tell people when the broadcast is going to happen.

Treat Facebook Live as if you're hosting an event. Because you want people to show up, you should tell them exactly when it's going to happen. Don't just post something about the upcoming broadcast. You may also want to encourage people to enter your Live video subscription. To reach more people, consider promoting your broadcast in other social channels.

Check your connection.

There's nothing more annoying than lagging during a broadcast especially for a viewer. To avoid this issue, make sure to check your connection and that you have a strong signal before going live. Use a speed test app to ensure that your internet speed is fit for live streaming.

Make your description compelling.

Catch your audience's attention with an informative and compelling description. Give them context. Make sure you offer them a good reason to tune in.

Tag your location.

You can reach people through notifications but you can also broaden your reach further by appearing on Facebook Live Map. You can reach new viewers by being discoverable on the Map. All it takes is to tag your location.

Encourage your viewers to follow you.

To ensure the number of your future viewership keeps growing, you can offer your viewers the option to subscribe to your Facebook Live videos. This way, they get automatically notified when you broadcast. They may not be aware of the option so make sure they are informed.

Be responsive to comments.

Engagement is essential in the success of your social content. With Facebook Live video, you have the best chance to engage your viewers. Read and respond to their comments in real time. Mention your viewers by their name. Make them feel involved and included.

Broadcast for extended periods of time.

The longest you can broadcast on mobile is 90 minutes. You don't have to consume that much time but spend at least 10 minutes live. It will give you more time to reach people and interact with them as you get your message across.

Finally, be resourceful and creative with your broadcasts. Do not be afraid to experiment. Explore different kinds of broadcasts. This is the best way to find out what resonates the most with your audience.

When is it best to use Facebook Live?

Depending on your strategy, the requirements of your campaign and your objectives, Facebook Live video can be quite useful. However, there are a couple of situations that call for live streaming and such situations include the following.

- Discuss hot topics
- Do a Q&A session
- Present breaking news
- Broadcast performances and live events
- Show behind-the-scenes
- Product demonstration
- Make announcements or launch campaign

As long as it is relevant and useful to your brand or business, go for it!

Facebook Creative Hub

This is the destination to help with your creative process from learning about, creating a mock up and a preview to testing your Facebook and Instagram ads. The Hub is a resource within Facebook Ads that allows advertisers to explore, share and create.

How exactly can Creative Hub help you in creating more effective Facebook ads?

There are a lot of ways that Creative Hub can be of assistance from learning about the most successful and most creative ad campaigns to sharing ideas that'll help you manage your own ad. Below is a list of the biggest benefits and the best ways to maximize the use of the hub.

Get inspired by big brands.

Access tons of examples of every ad type using the Get Inspired button.

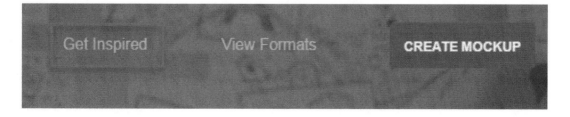

Create a concept and edit your idea with a mockup.

Some people forego the step of creating a mockup for their ads simply because it can be challenging. With this feature in Creative Hub, it's easier to create a mockup and bring your ideas to life until you are able to come up with the most effective and relevant ads for your campaigns.

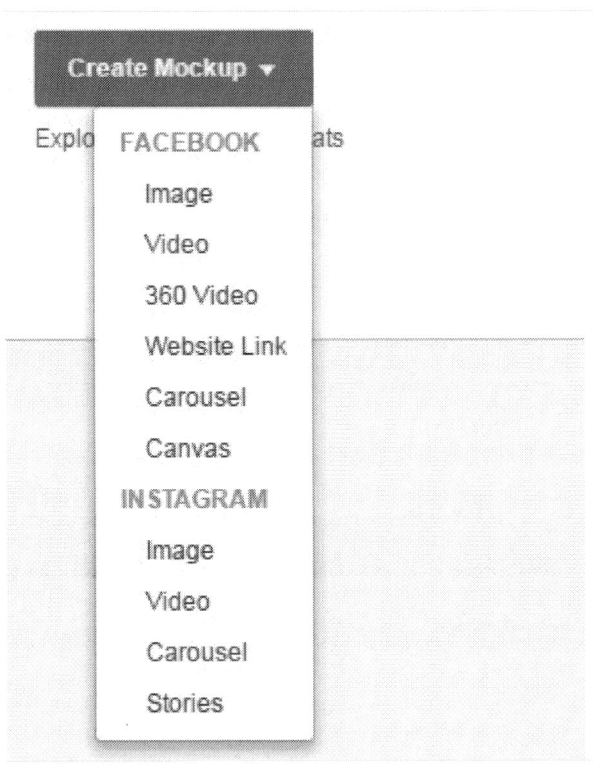

Test your images to make sure they are approved.

Another cool feature of Creative Hub is that it allows you to add images in your mockup ads using a built-in checker. So even before you devote your time to creating your final draft, you have a good idea with regards to whether or not your images will be approved. On top of this, Facebook can also gives you a rough idea on how the use of your image can contribute to the performance of your ad.

Discover new ad formats.

There are tons of things to learn from Creative Hub. You can get creative ideas even with new ad formats. You can get more of this from **Facebook Collections** and **Instagram Stories**.

Discover Instagram.

If you're not using Instagram ads yet, Creative Hub is a good place to start exploring this idea. You can learn from the Instagram pros and create your own mockup too until you are comfortable enough to put it out there and reap the benefits of using this format.

Improve your mobile presentation.

It is undeniable how people rely on their mobile phones for any task possible including browsing and shopping. With Creative Hub, you can get an idea how your content is presented on mobile devices. View the content the way mobile viewers see it and make the necessary adjustments.

You can also use Creative Hub for sharing ideas with your group or clients. You can preview your ads before they go live. Creative Hub also makes it easier to manage, edit and export your content.

Congratulations!

The fourth character of the password required to unlock the Answer Booklet is letter u.

Chapter 6 Quiz

Please refer to the Answer Booklet for the solution to this quiz

1. This is a fictional identity that you can use to guide your decisions about selecting your target audience.

   A) Facebook Audience
   B) Facebook Avatar
   C) Custom Audience
   D) Customer Avatar

2. What are the benefits of creating a customer avatar?

   A) It can help you create a better connection with your customers when you understand them well enough
   B) It will guide you in the process of producing highly targeted messages that can get better conversion rates.
   C) It can inspire your ad and content ideas and will allow you to find the audience your product will most likely appeal to
   D) It can help you in driving more sales and increasing customer retention

3. What are the essential information that will help you in the process of creating a customer avater?

   A) Background and Demographics
   B) Characteristics
   C) Pain Point
   D) Gain

4. With this feature, you get access to aggregated information about different groups of people starting with Facebook users to users who have connected to your Page to people that belong in Custom Audience.

   A) Customer Avatar
   B) Lifestyle
   C) Audience Insight
   D) Target Audience

5. What are the two things you need to prepare for before you head on to creating a Custom Audience?

   A) Customer File
   B) GDPR Compliance
   C) Existing Audience
   D) Facebook Users

6. This feature allows all users including Pages, people and public figures the ability of sharing live video with friends and followers.

A) Facebook Live
B) Facebook Video
C) Facebook Streaming
D) Facebook Messenger

7. Which of the following statements is not true.

    A) Facebook Live has its own notification system
    B) Facebook Live notifications are set to on by default
    C) Any person who have recently or frequently interacts with the broadcaster's Page can receive notification.
    D) There is no subscribe option to Facebook Live notifications.

8. This feature is designed to allow users to discover Live videos easily by displaying all Live videos currently broadcasting.

    A) Facebook Live Notifications
    B) Facebook Live Map
    C) Facebook Live Recording
    D) Facebook Live Filters

9. Which are included in the list of metrics used by Facebook in measuring the success of live video broadcasts?

    A) Peak concurrent viewers
    B) Viewers during the live broadcast
    C) Viewer engagement
    D) Metrics for video through Facebook Insights

10. This is the destination to help with your creative process from learning about, creating a mock up and a preview to testing your Facebook and Instagram ads

    A) Creative Center
    B) Command Center
    C) Creative Hub
    D) Creative Ads

Did You Know?

Video will be more important for social media content marketing than ever. According to Smart Insights, 90 percent of all content shared by users on social media in 2017 was video.

Chapter 7

Facebook Ad Campaign

There are 3 parts to the Facebook campaign structure and they include the following.

Campaign - A group of ads and ad sets makes a campaign. Each campaign is guided by one advertising objective.

Ad set - A group of ads makes an ad set. Targeting, schedule, budget, placement and bidding are defined at this level.

Ad - Your creative content makes an ad.

By making these components work together, you can run your ads exactly the way you want to run them and reach who you want to reach.

Choosing the Right Objective for Your Ads

Granted, your campaign goals will more likely evolve as your business expands. However, the starting point is always on building awareness for your brand or business and acquiring new customers. You will eventually want to compel people to purchase a product or service. You may also want to encourage them to sign up and join an event you're organizing.

There are various objectives that can go hand in hand with your business goals. Let's explore them one by one.

Goal 1: To raise public awareness of the business

If you want to increase public awareness of your business or brand, you need to tell people what it is that makes your brand or business valuable. People must be made to understand the overall value of your business that makes it unique among others i.e. your unique selling or value proposition.

The complementary advertising objectives to this main goal are Reach and Engagement.

- **Reach** - To achieve this your ad needs to be shown to people either residing nearby or around the general location of your business.
- **Engagement** - To drive engagement, you must connect with people you have already reached and boost your post to further grow your reach.

Goal 2: To find more potential customers

To achieve this objective, you need to find different ways to capture people's interest in your product or service. A couple of things that can work effectively include newsletter sign-ups or attendance in local events hosted by your business.

For instance, a newly opened local grocery delivery service aims to attract customers. To achieve this goal, they created a lead ad and had people sign up in their notification of the delivery service. They had an event launch and awarded attendees by giving them 20% off in their order.

The complementary advertising objectives to this main goal are Conversions and Lead Generation.

- **Conversions** - To improve conversion rates on your website, you will need to run ads that compels people to visit.

- **Lead generation** - To be able to gather leads for the business, you need to run ads that can collect people's information. A good example is a sign up for notifications and newsletters.
- **Engagement** - Increase your event's attendance by creating ads that can promote your event.
- **Messages** - To start communication with your potential customers, you need to run ads that are compelling enough to start a conversation, as well as, encouraging enough for your customers to respond.

Goal 3: To increase sales of the products or services

To measure the success of your campaign, you need to keep track of the number of people who viewed your ad, visited your website and purchased your product or service.

The complementary advertising objectives to this main goal are Engagement and Conversions.

- **Engagement** - When you make an offer, you would want people to sign up and claim it. To do this, you need to create ads with discounts, coupons and other special offers.
- **Conversions** - Interaction and engagement is essential for conversions. Find a way to build communication with your existing audience.
- **Messages** - Connect with your customers by creating ads that can keep them interested and compel them to purchase your products or services.

Setting Your Advertising Objectives

When people see your ads, you want them to respond accordingly. This is why before you create your ad, you need to have a clear objective. Allow this objective to guide your creative process. And this objective should be perfectly aligned with the overall goals for your brand or business. For instance, if you're aiming to get interested people to visit your website, you must create ads that encourage them to go.

Advertising objectives can be grouped into 3 categories. They are awareness, consideration and conversion.

Awareness

These are objectives for generating interest in your brand or business. There are two items in this group: Brand Awareness and Reach.

1. Brand Awareness – This basically entails increasing the awareness of your products or services. As well as, reaching people who are more likely to recall/ remember your ads

Platforms that support this objective	Ad formats to utilize
Facebook	Single image
Instagram	Carousel
Messenger	Single video
	Slideshow

2. Reach – This entails creating ads that can reach as many people from your audience

Platforms that support this objective	Ad formats to utilize
Facebook	Single image
Instagram	Carousel

Messenger	Single video
	Slideshow

Consideration

These are objectives that aim to put your business in the mind of people. When they start thinking about the business, the next goal is to compel them to seek more information about it.

1. Traffic - To increase your website's visits. To have people use your app

With this objective, you can send more people to the website or build their engagement in the app.

Platforms that support this objective	Ad formats to utilize
Facebook	Single image
Instagram	Carousel
Messenger	Single video
Audience Network	Slideshow
	Collection

2. App installs - To direct people to the app store where your app can be downloaded

Platforms that support this objective	Ad formats to utilize
Facebook	Single image
Instagram	Carousel
Messenger	Single video
Audience Network	Slideshow

3. Engagement - To have more people see and engage with your Page and posts

With this objective, you can do the following.

- Boost your post and improve post engagement
- Promote your Page and get more Page Likes
- Have more people claim an offer from your Page and receive more Offer claims
- Increase the attendance for an event on your Page and increase Event responses

Platforms that support this objective	Ad formats to utilize
Facebook	Single image
Instagram (except event ads)	Single video
	Slideshow

4. Video Views - To promote videos for product launches, customer stories raising brand awareness or showing behind-the-scenes footage

Platforms that support this objective	Ad formats to utilize
Facebook	Single image
Instagram	Carousel
Audience Network	Slideshow

5. Lead Generation - To collect lead information from people who are interested in the brand or businesses

Platforms that support this objective	Ad formats to utilize
Facebook	Single image
Instagram	Carousel
Messenger	Slideshow
	Single video

6. Messages - To have more conversations with more people and offer support, answer questions, generate leads and drive transactions

Platforms that support this objective	Ad formats to utilize
Facebook	Single image
Instagram	Carousel
Messenger	Slideshow
	Single video

Conversion

These are objectives encouraging people who expressed interest in your business to use and purchase your product or service.

1. Conversions - To have more people use your website, mobile app or Facebook app. To monitor and measure your conversions, use app events and use Facebook pixel

Platforms that support this objective	Ad formats to utilize
Facebook	Single image
Instagram	Carousel
Messenger	Slideshow
Audience Network	Single video
	Collection

2. Catalog Sales - To show the products from your catalog to your target audience

Platforms that support this objective	Ad formats to utilize
Facebook	Single image
Instagram	Carousel

Messenger	
Audience Network	

3. Store Visits - To promote multiple business locations to nearby people

Platforms that support this objective	Ad formats to utilize
Facebook	Single image
	Carousel
	Single video
	Slideshow
	Carousel

How to Set Up an Ad Account in Business Manager?

- Access your **Business Manager Settings**.
- From the **People and Assets tab**, choose **Ad Accounts**.
- From the right side section, click on **Add New Ad Account**.
- Pick from any of these options: **Create a New Ad Account**, **Claim Ad Account** and **Request Access to an Ad Account**.
- If you pick any of the last two options, you must enter the corresponding **Ad Account ID**.

After setting up the ad account, you are required to provide additional account information and credit card data before you can begin advertising.

How to Add your Ad Account Info?

- From the Business **Manager Main Menu**, go to **Ad Account Settings**.

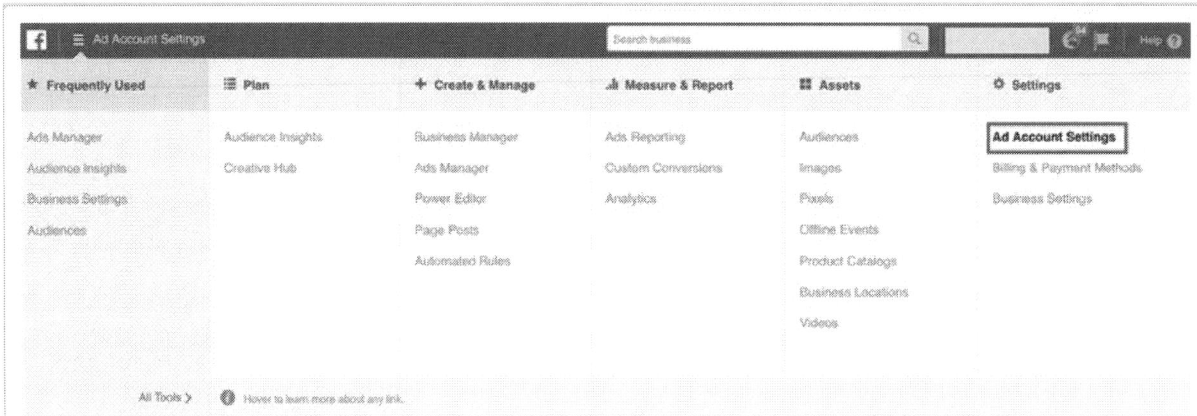

- Enter details including your company's name, address and other pertinent information.

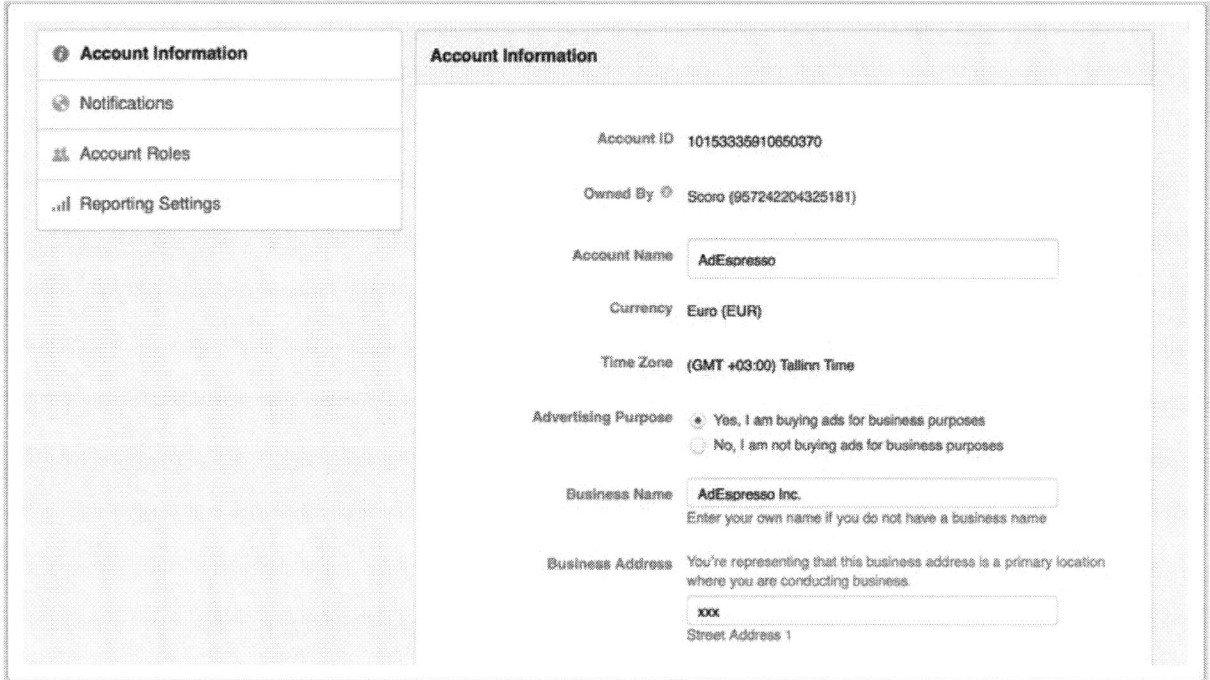

- Under **Payments tab**, choose **Add Payment Method**.
- Fill in your billing information.
- Enter your time zone and select your billing currency.
- After completing your ad account information, click on **Save Changes**.

How to Set Up your Billing and Payment Information?

- From the **Business Manager Menu**, click on **Billing & Payment Methods**.

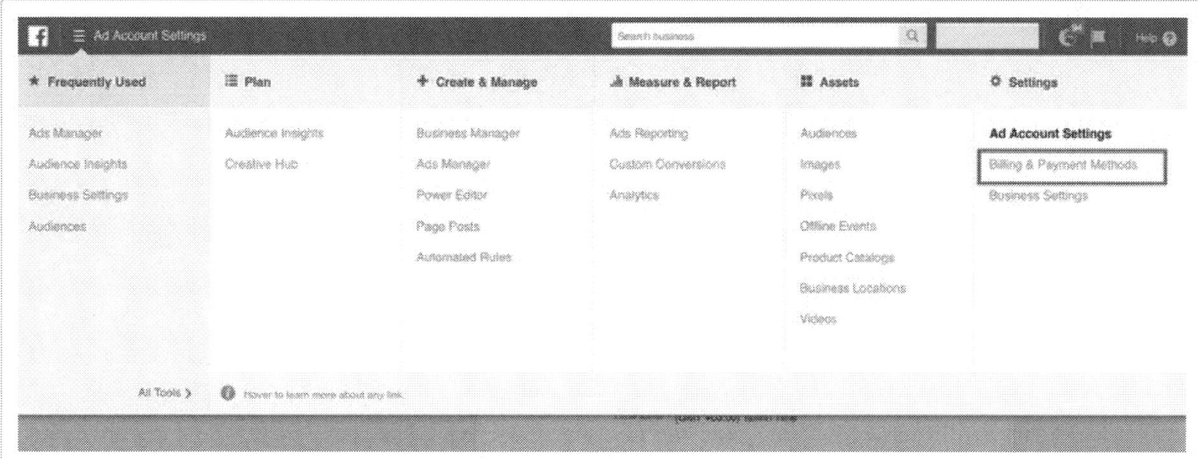

- You can do the following on the Billing page:

- Add a new payment method.
- Edit existing payment methods.
- Set your ad account's spending limit.

How to add new payment method?

- Click the green button for **Add Payment Method**.
- Select your preferred method.

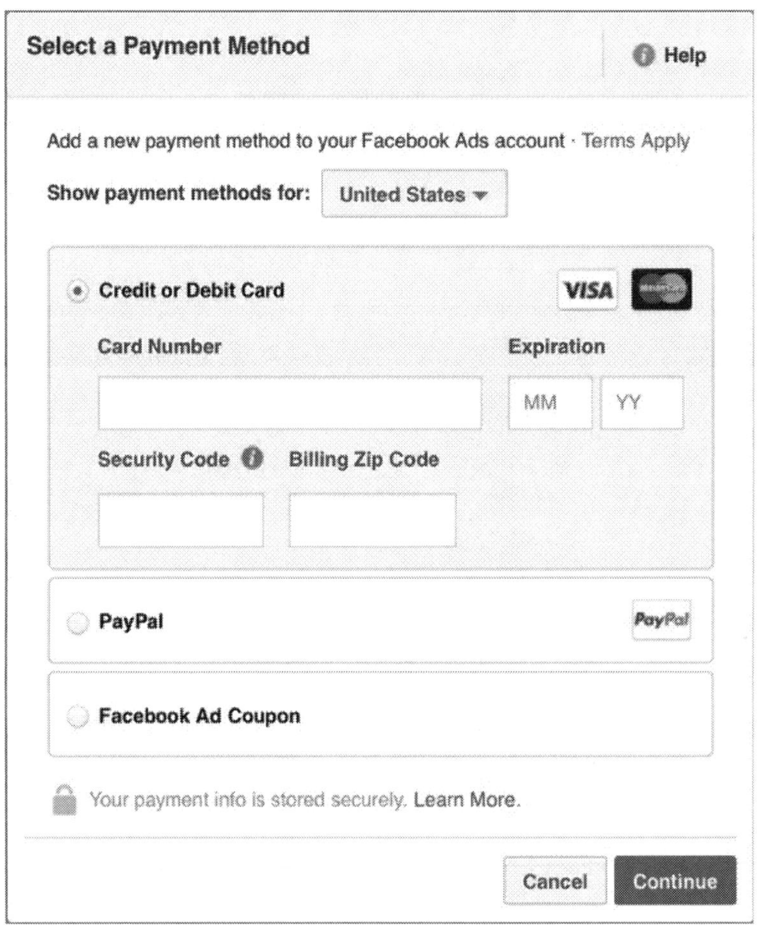

- Enter your information.
- Click Continue.

Adding Multiple Payment Options

There are multiple payment options accepted including Paypal payments and credit card payments. You also have the option to **Add multiple payment options**.

This is not necessary but as you grow your advertising efforts and push through your campaigns, adding a secondary payment method can help you avoid any issues.

This backup method will be useful in certain instances such as your primary card expiring or reaching your monthly limit or your card being blocked for any reason. This way, your advertising campaign won't be jeopardized and you won't be prevented from delivering your message and reaching your potential customers.

If you don't have any backup in place, then in the instance that your primary card fails, your campaign will suffer. Everything will be paused immediately until the outstanding balance is settled. After that, you will have to restart everything in your campaign manually one by one. This can be such a grueling task if you're running multiple campaigns. A secondary payment method can help you avoid the hassle.

How to Set Spending Limit?

You have the option to put a cap on your ad account spending. This way, you can ensure that you don't exceed your monthly advertising budgets.

Setting up an **Ad Account Spending Limit** is especially useful when you're working with agencies. It is important to ensure that your agency won't spend more than you're ready for.

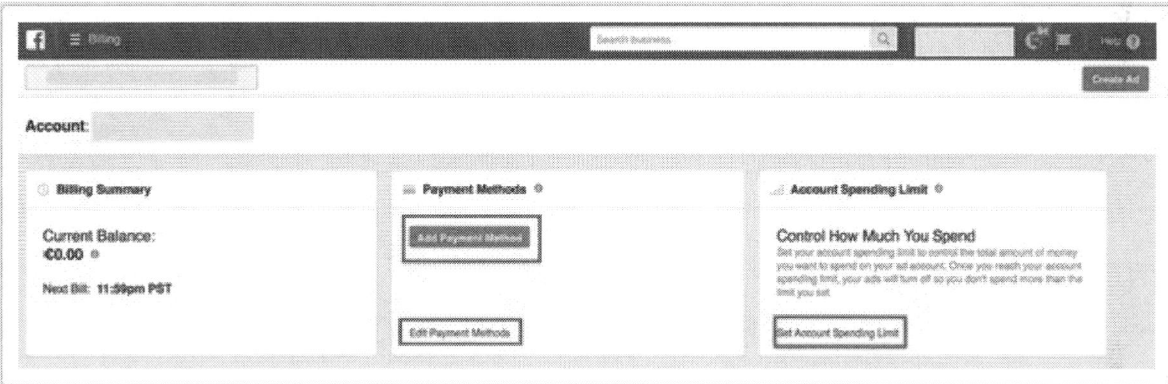

It's quite simple to set your account limit. All you need to do is click on the option to **Set Account Spending Limit**. Enter the amount and you're done.

The key to setting the limit is finding the sweet spot. You don't want to go way beyond but you should also avoid setting the amount too low. When you do, you may face a couple of challenges along the way. Every time you reach the limit, your accounts will be paused. It will stay on pause for 15 minutes or more. Losing time and momentum is not ideal when you want to reach as many people as you want.

Limits on Facebook Ad Accounts

There are certain limitations to your Facebook ad account you need to be mindful of. Among them are the following.

- Each user can manage a maximum of 25 ad accounts.
- Each ad account can manage up to 25 users for every account.
- Each regular ad account is allowed a maximum of 5,000 ads which are not deleted.
- Each regular ad account is allowed a maximum of 1,000 ad set which are not deleted.
- Each regular ad account is allowed a maximum of 1,000 campaigns which are not deleted.
- Each ad account is allowed to have a maximum of 50 ads per ad set which are not deleted.

Note that the limits apply to current and non-deleted campaigns and ads. In which case, when you reach the limit, you can delete your old ads and campaigns to make room for new ones.

Reviewing Your Notification Settings

Facebook Notifications allow you to stay on top of your campaigns. When a lot goes on with your campaigns, your inbox can get flooded very quickly. To avoid this, you can edit the frequency of email notifications.

How to edit your notification settings?

- Access your **Ad Account Settings** page.
- From the left side of the menu, go to Notifications.
- Add or take out the checkmarks next to the notifications according to the ones you want to keep receiving.

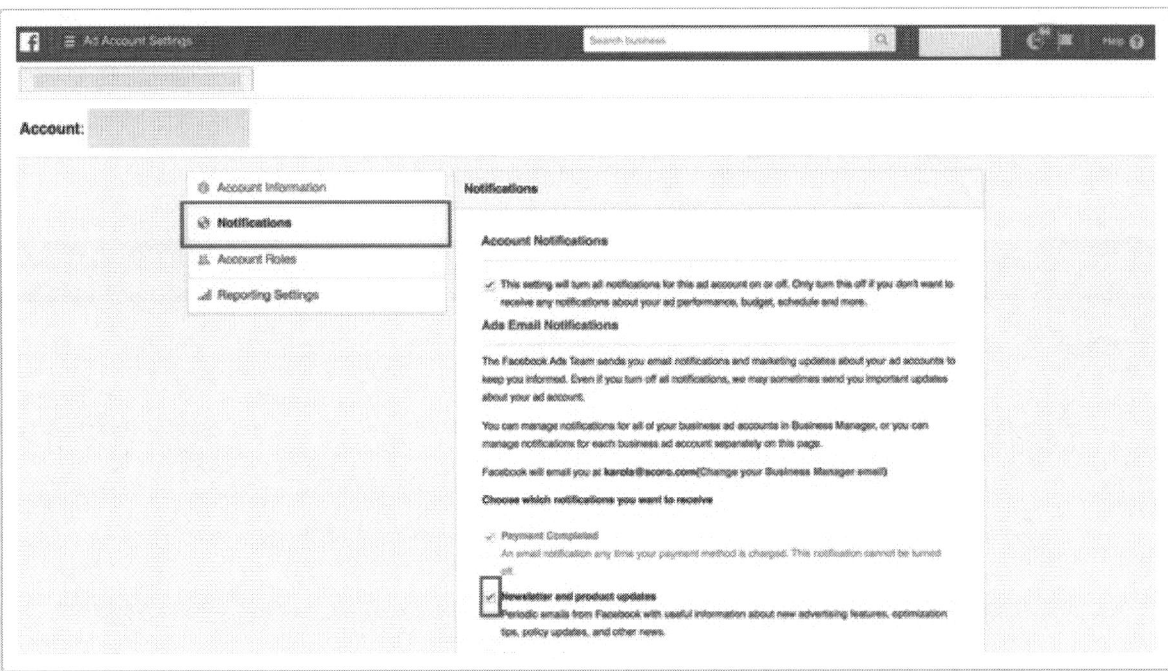

Creating an Effective Ad

Advertising is different for every business. It depends on the nature of the business and each business' specific goals. But the following pointers can help you create an effective ad according to your individual requirements.

Always begin with your goal.

Your goal should always be your starting point. It is crucial that you choose the right objective to guide your ads. Tailor your creative content and format around this objective. There are plenty of ways to increase awareness for your brand. One way of doing it effectively is by telling a story.

Do not just present your products or services the way people usually do. You can try telling a story behind them. It's also a great way of humanizing your business by letting people get to know your brand in a deeper way.

Use your goals to create different audiences.

Use your goal as the driving force in defining your audience. Also consider the possible objectives. Take into account what's important to your audience.

Build a custom ad experience for your audience.

Your approach to new customers should be difference from your existing ones.

Try using less text.

If you decide on using images on top of texts, it may be a good idea to downplay the amount of text you put into the ad. Make the copy short but compelling.

Create a focused message.

Avoid putting too much information in a single ad. Decide from the very beginning what your message will be. Stick and focus on that. If you must display information, you may want to consider using Carousel in order to show multiple images in one ad.

Choose your ad images carefully.

The right image can create a compelling visual message. It is also important to use high-resolution images. Use the size recommendations from the ads guide to make sure your ad images are presented properly. More importantly, it is essential that you follow a consistent theme for your images.

Include call-to-action.

Take advantage of the call-to-action buttons. Use them strategically to drive people to take action upon seeing your ads.

Play around.

Utilize the Creative Hub to explore different formats and images. Create your mock-ups, get as many useful feedbacks as you can and apply them.

Split Testing

This process gives you an opportunity for testing different variations of your ads. This way, you get to find out what works best. You can also learn a thing or two that'll help you improving your future campaigns.

When a split test is created, the audience is divided by ad sets and tested out with one variable to check out which ad set can perform better. The winning version of the ad is determined according to which achieved the lowest cost per result.

Before this, we emphasize on the importance of choosing the right target audience. A customer avatar plays a huge role in this regard. We've looked into the essential things you need to create one in the previous chapter. We will now look further into the process of building this profile essential to your business campaign success.

Here's a step by step guide to the process.

1. Create a profile for your ideal audience.

Whether you've already created one or still in the process of building it, you will find these guide questions useful either to create a new one or improve the one you already have.

- What is the age range of your ideal audience?
- Where do you think they're located?

- Are most of them married?
- Are most of them college educated?
- Is your ideal audience predominantly male or female or both?

These questions pave the way to defining the demographics of your ideal audience. It will help you jumpstart the process of creating a detailed picture of your audience.

2. Develop a series segmented custom audiences that are narrowly defined.

Rather than using big audience segments to create a single custom audience, you actually have the option to build multiple custom audiences.

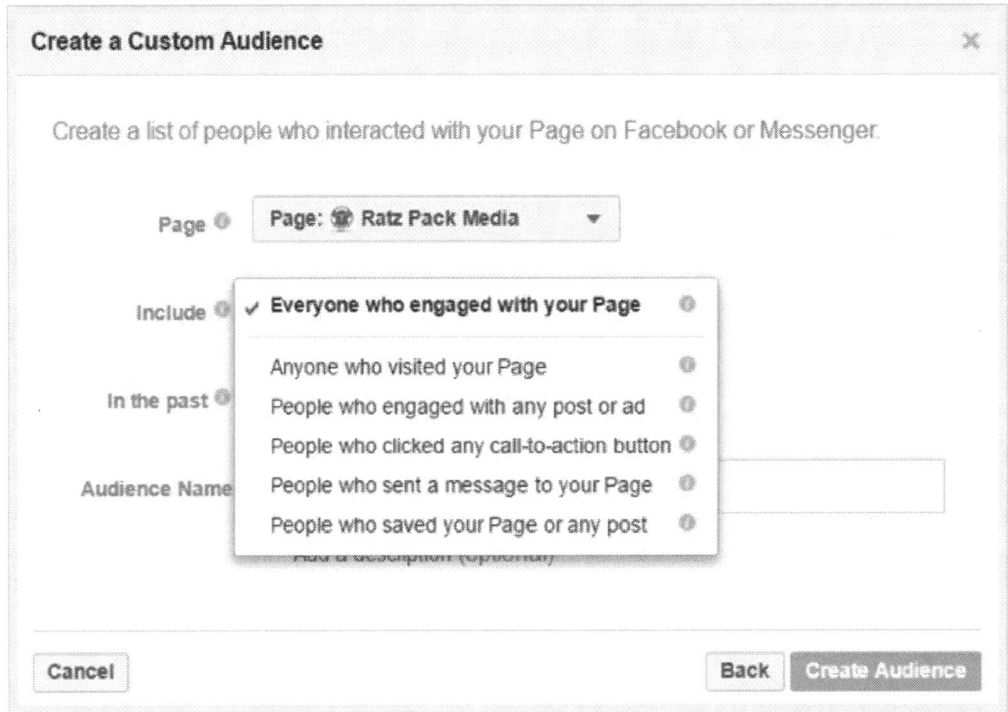

To give you an idea about the custom audience segments to create, here are a couple of examples.

- Video viewers
- Website visitors
- Previous purchasers
- Email subscribers
- People who engaged with posts
- Facebook likes
- 4-5 similar interests
- Lookalikes to any of these audience segments

3. Analyze your custom audience's characteristics using Audience Insights.

At this point, you can check if who you think your audience is aligns with the people that they really are. Compare your impression about them with the data on Audience Insights.

Access **Audience Insights** and go to the **Custom Audience section**.

Choose **Purchasers Audience**. If you have a big enough number like 1,000 in the list, you will have sufficient data to use.

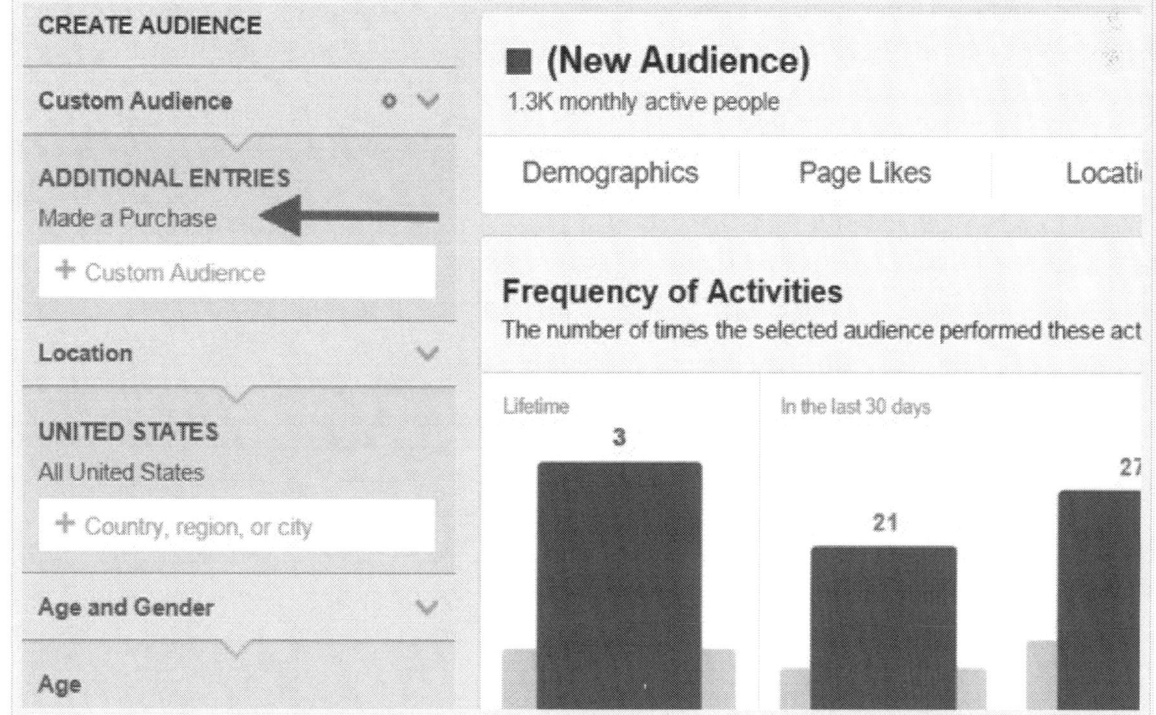

With a smaller number, you can pick another audience big or deep enough from your funnel. If there's not enough purchasers in your list, you may consider choosing **Website visitors** or **Email Subscribers** instead. This may mean the insights you get are not as powerful as those that may come from actual buyers. However, you will still gain some helpful information.

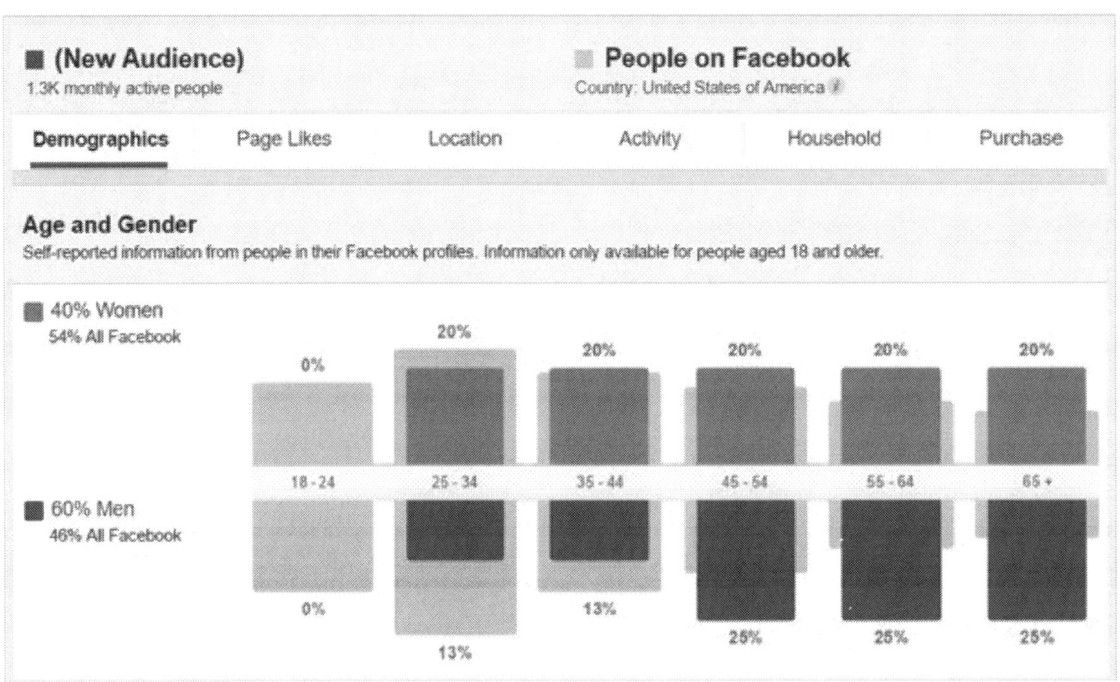

Check out what you have on the **Demographics tab**. Look at how large the audience is. Find out if the information displayed in this section matches your definition of ideal customers.

If you have a match between what you have initially and what audience insight tells you then you're in the right track. Identify any differences if there are any and use what you learn to better define your target audience.

Access the **Activity tab** and check if your buyers are avid Facebook users. If they are regular Facebook users, are they likely to engage with your ads? Do they log in to Facebook using their mobile devices or on desktop?

If your buyers are rarely clicking on ads, then it means that cost per click will not be cost efficient. If they are mobile users, then you need to create an excellent mobile experience for them.

(New Audience)
1.3K monthly active people

People on Facebook
Country: United States of America

Demographics | Page Likes | Location | Activity | Household | Purchase

Frequency of Activities
The number of times the selected audience performed these actions on Facebook. Based on Facebook user activity and environmental data.

Lifetime
In the last 30 days

Pages Liked	Comments	Posts Liked	Posts Shared	Promotions Redeemed	Ads Clicked
3	21	27	7	1	30

Device Users
How the selected audience accessed Facebook in the last 30 days, based on user activity and environmental data.
All Devices Used

Desktop Only	Desktop & Mobile	Mobile Only
8%	75%	17%

Computer	iPhone/iPod	iPad	Android	Blackberry	Mobile Web	Feature Phone	Unknown
100%	0%	0%	0%	0%	0%	0%	0%

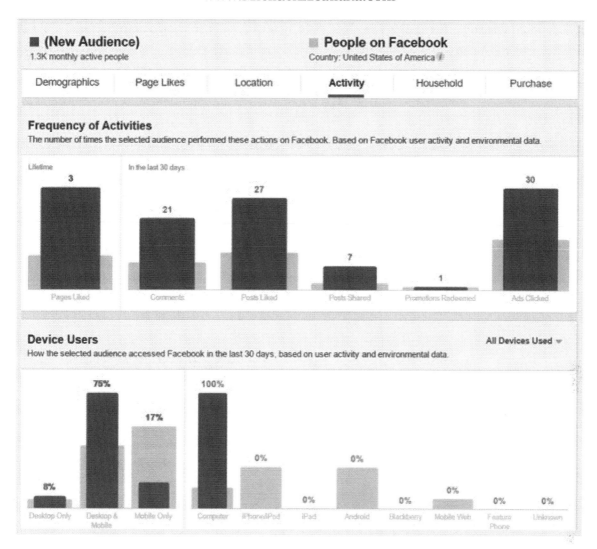

Check out the **Location tab** and find out where your buyers are. Are you thinking of targeting these areas? If you're just starting out, it will make sense to stick with your current target areas and branch out when you're ready.

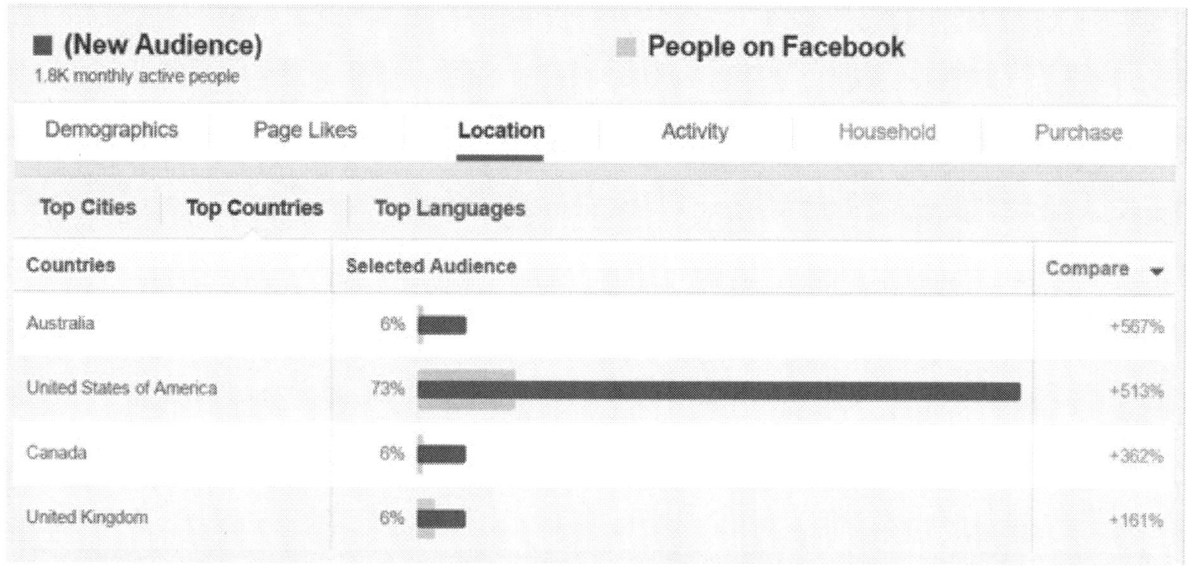

(New Audience)
1.8K monthly active people

People on Facebook

Demographics | Page Likes | Location | Activity | Household | Purchase

Top Cities | Top Countries | Top Languages

Countries	Selected Audience	Compare
Australia	6%	+567%
United States of America	73%	+513%
Canada	6%	+362%
United Kingdom	6%	+161%

Move next to the section for **Page Likes**.

Does the niche in your ideal audience fit with the pages? You may also want to check out other pages in the same niche as yours. You can learn about the frequency of their posts. And more importantly, you can find out what posts audiences are likely to engage with. This will help you as far as organic reach is concerned.

Page Likes

Facebook Pages that are likely to be relevant to your audience based on Facebook Page likes.

Page	Relevance	Audience	Facebook
Tasty	1	24.9m	83.3m
Walmart	2	23.8m	28.5m
Amazon.com	3	21.2m	25.2m
Target	4	19.2m	21.4m
Facebook	5	19m	48.4m
Family Guy	6	16.3m	40.9m
Eminem	7	16.2m	70.9m
Starbucks	8	15.6m	33.3m
Samsung Mobile USA	9	15.1m	22.6m
Subway	10	14.6m	22.6m

After your analysis of your purchasers, you need to move on to the other custom audiences. Follow the same flow of thought and questioning and get all the much needed information to understand your real target customer better.

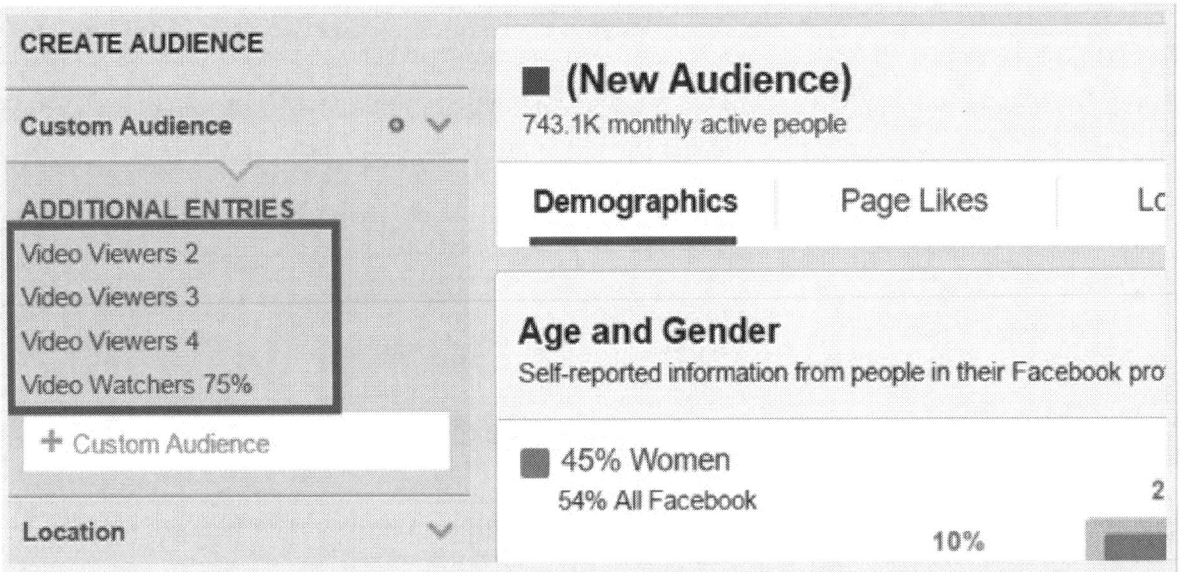

4. Optimize your Facebook targeting by comparing your Custom Audience segment data.

After learning about all the different audience segments, you can now make a full comparison. How close is your audience segment to the actual customers? Are there differences or any disconnect among the types of Facebook users you're targeting, from the people in your email newsletter to your purchasers?

Comparing the data you gathered will allow you to identify the audiences worth targeting. In case of major differences among your actual buyers, Facebook Likes and email subscribers, you may need to rethink your strategy and build a new one.

By the end of this exercise, you should already have found the audience that looks more like your purchasers. You should have already identified other Facebook Pages within your niche. From all this information, you will be able to create ad sets targeted to the right audiences and develop lookalike audiences from your custom audiences who are most like your buying customers.

5. Create multiple ad variations and put them to test.

Create and run ads separately for each of the identified audiences to determine the best-performing groups. Set your daily budget and let that determine the size of your ad sets.

Let's look at the different parts of a Facebook ad. There are 3 areas for your text including the following.

Text Post - This is the area above an image or a video

Headline - Below the image, the headline is that large black bold text.

Description - Below the image, the description is the smaller gray text.

Within the **Power Editor**, start with the ad creation process.

- Write 2 short sentences placed in different locations.
  - Sentence 1 for the Headline
  - Sentence 2 for the Text Post
  - Sentence 3 for the Description
- Choose an image or video.
- Duplicate the ad.
- Change up the placement of the sentences.
- Keep switching the elements until you've come up with multiple combinations of text placements.
- Duplicate your ad set and switch up the targeting.
- Repeat the process until you end up with 5 or about 10 ad sets with 48 ads each.
- Duplicate the combinations and change the image. Use about 4 images or videos or use the same video but use 4 different thumbnails.
- Write 3 new sentences.
- From all these combinations, you should be able to come up with 48 versions. You have a limit of 50 ads for every ad set.

6. Run your ads and track your results.

Give Facebook full 48 hours to run your ads before comparing their performance. For comparison, you can focus on these data points.

Cost per impressions or CPM

A higher CPM for a specific ad set can mean either of these two things.

You have a good content but it's not appealing to the audience. To remedy this issue, you need to try and test out new audiences.

You're targeting the right audience but the content is not good. To remedy this issue, you need to create another content.

Cost per Click or CPC

A higher than average CPC means you need to improve your ads and make them more compelling. Your message and targeting is spot on but your audience is not compelled to take action. Change up the call to action to get more clicks. You can add a phrase like **Click for more information** or write a more compelling **Call to Action** statement.

Time on Site

Getting thousand clicks is good but it can be an issue if the time on site is counted at 12 seconds. This can happen because of the following reasons.

- You're focusing too much of your spending on **Audience Network**.
- You're not reaching the right audience.
- There is no clear connection between the ad and your landing page.

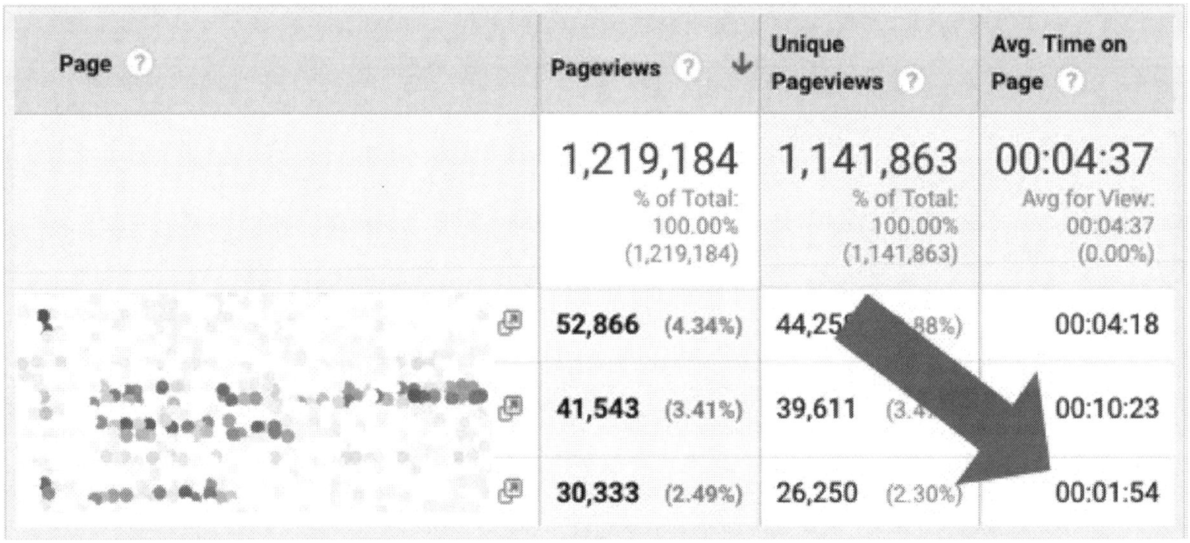

Page	Pageviews	Unique Pageviews	Avg. Time on Page
	1,219,184 % of Total: 100.00% (1,219,184)	1,141,863 % of Total: 100.00% (1,141,863)	00:04:37 Avg for View: 00:04:37 (0.00%)
[illegible]	52,866 (4.34%)	44,25[illegible] ([illegible]88%)	00:04:18
[illegible]	41,543 (3.41%)	39,611 (3.4[illegible])	00:10:23
[illegible]	30,333 (2.49%)	26,250 (2.30%)	00:01:54

You can remedy the issue by testing out different landing page layouts, images and header text. These changes may help in increasing the time spent on your page. You can also try breaking down your desktop and mobile traffic to check if these visitors behave differently.

Landing Page Conversion Rate

In some cases, you may have a good content, reaching the right audience, getting clicks and people spend time on your landing page but the conversion rate is less than satisfactory. This may happen for the following reasons.

- Your audience may not like your offer. To remedy the issue, try a different offer.
- You ask them to give too much information. To remedy the issue, keep your info requirements to 3-4 fields.
- You ask them for information they are not comfortable sharing.

With these data points, you will be able to compare the performance of your ads and ad sets. The information you obtain from the comparison can be used to fix what needs to be fixed, to adjust your spending and choose which ones to turn off or further optimize.

Ad Budgeting

How much do you want to spend showing your ads to people? Determining a budget is not just about deciding on the amount of money you're ready to spend. It also serves as a cost control tool. Setting a budget keeps you on top of your overall spending.

Here are a couple of reminders.

Your budget isn't about paying for the ability to display your ads. It isn't about buying ad placements. Rather, by setting your budget, you're telling Facebook the amount of money you're willing to spend in showing your ads.

A distinction must be made between budget and amount spent. In some cases, Facebook may not spend all of your budget. When it is determined that your ad set is able to compete in ad auctions consistently, your full budget may be spent. Otherwise, your full budget won't get used. Any unused budget won't be billed to you.

If you're not setting a campaign budget, each of your ad set must have its own budget. In which case, if you have multiple active ad sets, you must individually set a budget for them.

What types of budgets you can avail yourself of?

Budget can be set either at a campaign or ad set level. You can choose any one of the levels and there are two kinds of budgets to choose from.

Daily Budgets - This is the average amount that you're ready to spend on a campaign or an ad set every day.

Lifetime Budgets - This is the amount you're ready to spend for the whole run-time of your campaign or ad set.

Switching budget types is not allowed after the campaign or ad set is created. You can however, duplicate your existing campaign or ad set, switch out your budget type and create a new campaign or ad set.

How to decide on a budget?

When setting your budget, it is helpful to think about what you want to control. Decide on your budget depending on whether you care about controlling cost per optimization event or managing your total spending.

Goal 1 - To control total spending

If this is your main goal, you can set the specific total amount you're ready to spend. Give Facebook the flexibility to target and bid.

For instance, if you want to drive traffic to your website with $1,000, you can set $1,000 as your budget. For your optimization event, choose link clicks. Select a broad target audience, set your bid strategy to the lowest cost and remove the bid cap. This will prompt the delivery system to achieve on your behalf the most number of link clicks at the lowest possible cost while spending your full budget.

Goal 2: To control your cost per optimization event

If this is your goal, you must choose a more constrained bid strategy. You can give Facebook the freedom to spend while meeting your cost goal.

For instance, say purchases are your chosen optimization event. If you make a profit worth $10 and the cost of purchase is at $100 or lower, you can set a higher budget when it's paired with a bid.

When using a cost target for your conversion-optimized ad set or a bid cap, you can set your budget to at a minimum of 5 times as high as your cost target or bid cap. With this strategy, you are more likely to achieve 5 conversions a day at least.

What is the approach used for spending the budget?

The way Facebook spends the budget you set will depend on the delivery type you select. You can choose between standard or accelerated delivery. The latter option is only available when you use a bid cap.

Standard Delivery - In this delivery option, Facebook spends the budget evenly throughout the course of the campaign. This is referred to as pacing. This is the recommended option in most situations.

Accelerated Delivery - In this delivery option, Facebook will spend the budget you set as quickly as possible. This is the recommended option if your campaign is time-sensitive. In this option, your daily budgets may be spent in an hour or less. Your lifetime budget may be spent in a day or less. The spending won't resume until the next day. This is why accelerated delivery must also be used with caution.

How to edit budgets?

You are allowed to apply changes to your previously set budget. And you can do this at any time. To change your budget, you can follow these steps.

- Access the Ads Manager.
- Go to the campaign or ad set you like to edit.
- Choose the option to Edit.
- Change the budget as you please.
- Click on Confirm and Close.

After making changes to your budget, the delivery system will take 15 minutes to update. The Facebook system will need to readjust in order to show your ad in the most effective manner possible.

Budget changes can affect performance.

The changes that can happen in performance after editing your budget depends on how your ad sets or campaign is performing in the first place.

For instance, if your ad set is performing well, increasing the budget is more likely to improve results further. However, if you increase it so much that Facebook can't get enough results that work within the constraints you've set, your budget may not be fully spent. A significant increase in budget with the lowest cost bid strategy may also increase your cost per optimization event. The reason for this is that there's not much low-cost optimization events to use. In order to spend a much higher budget, chasing after higher-cost optimization events will be necessary.

On the other hand, if you lower your budget while getting your desired results, you are likely to continue spending your full budget. However, you are also more likely to achieve fewer results.

What happens if you change the budget while your ad set is not on the right track of spending the full budget? Increasing the budget may not make a lot of difference. However, you may spend a lower percentage of your set budget. On the other hand, reducing your budget may not do much except that a higher percentage of the budget may be spent.

Instagram Advertising

Although Instagram has not kept up with Facebook as far as the number of active users is concerned, it is definitely among the fastest growing apps in the world. Because Instagram users tend to be engaging, the platform also offers plenty of opportunities for advertisers.

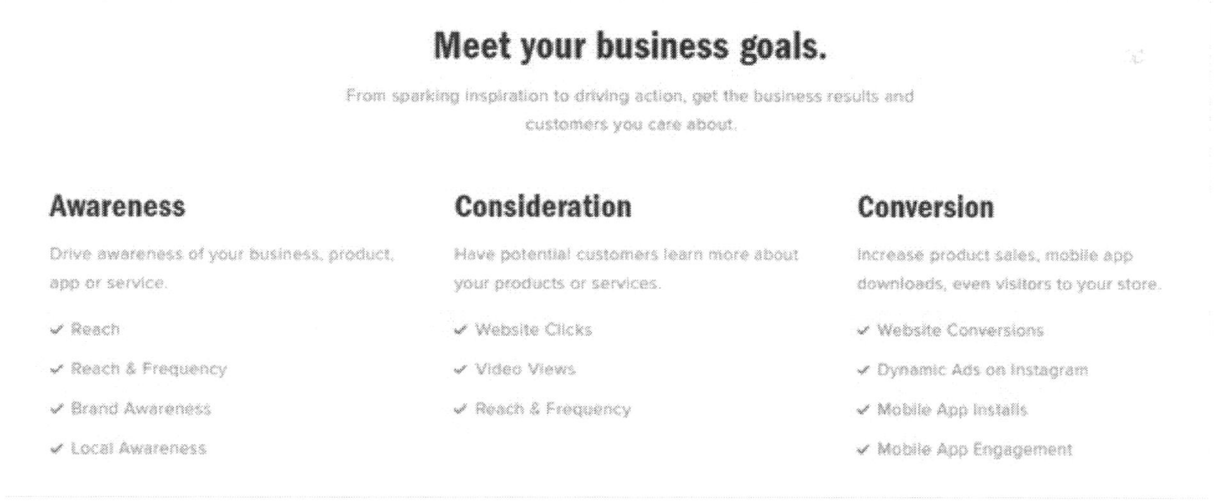

Meet your business goals.

From sparking inspiration to driving action, get the business results and customers you care about.

Awareness

Drive awareness of your business, product, app or service.

- ✓ Reach
- ✓ Reach & Frequency
- ✓ Brand Awareness
- ✓ Local Awareness

Consideration

Have potential customers learn more about your products or services.

- ✓ Website Clicks
- ✓ Video Views
- ✓ Reach & Frequency

Conversion

Increase product sales, mobile app downloads, even visitors to your store.

- ✓ Website Conversions
- ✓ Dynamic Ads on Instagram
- ✓ Mobile App Installs
- ✓ Mobile App Engagement

What are the advantages of Instagram advertising?

Detailed Targeting - Instagram is under the same wing as Facebook which means you have a great chance of targeting the right audience whether you target them according to their demographics, interests or behaviors.

Definitely Eye-Catching - Among the most visual platforms, Instagram advertising is ideal for both photo and video content. Another advantage is that even low budget advertisers can do well in the platform. Because a huge number of the content uploaded on Instagram are shot on mobile phones, creating an expensive and highly technical content is not necessary.

Increase Sales - Users can make purchases within Instagram itself. Because the platform is highly visual, advertisers can showcase their products and services in a compelling way.

Unique Ad Formats - Brands and businesses can further maximize their content by taking advantage of Instagram's various ad formats including photos and videos, carousel and story ads.

What are the things to consider before getting into Instagram advertising?

This platform does offer great opportunities for advertisers. However, there are a few issues to consider before jumping into it. The following are a few of them.

Limited Audience - With around 800 million active monthly users, Instagram seems like a dream choice for any advertiser. However, for those targeting an older audience, it may not make much sense to use the platform. That's because Instagram users primarily consist of people from ages 18 to 29.

Not Very Text-Friendly - Advertisers can use the platform for tease content or to get users to their sites. For everything else however, it may be a challenge especially for advertisers promoting high engagement products and services that require a lot of written content.

Time Consuming - Instagram ads require time to manage and constantly update. This goes for all advertising efforts on social media but more so for a platform that is so visual.

Consider all these things before you take action.

Facebook Advertising Do's and Don'ts

Facebook Advertising Policies are meant to regulate content and make sure they are appropriate for the users. In this section, we'll look into the do's and don'ts of Facebook advertising.

1. Do stay away from prohibited content.

There's a list of content Facebook doesn't allow. The list is long and it includes the following.

- Ads that violate the Community Standards
- Ads that promote illegal products and services. This includes inappropriate content intended to mislead, exploit and put undue pressure on targeted age groups
- Content promoting discriminatory practices
- Content that either sell or promote the use of tobacco products
- Ads that either sell or promote the use of drugs and related products
- Ads that either sell or promote the use of unsafe supplements
- Content that either sell or promote the use of explosives, ammunition and weapons
- Content that either sell or promote the use of adult products and services

- Ads with adult content including those that depict people in suggestive or explicit positions, nudity or those that are sexually provocative and overly suggestive
- Third-party infringement
- Sensational content
- Content that feature personal attributes
- Misleading or False Content
- Controversial Content
- Content that directs users to non-functional landing pages
- Ads that sell surveillance equipment
- Content with bad grammar and profanity
- Ads with images that depict nonexistent functionality.
- Content that promote negative self-perception such as before and after images
- Ads promoting cash advance and payday loans
- Ads for Multilevel Marketing
- Content that promote penny auctions
- Ads for counterfeit documents
- Low Quality or Disruptive Content
- Ads with Spyware or Malware
- Audio and flash animation that automatically plays without user interaction
- Content promoting unauthorized streaming devices
- Ads using tactics that circumvent Facebook ad review process
- Ads promoting prohibited financial products and services

2. Do exercise caution with restricted content.

The items in the restricted content section requires certain prerequisites. Most of them require prior written permission. Others must absolutely abide by local laws. There are many in this list that are restricted for minors. The restricted section includes ads and content that promote the following.

- Alcohol
- Online Dating Services
- Gambling with real money
- State Lotteries
- Online and Offline Pharmacies promoting prescription pharmaceuticals
- Dietary and Herbal Supplements
- Subscription Services
- Financial Services or credit card applications
- Branded Content
- Student Loan Services
- Political Advertising
- Cryptocurrency Products and Services

3. Don't use video ads with disruptive content.

Video ads are encouraged because they can engage users the way that a *still image* or a plain text can't. However, Facebook doesn't allow videos with disruptive content like flashing screens. Trailers for TV shows, movies, video games and similar content must not target users under the age of 18. Entertainment related video ads that feature excessive depictions of violence, profanity, adult content, drugs and alcohol use are not allowed.

4. Do use targeting options properly.

This means targeting options should not be used for predatory advertising tactics and discrimination. Although Facebook allows you to create an audience, it is important to abide by their terms.

5. Do use positioning accurately.

Your content must be relevant and appropriate to either the product or service you're promoting. All pieces of information must be accurate. Also, the promoted products or services in the ads should match the landing page users are directed to.

6. Don't overdo text in ad images.

Facebook advises against the use of too much text in ad images. It will not only compromise ad reach, it may also get rejected. As much as possible, limit it to a little or zero image text.

7. Don't use lead ads questions.

Content must not contain questions that are intended to obtain sensitive information from users such as the following.

- Account information
- Criminal records
- Financial data
- Government Issued Identifiers
- Health records
- Insurance records
- Political affiliation
- Ethnicity or Race
- Religion
- Sexual orientation
- Membership in trade unions
- Usernames and Passwords

Facebook reserves the right to reject an ad or content that they deem unfit or in violation of their terms and conditions. You will find more information about Facebook advertising policies on their website.

Chapter 7 Quiz

Please refer to the Answer Booklet for the solution to this quiz

1. What are the parts of a Facebook campaign structure?

   A) Campaign
   B) Ads
   C) Ad Sets
   D) Carousel

2. What are the parts of a Facebook campaign structure?

   A) Awareness
   B) Consideration
   C) Conversion
   D) Purchases

3. These are objectives that aim to put your business in the mind of people. When they start thinking about the business, the next goal is to compel them to seek more information about it.

   A) Awareness
   B) Consideration
   C) Conversion
   D) Purchases

4. These are objectives encouraging people who expressed interest in your business to use and purchase your product or service.

   A) Awareness
   B) Consideration
   C) Conversion
   D) Purchases

5. If you want to collect lead information from people who are interested in the brand or businesses, which advertising objection should you choose?

   A) Traffic
   B) App Installs
   C) Engagement
   D) Lead Generation

6. What are the things you can do with Engagement as your advertising objective?

   A) Boost your post and improve post engagement

B) Promote your Page and get more Page Likes
C) Have more people claim an offer from your Page and receive more Offer claims
D) Increase the attendance for an event in your Page and increase Event responses

7. Which of the following statements is not true.

A) Each user can manage a maximum of 25 ad accounts.
B) Each ad account can manage up to 25 users for every account
C) Each regular ad account is allowed a maximum of 5,000 ads which are not deleted
D) Each regular ad account is allowed a maximum of 100 sets which are not deleted

8. Which of the following are examples of custom audience segments?

A) Facebook likes
B) Website visitors
C) Previous buyers
D) Email subscribers

9. How long does the Facebook system need to update after editing your budget?

A) 5 minutes
B) 10 minutes
C) 15 minutes
D) 20 minutes

10. What are the ad formats available on Instagram?

A) Photos and videos
B) Carousels
C) Story ads
D) Canvas story ads

Did You Know?

When asked to choose one social network "if trapped on a deserted island," 44 percent of teenagers chose Snapchat, ahead of Instagram (24 percent) and Facebook (14 percent). (recode)

Chapter 8

Sales Funnels and Leads

Capturing your audience's interest is only the beginning. More often than not, most of them are not ready to purchase yet. You need to build goodwill and nurture that relationship until they are ready to give you their business. And you can do this with Facebook sales funnel.

There are various stages to take into consideration. In every step of the way, relevant messages must be used to appeal to these users and bring them a little closer to conversion. Organic posts can do this. However, you can push it further by reinforcing or spearheading Facebook ads that are highly targeted and appeal to these users at various stages of the funnel.

Facebook is used by a lot of people not exactly to purchase random products or avail themselves of services. They log in for recreation and social purposes. Savvy advertisers can leverage sales funnels to generate demand. They can remind Facebook users about needs or pain points they may not have been aware of in the first place. With the help of Facebook sales funnel, you can possibly stand out, get through the noise and obtain the conversions you have been hoping to get.

There are four stages in the Facebook Sales Funnel.

- The user is made aware of your product or service.
- After being introduced to your product or service, the user develops interest and considers a purchase.
- The user is prepared to make the purchase.
- The user has already completed the purchase. The goal now is to nurture the relationship and turn the user from a one-time purchase to a long-term customer.

How to create a Facebook Sales Funnel?

Facebook advertising uses a proactive approach. And you can take advantage of this by creating interest and drive sales. Let's go through the process step-by-step.

1. Generate Awareness

The first step is to get users into the sales funnel. There are different strategies that can be used to generate awareness including the following.

- **Run Facebook ads** - Target users who may be interested in your products or services. You do have to target users that are not yet connected to your business Page. You can revisit your custom audiences and choose the high value ones. Create lookalike audience based on this. When you create your ads, write a quick introduction and tell users why they need your products or services.
- **Create a referral contest** - Hosting a contest or making an offer for extra entries by referring a friend can certainly increase your sign up. You can possibly have second to third degree level of awareness. When you have their email addresses, you will also be able to run retargeting campaigns.
- **Run engaging posts** - Organic posts that are engaging is another way of introducing your brand or business. To do this, you can write posts asking for your audience's opinions. As they respond, the whole post will also show up in their feeds for their friends to check out.

2. Address their pain points and overcome any objections.

Moving from awareness to generating interest, you need to start letting these users know how and why they need your product or service. You need to address their pain points and at the same time, find a way to overcome their objections. There are several ways to do this but you can consider the following strategies too.

- **Create a retargeting campaign** - From the interest you have built in the previous stage, you need to build it up further. This means you need to retarget the users who have previously expressed their interest in your products or services. They need to be reminded about your offers and you must make a more compelling material at this point.
- **Respond to all comments** - With your ads, you can address any comments or hesitations these users may still have. You can also use testimonials to help validate your claims.
- **Testimonials** - You can also use testimonials from satisfied customers to help validate your claims.
- **Use organic posts and ads** - Educate users about the features and benefits of your products and services. You can do this to remind them why they absolutely need what you're offering.

3. Offer incentives for purchases.

If you get the users to the point of considering a purchase, all you need to give them is a little push. You can accomplish this by offering them immediate incentives.

Incentives can come in the form of special discounts. For instance, you can offer 20% off discount on the first purchase. Offer them information for your flash sales in the future. You can also offer free shipping. To make this more compelling, you should create a sense of urgency. For example, add a deadline to the special discount or special promotion. Display the stocks left or put a timer on the sale.

4. Keep your customers engaged by upselling and referral incentives.

After their first purchase, you now have to think about converting these one-time customers to long-term ones. Encourage referrals and drive continuous sales through upselling.

- Retarget customers with loyalty perks
- Remind your customers about your referral programs
- Offer complementary products or services

ClickFunnels on Facebook

ClickFunnels is a software that can help you design and build sales pages and landing pages. It also helps you manage the entire sales funnel. And you can integrate it with your Facebook Page.

Before you can integrate ClickFunnels with your Facebook Page, you need to meet two major requirements.

- Your Facebook Business Page must have at least 2,000 fans (according to Facebook policy).
- You have an existing funnel that's built in ClickFunnels.

Let's begin with creating a sales funnel in ClickFunnels.

How to set up a sales funnel in ClickFunnels?

- Access ClickFunnels and register.
- Click on the option to **Create Funnel**.

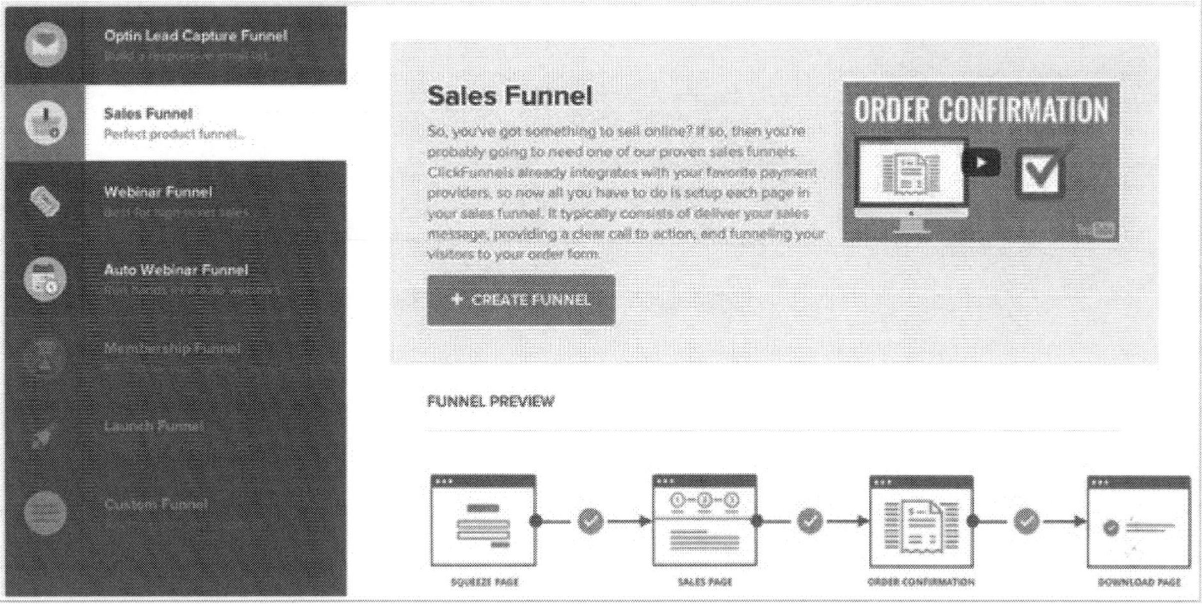

- Choose **Sales Funnel**.
- Click on **Create Funnel**.
- Enter a name for the funnel and add a tag to keep your funnels organized.

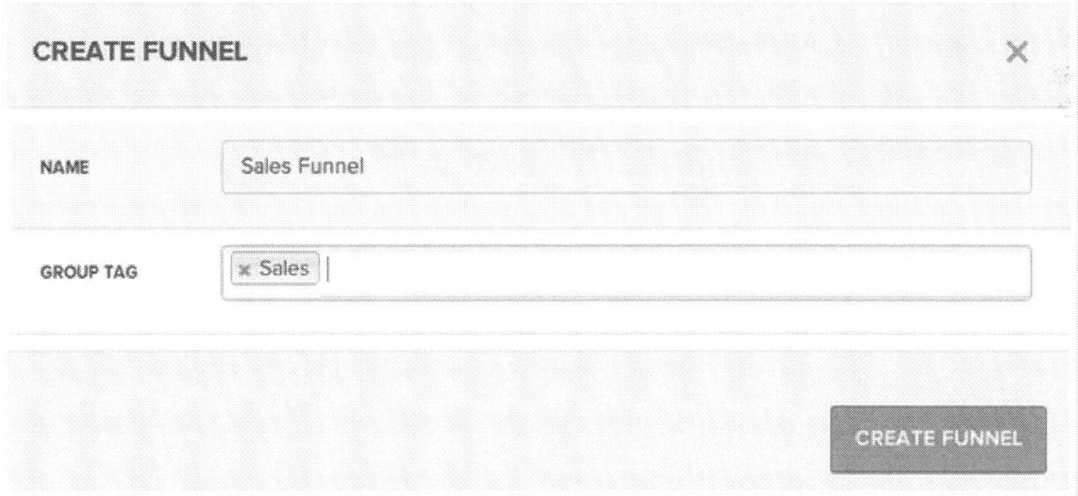

- After creating your first sales funnel, choose your template for each page. You can change the template any time but this will make you lose any edits you've applied.

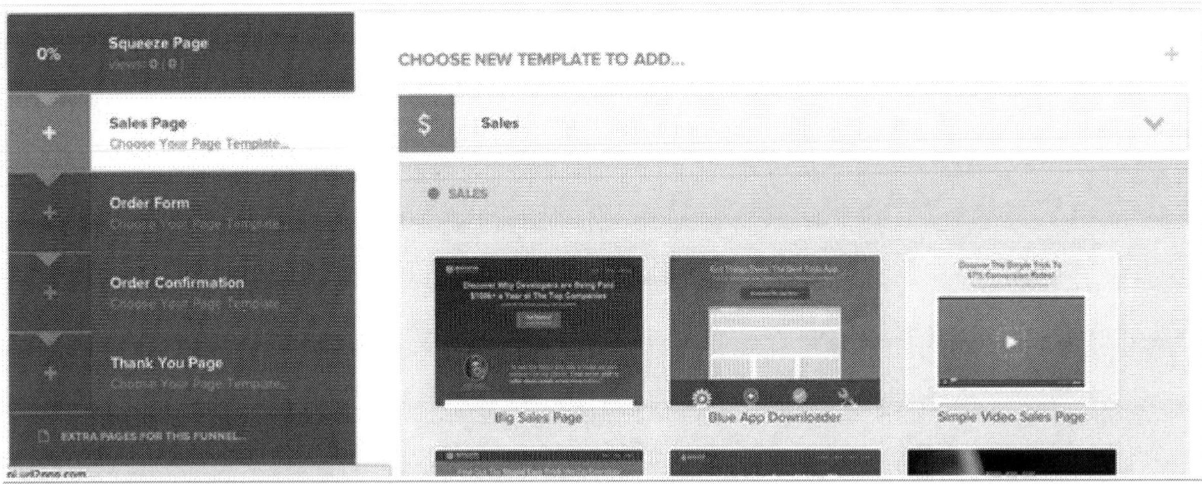

- Use the editor to edit the content and look of your selected templates.

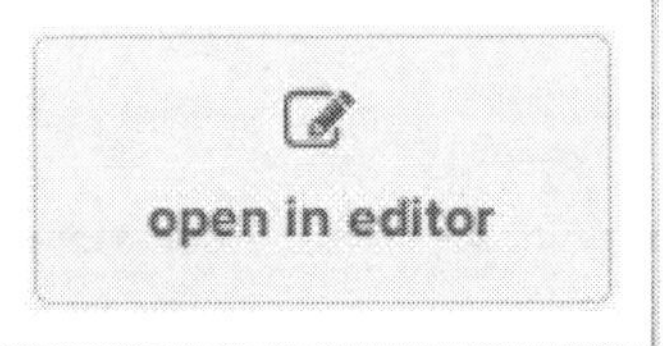

- Go to the **Order Form**, choose the **Product/Sales tab** and click on **Add product**.

- Enter a name for your product, choose your billing integration and set the amount.
- Choose either **Subscription** or **One-time** payment at the bottom of the page.

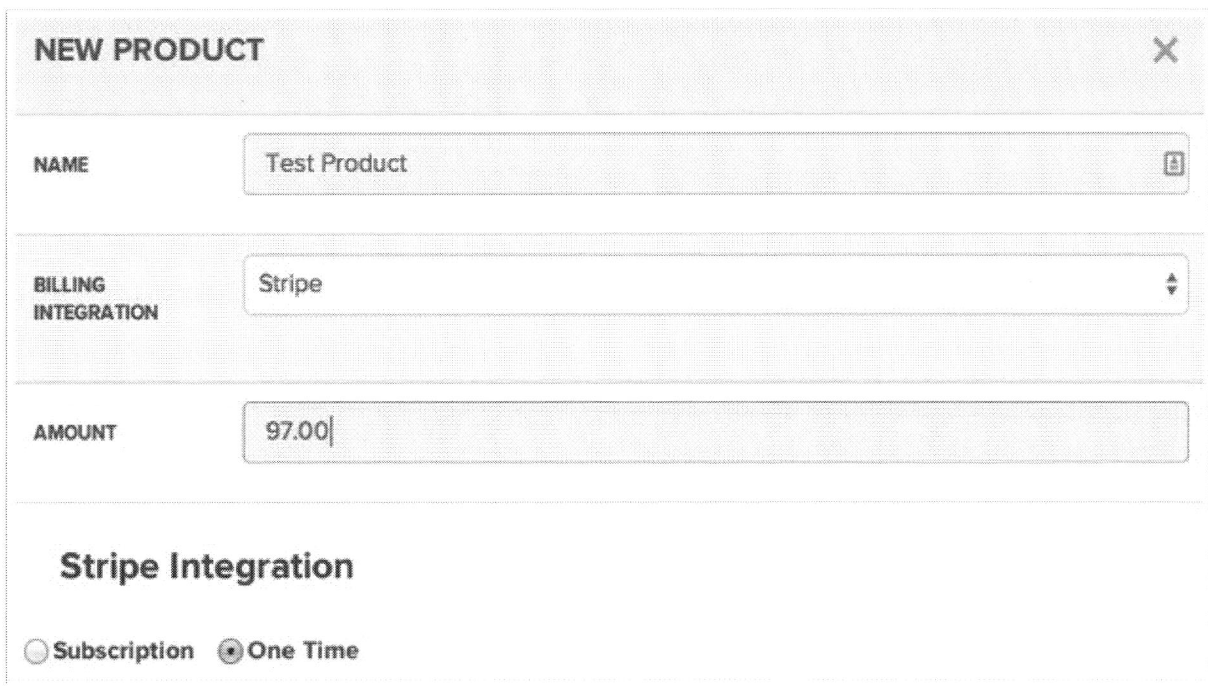

- Create a fulfillment email. This email will be sent to the customer after a purchase. Do not remove the Merge tag below after making your changes.

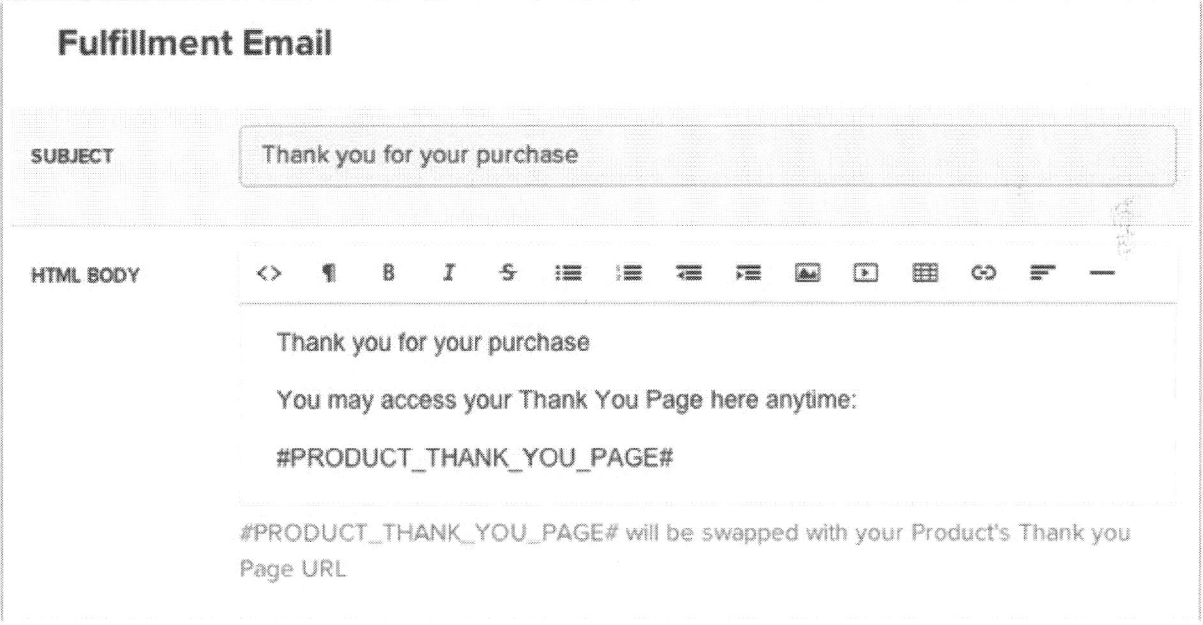

- **Activate the Integrations**. This applies only if you are shipping physical products.
- Click on the **Create Product** button below the page after making the changes.
- This will automatically add the product to your **Order Form**.

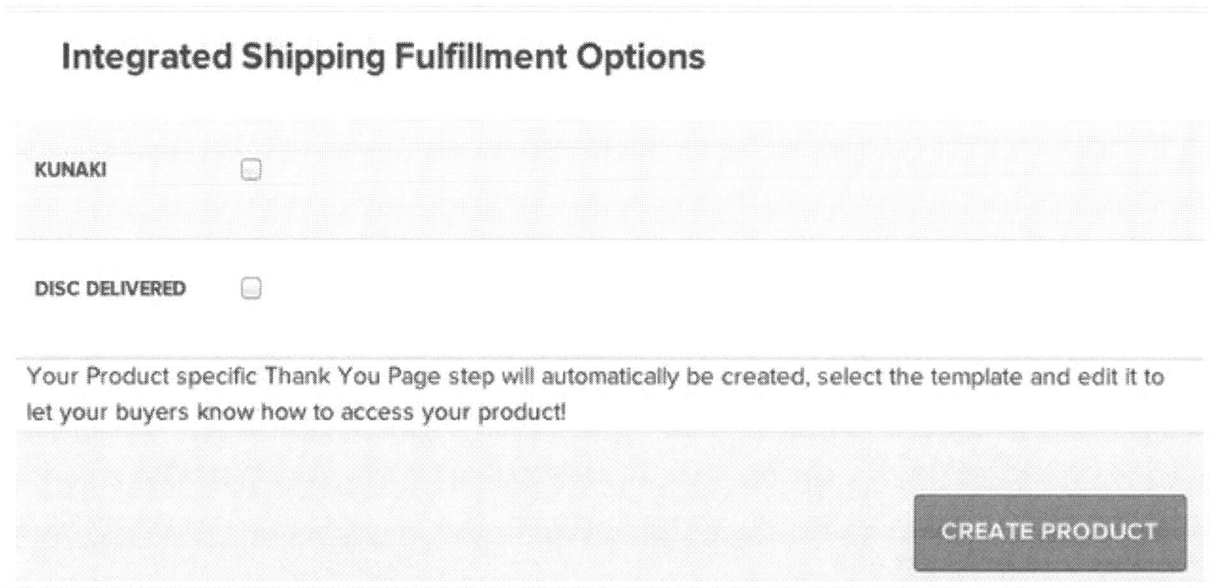

- Get the link for the **Order Form** page.

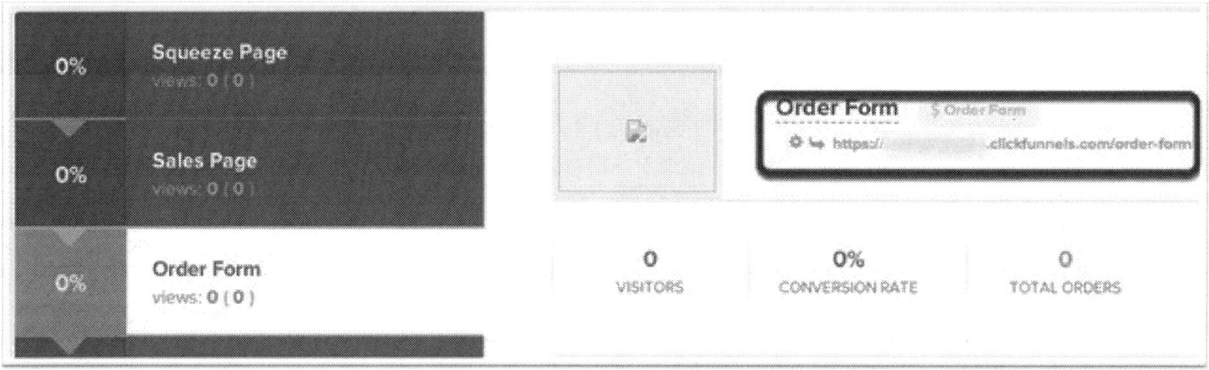

- Go to the Editor of the Sales Page. Access the **Buy Button** settings and attach the link of the Order Form to the **URL/Action** field and save.

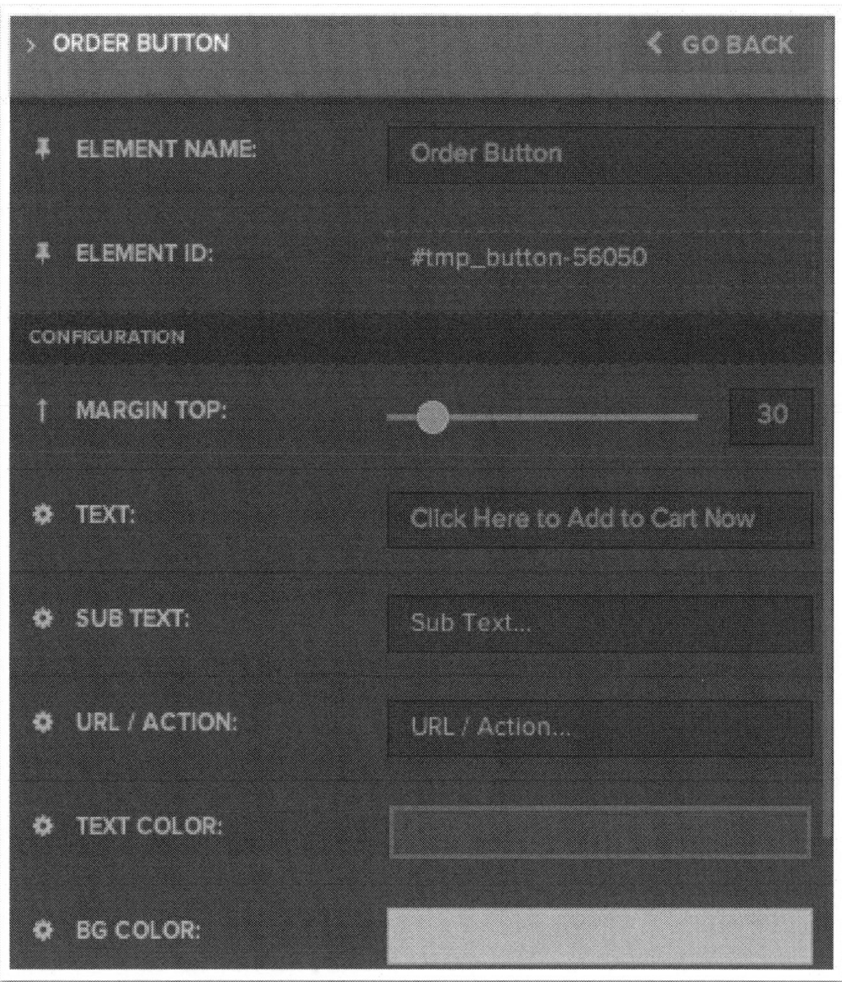

- Adding a product to the Order Form will automatically create a **Product Specific Thank You page**. This will be used for delivering your products. At this point, you can select a template and edit the details on the page. You can allow customers to download what they purchased or receive confirmation for shipping if you're selling a physical product.

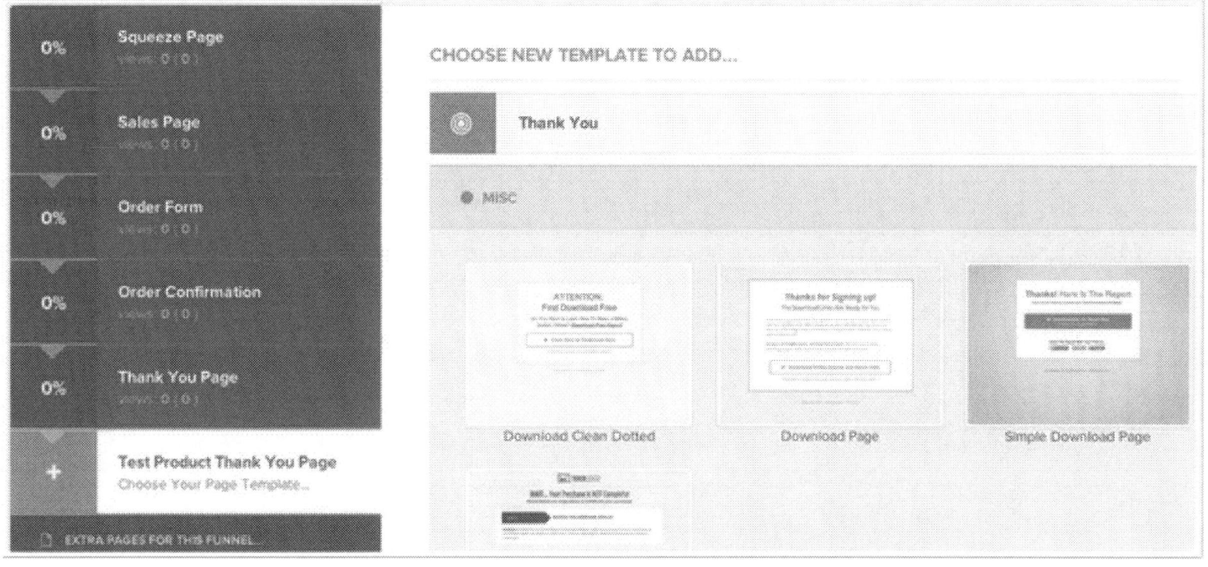

- Test your funnel by going to the **Funnel Settings** page. Edit the Funnel by clicking on the gear icon.

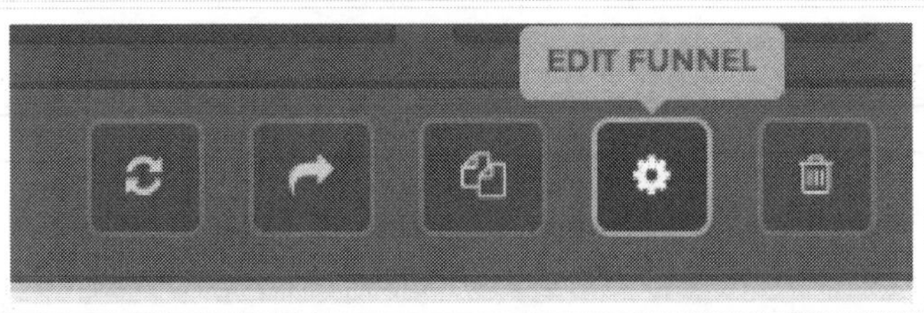

- At the bottom of the newly opened window, **Enable test mode**. This step will allow you to go through each of the pages you have just customized and make sure everything looks ready.

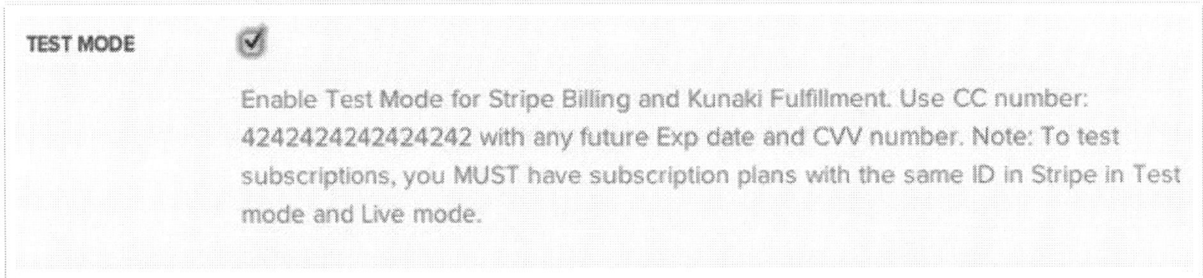

- After this step, disable the test mode so you can start receiving purchases from real customers.

How to add your Funnel to your Facebook business page?

Now that you've created your Funnel in ClickFunnels, you're ready to integrate it with Facebook.

- Access your list of Funnels within **ClickFunnels**.

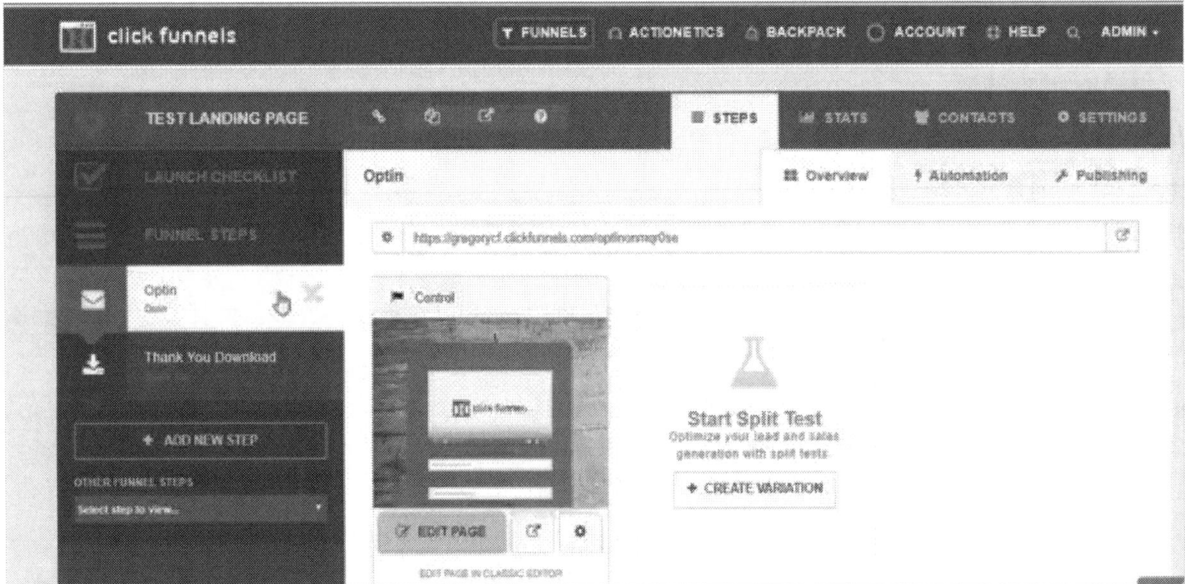

- Choose the one you want to edit.
- Click on the **Publishing** tab of the funnel.
- Choose the option to **Add to Facebook**.

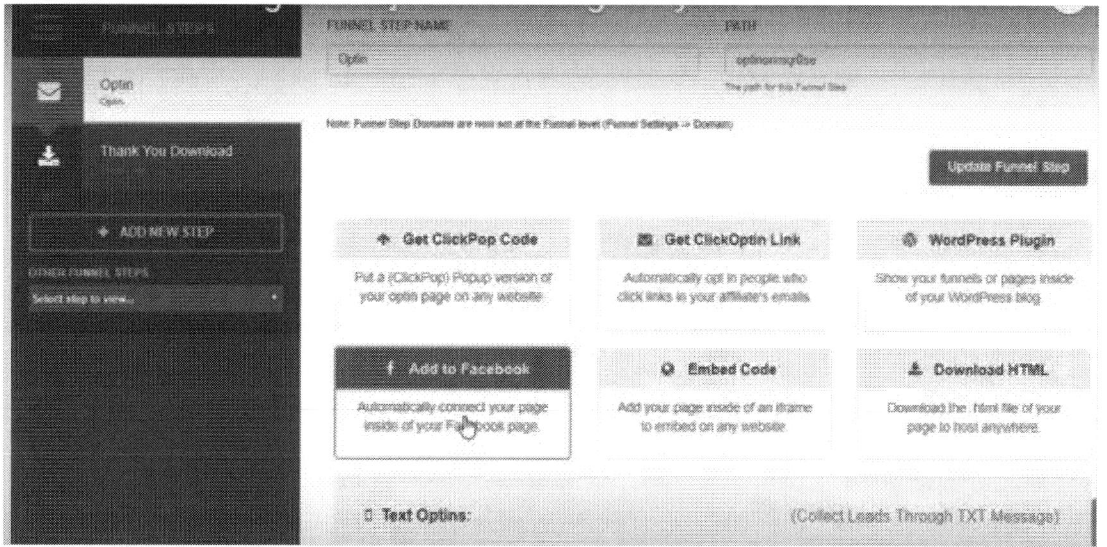

- Click on the dropdown menu to choose your Facebook Business Page.
- Click on Add Page tab.

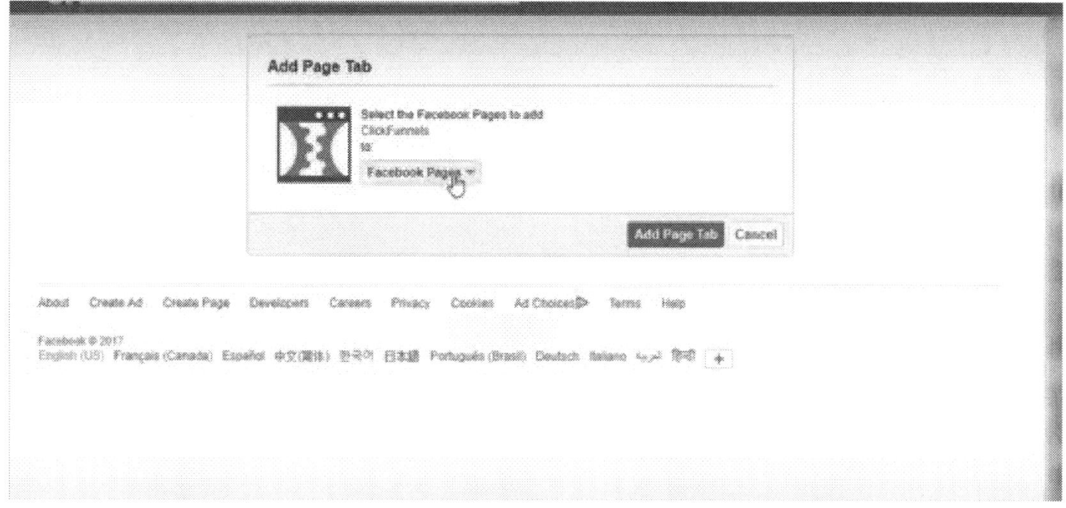

- Verify that Clickfunnels has been added by opening your Facebook Page.
- Click on **See More**. You should be able to check the addition of ClickFunnels here.
- Edit the Clickfunnels tab by going to Settings.
- Choose the option to Edit Page.

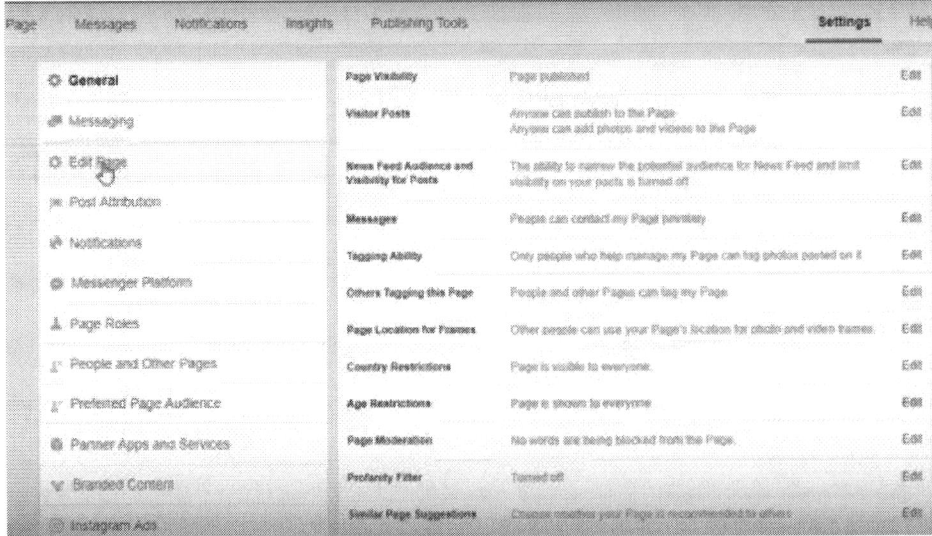

- Scroll down to the bottom and click on Settings.
- Select Edit Settings.

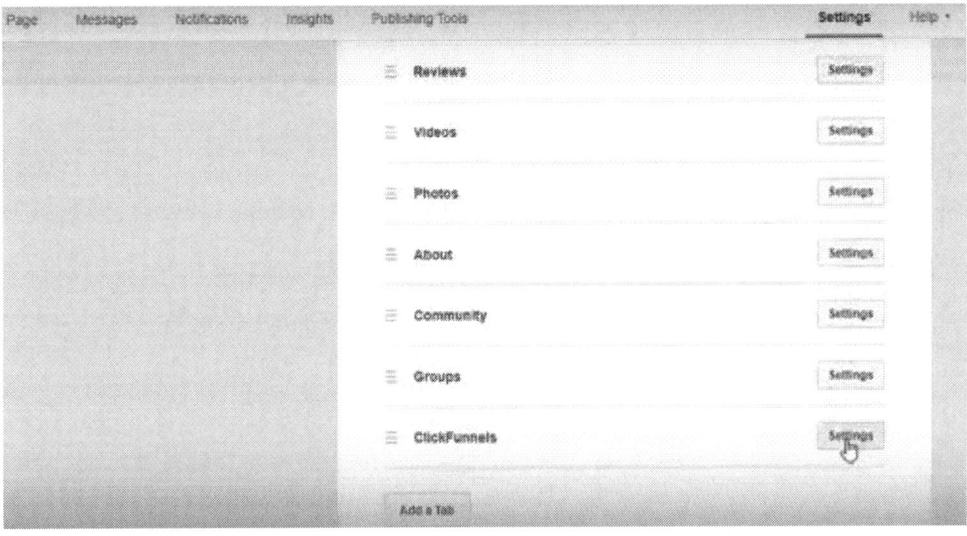

- Add the **Custom Tab Image** you prefer.

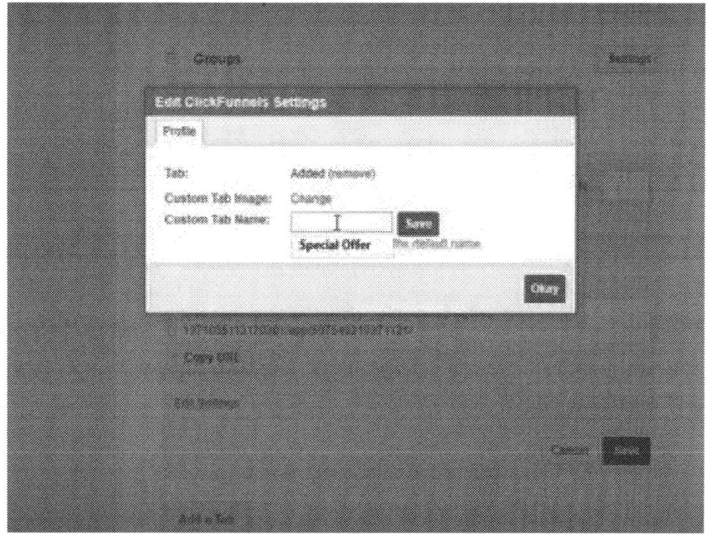

- Enter your preferred tab name on the field that says **Custom Tab Name**. Save your changes.

Lead Magnet

We've been talking about creating compelling messages and coming up with irresistible offers to get sign ups from your target audiences. Lead magnet is about offering an incentive for potential buyers to sign up using their email addresses and other contact info. More often than not, marketers usually offer lead magnets in the form of digital content including eBooks, videos, reports, PDF checklists, etc.

Email is a personal thing. This means people are less likely to openly share it. With the right incentive however, they may find a compelling reason to give it to you. And this is why you need a lead magnet. This is essential if you want to generate leads. You can incorporate it to your lead generation campaign.

What will make a lead magnet irresistible?

There are a couple of things you can do to make great lead magnets that attract signups. You can use the following guidelines in coming up with excellent lead magnets.

- Find a real problem and solve it with your lead magnet.
- Help your audience achieve something easily.
- Be as specific as possible to convert leads.
- Offer lead magnets that are easy to digest. If you're offering free reports or eBooks, make it easy to read.
- Offer high-perceived value with high actual value.
- Lead magnets should be instantly accessible.
- Use a lead magnet that demonstrates your expertise or represents your unique selling proposition.

Keep these things in mind when building your lead magnets and you'll achieve great results.

Aweber Email Autoresponder

An autoresponder is a computer program that automatically answers e-mail sent to it. Automating tasks is necessary if you want to handle things more efficiently. When you experience an exponential growth in email subscriptions and your email requirements become a bit more challenging to manage, you will need a tool that allows you to automatically send responses instead of doing them manually and individually.

Aweber is a software that can help you in creating and managing autoresponders. This way, you can communicate with your audience in a timely manner.

Domain Name with GoDaddy

You've chosen your sales funnel and you have your email autoresponder set up. It's now time to think about getting a domain name.

A domain name is a human-readable and recognizable address for your website. While ecommerce sites offer free domain names, you may want to get your own as this will further set you apart. You can choose a domain name that fits your brand or business perfectly. Here are a couple of things to consider when purchasing a domain name.

- A **.com** domain name is among the most prestigious and also among the hardest to find. Most **.com** names are already taken but because it's the most recognizable, you may still want to try just in case the one you have in mind happen to be available.
- Don't be afraid to try other variants of your preferred domain name using other suffixes. If a **.com** name is unavailable, consider other suffixes e.g. **.net, .org, .co.uk** etc.
- Create a domain name that is short and memorable.
- As much as possible, avoid domain names with hyphens.

When it comes to domain names, NameCheap and GoDaddy are great with the later being the most popular. It's a go-to choice for most people for a lot of reasons including the following.

- It's affordable. For $7 a month, you can get a domain name with GoDaddy.
- It has a good integration with products.
- It offers good security.
- GoDaddy provides excellent support with little down-time.

How to register a domain name with GoDaddy?

- Access the GoDaddy website.
- You will be asked if you prefer a .com suffix. A **.com** name is the default but you will be offered other variants too.
- Enter the domain name you want to check for availability.
- Choose the domain type you prefer by clicking on the corresponding checkbox.

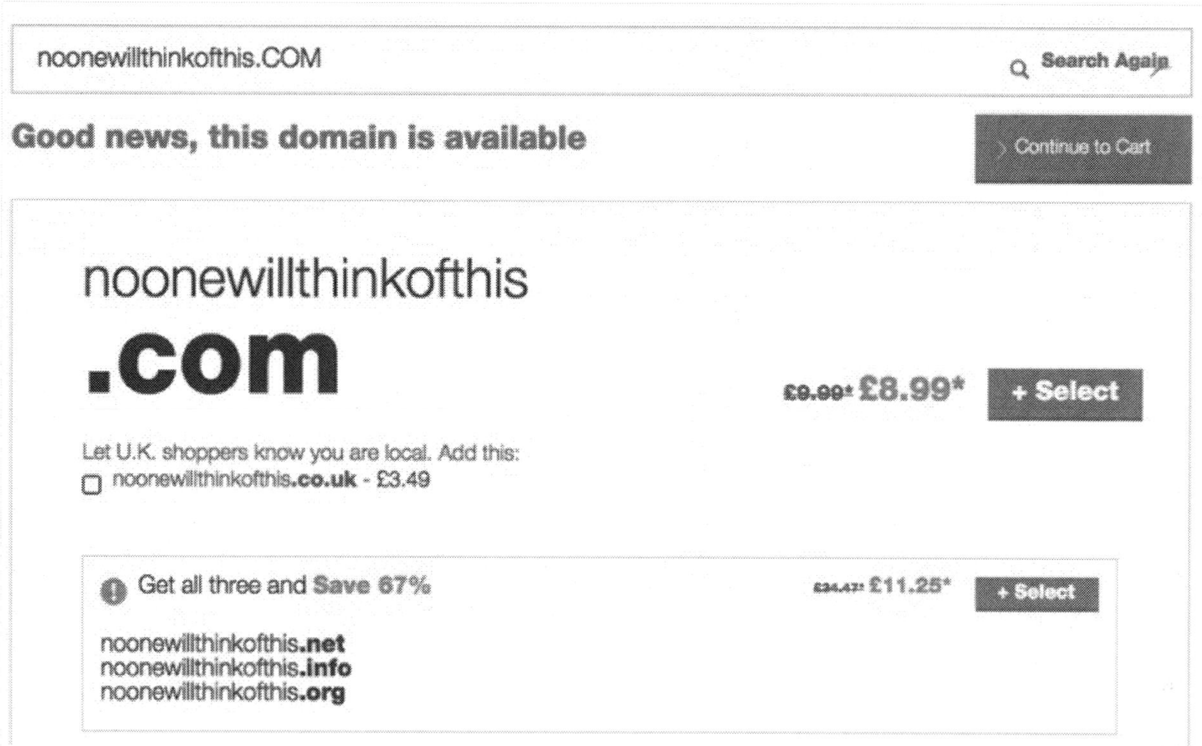

- Decide if you want a domain privacy for additional cost. You will also be offered hosting and email options. If you don't want any, skip them.
- Move on to registration and create an account. Enter the necessary information and click on Submit.

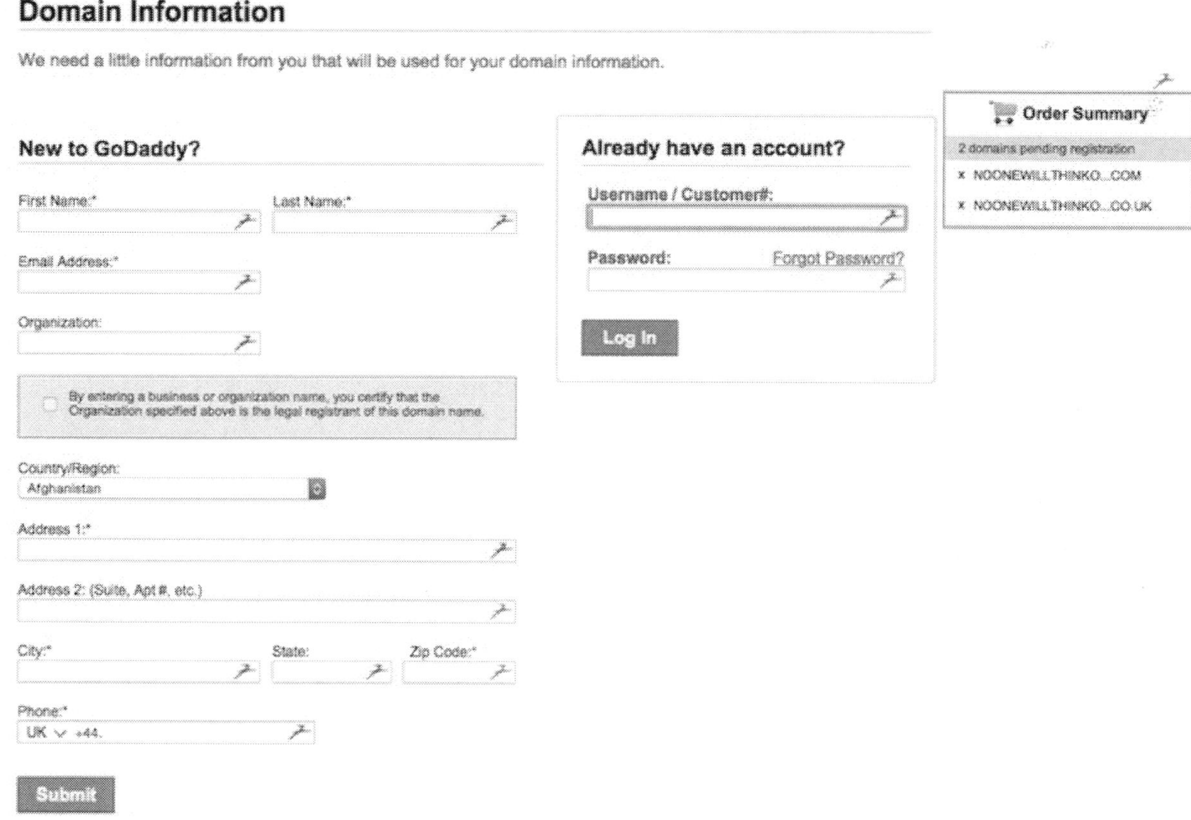

- Review your purchase and make sure the correct domains are entered.
- You will be asked to register the domain for a certain timeframe. The default is set to 2 years. Other options available are 1, 3, 5 or 10.
- You will get offered other add-ons, skip if you don't want any and proceed to checkout.

Throughout this chapter, we've looked into several ways to improve the effectiveness of your Facebook advertising. To clarify things further, let's list a concise summary of some of the most common mistakes you should avoid and some of the frequently asked questions. We also debunk some common myths about Facebook advertising.

20 Common Facebook Advertising Mistakes

1. Not fully understanding the ad objective

2. Choosing a very broad audience or keeping it too narrow

3. Not targeting the right audience

4. Failing to create compelling headlines

5. Creating ads that are too wordy

6. Missing the mark on the quality of images

7. Failing to make a clear value proposition

8. Ignoring the advantages of using Facebook Pixels

9. Forgetting to add captions for video ads

10. Not delivering the ad at the right time

11. Failing to check in with performance on a daily basis

12. Forgetting to test the landing pages

13. Not maximizing the use of Facebook Insights

14. Failing to optimize the ad creative for clicks and attention

15. Not investing enough or at all in audience research upfront

16. Mismatching the offer with the audience

17. Relying too much on Interest targeting

18. Not using the right ad type for the circumstances

19. Failing to take advantage of optimization rules

20 Being impatient about results

20 Frequently Asked Questions about Facebook Advertising

1. Where should traffic be directed after a user clicks on the Facebook ad?

Traffic can be sent either to an external website or to an internal Facebook Page. If you have a website capable of tracking actions, it can be used as a landing page for your Facebook ads.

2. How often should one update their Facebook ads?

To keep the audience interested and engaged, keeping content fresh is essential. Monitor your results regularly. When the response rate is becoming stale, your ad is due for an update.

3. How much targeted can ads be?

The biggest advantage of Facebook advertising is its ability to target people in a granular way. With Facebook, you can get as specific as possible with regards to choosing your audience. You can sort them out through demographics, interests, relationship status, income level, employment type, education level and other measures.

4. What is the recommended minimum budget per ad campaign?

This totally depends on your campaign objectives.

5. How should a headline text be written?

Headlines have to be straight to the point. To ensure that your headline text is effective and irresistible, you must keep on testing to see which one gets the most response.

6. How to create real engagement with Facebook ads?

There are several ways to create engagement with the audience. You can use questions, fill-in-the-blanks statements, contests and giveaways. Most importantly, you must have relevant and valuable content.

7. Is it possible to target previous customers using email addresses?

Yes. It is certainly possible to target former customers with their email addresses. This is referred to as Facebook custom audience.

8. Is a narrow audience generally more expensive?

Targeting smaller audience is generally more expensive. What you need to be especially mindful of is frequency because you wouldn't want to keep hitting the same person again and again using the same message.

9. What's the average CTR on Facebook?

The average Click-Through-Rate (CTR) varies according to the market and the industry but the average is somewhere between 0.4 and .5%.

10. Which is better, lifetime budget or daily budget?

One is not exactly better than the other. It all depends on what fits your business best.

11. How do I write better ad copy?

Your ad copy should be short, interesting and to the point. It is important to use the right tone of voice. Focus on the important message. And always write with your target audience in mind.

12. How do I check whether or not my ads design is working?

High quality ads are usually seen as more credible. Ad designs that spark positive emotions are also more likely to perform better. If your ad image is capable of attracting attention in users News Feed then it is more likely to work well. Finally, use split testing to your advantage and find out what works best for your target audience.

13. What are the things to absolutely avoid when writing the ad copy?

Avoid making it too long that it becomes difficult to read. Make sure to proofread and use the right spacing and punctuations. Otherwise, your ad may not seem trustworthy. Always present the unique benefit of your product and make an appealing offer.

14. What are the common bidding mistakes to avoid?

Changing your bidding methods so often that the Facebook system is not given enough time to optimize. You place manual bids that are too low that Facebook is unable to deliver the ads. You choose to bid on impressions when conversion is your objective.

15. How do I find the best target audience on Facebook?

The best way to find the best target audience is to explore different targeting options including: targeting by demographics, custom audiences, lookalike audiences and interest-based targeting.

16. How do I know my ad campaign is relevant to my target audience?

You can analyze the ad metrics relevance score to determine whether or not your ad campaign is relevant to your target audience.

17. How do I check whether or not I've selected the right ad placement for my campaign?

You can always check Facebook Ads Manager and access your campaign results by Placement. Analyze the data to find out if you're using the right ad placement or make changes when necessary.

18. What are the most recommended ad placements?

Your ad placement should be based on your campaign objective. Here are a couple of suggestions.

- For brand awareness, use Facebook and Instagram.
- For engagement, consider Facebook and Instagram.
- For video views, choose among Facebook, Instagram and Audience Network or use a combination
- For app installs, try Facebook, Instagram and Audience Network
- For traffic, consider Facebook and Audience Network
- For product catalog sales, use Facebook and Audience Network
- For conversions, try Facebook and Audience Network.

19. What are the most common landing page mistakes to avoid?

- You're creating a bad first impression.
- You're attempting to target everyone at once.
- Your usage of call-to-actions causes confusion.
- Your value proposition is unclear.
- You're giving your audience a poor mobile experience.
- Your ad designs and the landing page are not congruent e.g. message conveyed, color theme etc.

20. What do I do when my ad frequency is getting too high?

There are several options to consider when frequency is getting too high. Such options include the following.

- Put the ad campaign on a pause.
- Try switching your ad audience and attempt targeting new audiences.
- Edit your ad design and change your offer.

20 Myths about Advertising on Facebook

1. Facebook advertising is not right for Business-to-Business (B2B).

It is actually an effective channel for targeting professionals and businesses where you can specify your audience according to demographics, industry type, employment type, job tittle, income, etc.

2. Investing to get Page Likes is absolutely necessary.

Just because a user liked your page does not mean he or she will become your customer. Invest instead on Facebook ads with a clear objective and a compelling offer.

3. Retargeting all site visitors is essential.

It is indeed important to pay attention to retargeting visitors. However, using a one size fits all approach does not work. Instead of using single ad set to retarget them all, find out their reasons for visiting your website in the first place and retarget them accordingly.

4. Left side ads are more effective than right side ads.

Right side ads can be just as effective as left side ads when used correctly. Separate your right side ads into different ad sets, set them up to pay for link clicks instead of impressions.

5. The most important metric is relevance score.

It is important but what's more important is meeting your Return-on-Investment (ROI) target. Focus on end results and evaluate the cost for every acquired user and ROI.

6. You should always use images of smiling people in your ads.

It's more important to use images that are genuine and can help your audience understand instantly "what's in it for them."

7. You should not have over 20% written text in an ad.

Excessive copy may be shut down by Facebook during the holiday season but can get excellent distribution for the rest of the year. Focus on the quality of the text content instead.

8. A low relevance score will make you pay more for your ads.

Relevance score is only one of the ad metrics used in the auction system. There are other quality indicators considered.

9. Manual bidding is better than automatic bidding.

The algorithm has been designed to provide consistent delivery that yields the best results. More often than not, automatic bidding provides the best results.

10. It's bad to have a high frequency rate.

Although a high frequency rate is one of the signs of a campaign that's performing poorly, there are instances when the frequency may be high but the ROI remains in good standing. This is why advertisers have to look at the data as a whole and focus on ROI, instead of evaluating the performance of a campaign based on a single ad metric only.

11. Facebook ads only work for bottom-of-the-funnel.

Facebook ads can work effectively for every stage of the funnel. When creating your ad campaigns, keep the funnel in mind.

12. Facebook ads are mostly used for increasing followers and engagements in posts.

Facebook advertisers are in fact, creating more and spending more on website conversion ads among other ad types.

13. If you're paying just for clicks, it's perfectly fine to spray and pray you'll get some.

To get most value for what you pay for, it is best to pay attention to ad targeting. It's always important to get your ads in front of the right audience. Otherwise, it will be a total waste of your ad budget.

14. The competition is very fierce for Post engagement ads and page likes.

According to Socialbakers' Facebook ads data, CPC for Page Like ads and Post Engagement ads are actually decreasing. It appears Advertisers are beginning to spend less on these kind of campaigns.

15. Cost per Click on ad types are increasing.

CPC rates for most ad types are relatively steady and has not increased in recent years.

16. Because of Lead Generation ads, website conversion ads have become obsolete.

Advertising budget allocation spent on website conversion ads is steady while advertisers are still hesitant about investing in Lead Generation ads.

17. Advertisers are spending most of their money on video ads.

Video ads certainly have become quite popular. However, video ads still make up only less than 20% of total ad spend for advertisers.

18. Facebook ads are often ignored by users because they are annoying.

When an ad is irrelevant, users will most likely ignore it. This is why targeting is important and showing the ads relevant to your selected audience.

19. You need to spend on professional quality images.

Images on ads have to be attention grabbing and visually appealing but there are plenty of ways to achieve these requirements without spending too much. Striking graphics style can be a great attention grabber. Images with humor work too. Test out different images and see what works best.

20. Facebook advertising is too expensive

Facebook advertising certainly costs money but depending on your objective and available budget, anyone can advertise with as little as $5 a day and achieve great results.

Congratulations!

The sixth character of the password required to unlock the Answer Booklet is letter a.

Chapter 8 Quiz

Please refer to the Answer Booklet for the solution to this quiz

1. What are the steps to creating a Facebook Sales Funnel (in the right order)?

    A) Keep your customers engaged by upselling and referral incentives
    B) Address pain points and objections
    C) Offer incentives for purchases
    D) Generate awareness

2. Which of the following are good examples of generating awareness?

    A) Create a referral contest
    B) Retarget previous buyers
    C) Run Facebook ads for users who may be interested in your product or service
    D) Run engaging posts to introduce your brand or business

3. This is a software that can help you design and build sales pages and landing pages. It also helps you manage the entire sales funnel.

    A) ClicktheFunnel
    B) ClickFunnels
    C) ClickIt
    D) ClickSalesFunnels

4. What are the things you need before you can integrate ClickFunnels with your Facebook page?

    A) An existing funnel in ClickFunnels
    B) Facebook Business Page of at least 500 fans
    C) Facebook Business Page of at least 1500 fans
    D) Facebook Business Page of at least 2000 fans

5. This email will be sent to the customer after a purchase.

    A) Thank You email
    B) Come Again email
    C) Fulfillment email
    D) Subscription email

6. When do you need to activate Integrations in ClickFunnels?

    A) When you're selling ebooks
    B) When you're selling any physical products
    C) When you're offering subscriptions
    D) When you're offering a service

7. This is about offering an incentive for potential buyers to sign up using their email addresses and other contact info.

    A) Lead magnets
    B) Incentives
    C) Lead ads
    D) Lead audience

8. Which of the following statements are true about lead magnets?

    A) An effective lead magnet is instantly accessible
    B) To get more signups, you should be as specific as possible to convert leads.
    C) To maximize lead magnets, you should use one that demonstrates your expertise or represents your unique selling proposition.
    D) An excellent lead magnet is one that helps your audience achieve something easily.

9. This is a software that can help you in creating and managing autoresponders so you can communicate with your audience in a timely manner.

    A) Aweber Autoresponsive
    B) Aweber Auto
    C) Aweber Autoresponder
    D) Aweber Autorespond

10. This is a human-readable and recognizable address for your website.

    A) Domain name
    B) Address name
    C) Website address
    D) Website domain

Did You Know?

Sixty-seven percent of consumers use Facebook and Twitter to find a resolution to issues, and 1 in 3 prefer customer care over social media to telephone or email. (Social Media Today)

Chapter 9

A Case Study

Product: High-Ticket Mastermind Events Valued at $2,000

Target Audience: Small Business Owners, Entrepreneurs and High Level Business Executives looking to grow their business

1. Defining the ideal audience

Kevin Miles is a 30-year-old CEO of Social Media-Marketing Agency – **Kevin Miles Promotions**. He's managed to secure a contract with ABC Ltd to promote one of their high-ticket network events worth $2,000 and he's set to earn 50% commission on each ticket sale. He doesn't have an existing customer base but he has a good idea about his ideal audience. Based on his initial research, he defined his ideal audience as follows.

Age range:

Gender: Men and Women

Education: College level

Job Title: Business owners and entrepreneurs

Interests: Grant Cardone, Rich Dad Poor Dad, Tony Robbins

2. Cross-referencing with Audience Insights

To find out more about his target audience, Kevin used Audience Insights particularly focusing on Interests to find real people that match his ideal audience. This is what he found out.

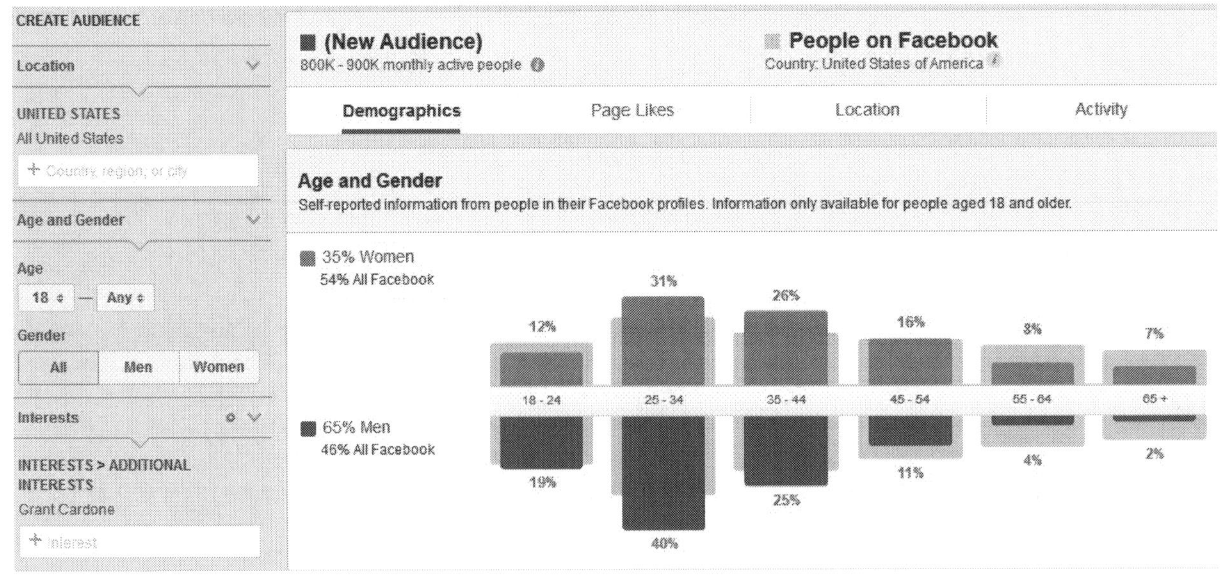

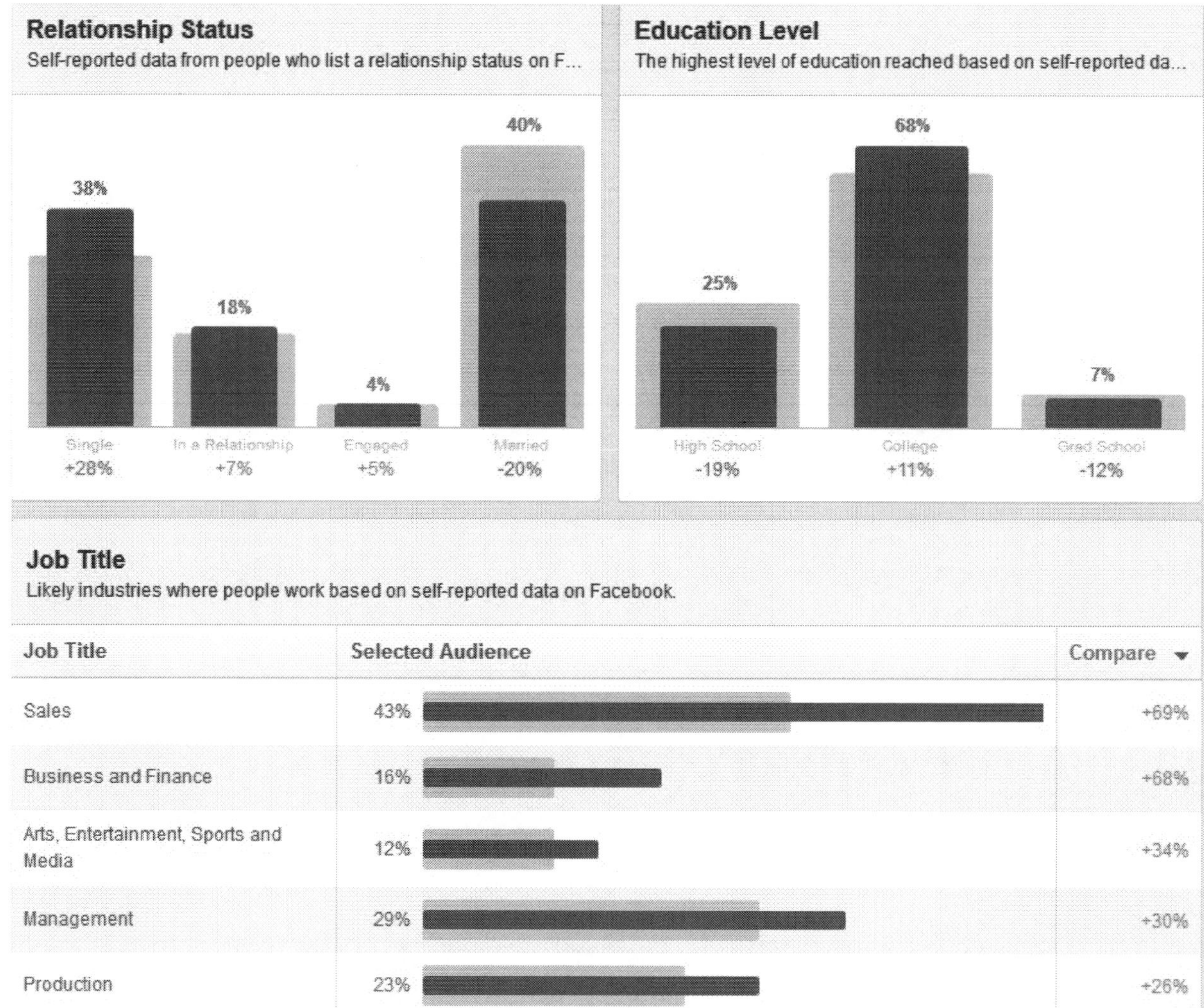

Aside from defining the audience demographics, he further dug in to the research by assessing the Page Likes of his potential audiences. He used this information to list 20+ additional interests that allowed him to narrow down his audience and find the right target.

3. Building the Page

Kevin is fully aware that he needed to build a reputation first in order to get people to buy into his high-ticket event. After defining his target audience well, he began building his page and adding appropriate and relevant content. He applied the knowledge he gathered from his research through Audience Insights to get attention and create awareness for his page.

He made sure that with every post he makes, he is able to add value for the audience. At the same time, he wanted to engage the users who have already liked his page to get information from them. To do this, he would ask his Page fans to rate statements relating to business and the challenges that come with it. He would ask them to give a score for the statements from 1 to 5.

1 - Strongly disagree
2 - Disagree
3 - Can't Say
4 - Agree
5 - Strongly Agree

*Among a few examples of the statements he would use are the following.

- *I have more leads than I can handle.*
- *Every business process is well documented.*
- *I have A-players working for me.*
- *I can run my business stress free.*

With these statements, Kevin puts forward a lot of the pain points of business owners and entrepreneurs. And he would be able to use this information later to position his high-ticket event.

4. Creative Hub

As Kevin was slowly building his page fan base, he explores Facebook Creative Hub to get ideas about content. After getting inspired, he was slowly building his content. He came up with a mockup and used the guidelines provided until he was satisfied with what he had. He created different variations for his ad for split testing later.

5. Buying a domain name.

Kevin knew he wanted a dedicated domain name for promoting the mastermind event so he decided to invest in a domain name. He used GoDaddy to register a domain and opted for the .com suffix which cost more but recognizable. He only needed to buy the domain name so he skipped on any add-ons. After going through the process, he was able to register <**www.jointhemasters.com**>

6. ClickFunnels registration.

Because Kevin did not have the technical skills required to write code or build a website or a sales funnel from scratch, he opted to use ClickFunnels. He would set it up as his landing page for his Facebook ads, the same place where he can add his high-ticket mastermind event as a product where his audience can get a digital ticket for.

He updated his GoDaddy account to add Clickfunnels and integrated the domain name to his funnel.

7. ClickFunnels with aweber

Kevin was slowly building up his customer base and gradually engaging his audience. He knew he would later on need an autoresponder to make email correspondence easier. He needed to automate the process so he signed up with aweber. To manage everything that has to do with his event in one place, he integrated ClickFunnels with Aweber.

8. Creating lead magnets

To create lead magnets, Kevin used the pain points he identified and addressed them, especially for the statements where users either "disagreed" or "strongly disagreed." He wanted to make the lead magnets as instantly accessible as possible. He used samples of topics from the mastermind events itself so he can give people an idea of the things to expect during the event.

Pain Points	Lead Magnet
I have more leads than I can handle.	A Blueprint for Lead Management, downloadable guide
Every business process is well documented.	Business documentation template.
I can run my business stress free.	A guide for automation tools

He used these incentives to position himself as an authority figure, as well as, give people an extra nudge so they would sign up with their email addresses. He offered more incentives for people who referred friends.

9. Integrating sales funnel with Facebook

Kevin had decided that he would be using Facebook primarily for marketing purposes but in order to direct his audience on Facebook to his landing page on ClickFunnels, he had to integrate the platforms together. After the integration, any clicks on his posts or ads will directly bring the users to either his subscription page or the high-ticket event page where they can purchase a ticket.

10. Testing out posts with Facebook Page audience

While his Facebook fan page is growing in numbers, Kevin decided to test out his ads to his existing Page audience. He rolled out a couple of variations and tried out different ad formats including story ads, single image ads and video ads. He took note of the ad content that his audience responded to the most. He used the information he gathered to roll out the event to a wider audience.

11. Lookalike audience.

As his email list was growing, Kevin could already create a lookalike audience. He used the custom audience and ran the best performing ad posts in his page to reach more people.

12. Exclusive Event

With a high-ticket event worth $2,000, Kevin expected plenty of objections. Among them was the high cost. He framed his copies in a way that emphasized the ticket cost is an investment to reach profit goals. For instance, when he asked his Page audience, how much profits they can expect when their pain points are addressed.

One user responded he can potentially earn $100,000 a month if his business operation becomes more efficient. For a $100,000 potential earning, a $2,000 investment doesn't sound that bad. It actually makes a lot of sense from a ROI perspective. Phrased this way, Kevin was able to grow his conversion rates.

He also made the event seem exclusive. To get in to the event, Kevin rolled out application forms. He was careful to keep the form short but sweet with basic info and a maximum of 5 evaluation statements similar to the ones he used for his lead magnets.

With this strategy, Kevin was making an impression about the mastermind event. The idea of applying for attendance to an event effectively invoked a sense of exclusivity among the audience. At the same time, Kevin was able to gather more insight which he can use to address any other possible objections and further grow his conversions.

13. Facebook Group and Email Reminders

Kevin was able to grow the event attendance. To keep the momentum, he decided to create a Facebook Group where only those who have confirmed attendance can have access to. As the event drew closer, he would use Facebook Live to interact with the attendees. He used the interaction to further build confidence in the benefits of the event. He also rolled out email reminders which he automated using aweber.

The event was a success. There was more attendance than Kevin had expected – 68 people attended in total. And with his campaign process well documented in Facebook, ClickFunnels and aweber, he already had valuable data which he can use for promoting other high-ticket mastermind events in the future.

To keep in touch with the attendees, he had automated emails sent through aweber asking them for feedback. He also continued to interact with the Group and Page fans to check with their results after applying the principles they have learned from the mastermind event.

Amount Spent on Marketing = $14,500

Total Revenue = 50% of $2,000 x 68 = $68,000

Net Profit = $68,000 - $14,500 = $53,500

ROI = 53,500/14,500 = 369%

Conclusion

I hope the above case study has put the entire process into perspective for you. The product marketed could have *anything* e.g. a golf club, an online course, a travel experience etc. The point is that the knowledge you've gained will allow you to effectively market pretty much anything. Now is the time to put into practice what you've learned and further consolidate your knowledge.

When it comes to Facebook, the sky is the limit. You have an opportunity to reach thousands if not millions of people. To get the most bang out of your buck with Facebook advertising, here are a few more reminders to live by.

Be straight with your goal.

What are you trying to achieve? Whether it is to increase traffic, raise awareness for your brand or business or boost your page likes, use this objective to guide your decisions from content creation to targeting to ad placements. Guided by your specific goals, you can create an appropriate call to action which will make your campaign effective.

Try different demographics.

If you're not getting the results you want, consider trying out different demographics. This will give you an idea how they perform until you find the perfect mix of parameters to reach your goals.

Also, don't be constrained by demographics. When using Audience Insight to define your customer avatar, take advantage of utilizing interests, Page likes, etc. Every person has a pain point and something that motivates him or her. You can use this motivation to push your products or services forward.

Be specific with your audience.

It is important to narrow the parameters. This may mean your number of reach decreases. However, it will help make sure that you are indeed targeting the right people.

Don't run ads for too long.

Variation is essential which is why you should not extend the duration of the campaign longer than you should. Once you see the results declining, take it as your cue to switch things around. If you still have budget to spend, choose another ad or ad set. Keep it fresh as much as possible.

Try out different content.

Experiment not just with your demographics but also with the kind of content you're putting out there. You can also choose different variations and audiences. Compare the performance of your ads and campaign.

Facebook gives you access to this data. Take your time to review the information so you can figure out what works best for your business or brand. With this in mind, you will be able to create more effective posts.

You can't expect to get things right the first time. However, as you get the hang of it and apply what you learn, you will be able to improve your results.

You will need to put in all the hard work in the beginning but once you've mastered a formula, you can automate and do less work for more profits.

You Are One Of A Kind

I want to share with you something that I find terribly sad. Once people start reading a book, they typically only read 10 percent of it before they give up or forget about it. Only 10 percent. What's sad about this is that from this statistic, we can see that very few people actually follow through on what they commit to (at least when it comes to reading). The reason for this is harsh but understandable: most people are not willing to hold themselves accountable. People "want" and "want" all day, but very few actually have the fortitude to put in the work.

So what's my point? First, I am trying to tell you that if you're reading these words, you are a statistical anomaly (and I am grateful for you). But here's the kicker: in order to become successful as a result of this book, you are going to have to be in the 1 percent. You need to take action.

So What's Next?

Now that you are fully aware of the tremendous opportunities available to you with regards to Facebook Advertising, what's the next step? Well, it's time to pull up your sleeves and get to work. It's time to take action. It's time to fire up that laptop and start getting things done. Many aspiring online entrepreneurs will never achieve their goals because they never get started. Don't be one of these dreamers. You have to take action.

I'll tell you right now that getting started is going to be difficult and often confusing. But that is part of the game. As the saying goes, the city of Rome wasn't built in one day. Generating a consistent stream of revenue with Facebook Advertising takes time and hours of hard work. It can take a lot of trial and error before you get the hang of things and begin to see some consistent revenue coming your way. This is why throughout this book, I've gone through the effort of providing simple, step-by-step instructions that'll guide you.

The concepts discussed in this book will assist you immensely whether you're a small business owner looking to grow his or her bottom line and online presence using Facebook Ads or an Affiliate Marketer looking to promote an online course or even the owner of a social media marketing agency who is looking to get into joint partnerships with local businesses in a bid to help promote their brand, a product or an event online. The opportunities are endless!

My last piece of advice for you is this: "Set your goals and don't stop until you achieve them." Don't let anything or anyone try to discourage or bring you down. Just focus on those goals and keep on working and hustling towards them. That's what most successful entrepreneurs would do. Work hard, work smart, and be patient. These are the keys to achieving your goals. It doesn't matter if these are short-term or long-term goals.

I wish you the very best of luck!

The End

Thank you very much for taking the time to read this book. I tried my best to cover as much information as I could without overwhelming you. If you found it useful please let me know by leaving a review on Amazon! Your support really does make a difference and I read all the reviews personally so can I understand what my readers particularly enjoyed and then feature more of that in future books.

I also pride myself on giving my readers the best information out there, being super responsive to them and providing the best customer service. If you feel I have fallen short of this standard in any way, please kindly email me at michael@michaelezeanaka.com so I can get a chance to make it right to you. I wish you all the best with your business!

Other Book(s) By Michael Ezeanaka

Affiliate Marketing: Learn How to Make $10,000+ Each Month On Autopilot

Are you looking for an online business that you can start today? Do you feel like no matter how hard you try - you never seem to make money online? If so, this book has you covered. If you correctly implement the strategies in this book, you can make commissions of up to $10,000 (or more) per month in extra income.

- WITHOUT creating your own products
- WITHOUT any business or management experience
- WITHOUT too much start up capital or investors
- WITHOUT dealing with customers, returns, or fulfillment
- WITHOUT building websites
- WITHOUT selling anything over the phone or in person
- WITHOUT any computer skills at all
- WITHOUT leaving the comfort of your own home

In addition, because I enrolled this book in the kindle matchbook program, **Amazon will make the kindle edition available to you for FREE** after you purchase the paperback edition from Amazon.com, saving you roughly $6.99!!

Available In **Kindle**, Paperback and **Audio**

Passive Income Ideas: 50 Ways To Make Money Online Analyzed

How many times have you started a business only to later realise it wasn't what you expected? Would you like to go into business knowing beforehand the potential of the business and what you need to do to scale it? If so, this book can help you

In Passive Income Ideas, you'll discover

- A concise, step-by-step analysis of **50 business models** you can leverage to earn passive income (Including one that allows you to earn money watching TV!)
- Strategies that'll help you greatly simplify some of the business models (and in the process **make them more passive!**)
- What you can do to scale your earnings (regardless of which business you choose)
- Strategies you can implement to **minimize the level of competition** you face in each marketplace
- Myths that tend to hold people back from succeeding in their business (**we debunk more than 100 such myths!)**
- Well over 150 Insightful tips that'll give you an edge and help you succeed in whichever business you chose to pursue
- More than 100 frequently asked questions (**with answers**)
- 50 positive vitamins for the mind (in the form of inspirational quotes that'll keep you going during the tough times)
- A **business scorecard** that neatly summarizes, in alphabetical order, each business models score across 4 criteria i.e. simplicity, passivity, scalability and competitiveness

- ...and much much more!

What's more? Because the book is enrolled in kindle matchbook program, **Amazon will make the kindle edition available to you for FREE** after you purchase the paperback edition from Amazon.com, saving you roughly $6.99!!

Available In Kindle, Paperback and Audio

Work From Home: 50 Ways To Make Money Online Analyzed

This is a **2-in-1 book bundle** consisting of the below books. Amazon will make the kindle edition available to you for FREE when you purchase the print version of this bundle from Amazon.com - **saving you roughly 35%** from the price of the individual books.

- Passive Income Ideas – 50 Ways to Make Money Online Analyzed (Part I)
- Affiliate Marketing – Learn How to Make $10,000+ Each Month on Autopilot (Part 2)

Get this bundle at a 35% discount from Amazon.com

Available In Kindle, Paperback and Audio

Dropshipping: Discover How to Make Money Online, Build Sustainable Streams of Passive Income and Gain Financial Freedom Using The Dropshipping E-Commerce Business Model

How many times have you started a business only to later realise you had to spend a fortune to get the products manufactured, hold inventory and eventually ship the products to customers all over the globe?

Would you like to start your very own e-commerce business that gets right to making money without having to deal with all of these issues? If so, this book can help you

In this book, you'll discover:

- A simple, step-by-step explanation of what the dropshipping business is all about (Chapter 1)
- 8 reasons why you should build a dropshipping business (Chapter 2)
- Disadvantages of the dropshipping business model and what you need to look out for before making a decision (Chapter 3)
- How to start your own dropshipping business including the potential business structure to consider, how to set up a company if you're living outside the US, how much you'll need to start and sources of funding (Chapter 4)
- How the supply chain and fulfilment process works – illustrated with an example transaction (Chapter 5)
- Analysis of 3 potential sales channel for your dropshipping business - including their respective pros and cons (Chapter 6)
- How to do niche research and select winning products – including the tools you need and where to get them (Chapter 7)

- How to find reliable suppliers and manufacturers. As well as 6 things you need to look out for in fake suppliers (**Chapter 8**)
- How to manage multiple suppliers and the inventory they hold for you (**Chapter 9**)
- How to deal with security and fraud issues (**Chapter 10**)
- What you need to do to minimize chargebacks i.e. refund rates (**Chapter 11**)
- How to price accordingly especially when your supplier offers international shipment (**Chapter 12**)
- 10 beginner mistakes and how to avoid them (**Chapter 13**)
- 7 powerful strategies you can leverage to scale up your dropshipping business (**Chapter 14**)
- 15 practical tips and lessons from successful dropshippers (**Chapter 15**)

And much, much more!

Finally, because this book is enrolled in Kindle Matchbook Program, the **kindle edition of this book will be available to you for free** when you purchase the paperback version from Amazon.com.

If you're ready to take charge of your financial future, grab your copy of this book today! Start taking control of your life by learning how to create a stream of passive income that'll take care of you and your loved ones.

Available In **Kindle**, **Paperback** and **Audio**

Dropshipping and Facebook Advertising: Discover How to Make Money Online and Create Passive Income Streams With Dropshipping and Social Media Marketing

This is a **2-in-1 book bundle** consisting of the below books and split into 2 parts. Amazon will make the kindle edition available to you for FREE when you purchase the print version of this bundle from Amazon.com - **saving you roughly 25%** from the price of the individual paperbacks.

- Dropshipping – Discover How to Make Money Online, Build Sustainable Streams of Passive Income and Gain Financial Freedom Using The Dropshipping E-Commerce Business Model (Part 1)
- Facebook Advertising – Learn How to Make $10,000+ Each Month with Facebook Marketing (Part 2)

Available In **Kindle**, **Paperback** and **Audio**

Real Estate Investing For Beginners: Earn Passive Income With Reits, Tax Lien Certificates, Lease, Residential & Commercial Real Estate

In this book, Amazon bestselling author, Michael Ezeanaka, provides a step-by-step analysis of 10 Real Estate business models that have the potential to earn you passive income. A quick overview of each business is presented and their liquidity, scalability, potential return on investment, passivity and simplicity are explored.

In this book, you'll discover:

- How to make money with Real Estate Investment Trusts – including an analysis of the impact of the economy on the income from REITs (**Chapter 1**)

- A step-by-step description of how a Real Estate Investment Groups works and how to make money with this business model (**Chapter 2**)
- How to become a limited partner and why stakeholders can influence the running of a Real Estate Limited Partnership even though they have no direct ownership control in it (**Chapter 3**)
- How to protect yourself as a general partner (**Chapter 3**)
- Why tax lien certificates are one of the most secure investments you can make and how to diversify your portfolio of tax lien certificates (**Chapter 4**)
- Strategies you can employ to earn passive income from an empty land (**Chapter 5**)
- Two critical factors that are currently boosting the industrial real estate market and how you can take advantage of them (**Chapter 6**)
- Some of the most ideal locations to set up industrial real estate properties in the US, Asia and Europe (**Chapter 6**)
- Why going for long term leases (instead of short term ones) can significantly increase you return on investment from your industrial real estate properties (**Chapter 6**)
- Why commercial properties can serve as an excellent hedge against inflation – including two ways you can make money with commercial properties (**Chapter 7**)
- How long term leases and potential 'turnover rents' can earn you significant sums of money from Retail real estate properties and why they are very sensitive to the state of the economy (**Chapter 8**)
- More than 10 zoning rights you need to be aware of when considering investing in Mixed-Use properties (**Chapter 9**)
- 100 Tips for success that will help you minimize risks and maximize returns on your real estate investments

And much, much more!

PLUS, **BONUS MATERIALS**: you can download the author's Real Estate Business Scorecard which neatly summarizes, in alphabetical order, each business model's score across those 5 criteria i.e. liquidity, scalability, potential return on investment, passivity and simplicity!

Finally, because this book is enrolled in Kindle Matchbook Program, the **kindle edition of this book will be available to you for free** when you purchase the paperback version from Amazon.com.

If you're ready to take charge of your financial future, grab your copy of This Book today!

Available In **Kindle**, **Paperback** and **Audio**

Credit Card And Credit Repair Secrets: Discover How To Repair Your Credit, Get A 700+ Credit Score, Access Business Startup Funding, And Travel For Free Using Reward Cards

Are you sick and tired of paying huge interests on loans due to poor credit scores? Are you frustrated with not knowing where or how to get the necessary capital you need to start your business? Would you like to get all these as well as discover how you can travel the world for FREE?

If so, you'll love Credit Card and Credit Repair Secrets.

Imagine knowing simple do-it-yourself strategies you can employ to repair your credit profile, protect it from identity theft, access very cheap and affordable funding for your business and travel the world without any out of pocket expense!

This can be your reality. You can learn how to do all these and more. Moreover, you may be surprised by how simple doing so is.

In this book, you'll discover:

- **3 Types of consumer credit (And How You Can Access Them!)**
- How To Read, Review and Understand Your Credit Report (Including a Sample Letter You Can Send To Dispute Any Inaccuracy In It)
- **How To Achieve a 700+ Credit Score (And What To Do If You Have No FICO Score)**
- How To Monitor Your Credit Score (Including the difference between hard and soft inquiries)
- **What The VantageScore Model Is, It's Purpose, And How It Differs From The FICO Score Model**
- The Factors That Impact Your Credit Rating. Including The Ones That Certainly Don't - Despite What People Say!
- **Which Is More Important: Payment History Or Credit Utilization? (The Answer May Surprise You)**
- Why You Should Always Check Your Credit Report (At least Once A Month!)
- **How Credit Cards Work (From The Business And Consumer Perspective)**
- Factors You Need To Consider When Choosing A Credit Card (Including How To Avoid A Finance Charge on Your Credit Card)
- **How To Climb The Credit Card Ladder And Unlock Reward Points**
- Which Is More Appropriate: A Personal or Business Credit Card? (Find Out!)
- **How to Protect Your Credit Card From Identity Theft**
- Sources of Fund You Can Leverage To Grow Your Business

And much, much more!

An Identity Theft Resource Center (ITRC) report shows that 1,579 data breaches exposed about 179 million identity records in 2017. Being a victim of an identity scam can cause you a lot of problems. One of the worst cases would be the downfall of your credit score. You don't have to fall victim to it.

This book gives you a simple, but incredibly effective, step-by-step process you can use to build, protect and leverage your stellar credit profile to enjoy a financially stress-free life! It's practical. It's actionable. And if you follow it closely, it'll deliver extraordinary results!

PLUS BONUS - because this book is enrolled in Kindle Matchbook Program, the **kindle edition of this book will be available to you for free** when you purchase the paperback version from Amazon.com.

If you're ready to take charge of your financial future, grab your copy of This Book today!

Available In **Kindle**, **Paperback** and **Audio**

N/B - For other books in the Business and Money Series, see page 4

Made in the USA
Middletown, DE
14 July 2019